AMERICA NEEDS A
SUPERHERO

*How We **Really** "Make America Great Again"*

ROSIE AVILA

LIBERTY HOUSE
PUBLISHING

First Printing, 2016

Liberty House Publishing
620 N. Main St.
Santa Ana, CA 92701

Set in Adobe Garamond Pro by Adobe.®

Front cover artwork by Jordan Avila. Prints available at JorArts.org

Book design by Bethany Guajardo using Adobe® InDesign.®
Orange County, CA • teambeth.com

Rosie Orula

AMERICA NEEDS A SUPERHERO

WHAT PEOPLE ARE SAYING

"Rosie's keen insight shows us how history can speak to our times. Simple, clear and passionate!"
—Nelson Duncan, US Chief Petty Officer, USN

"There are many books written about education, but not too many authors are as experienced as Rosie Avila, both as a teacher, school board member and an activist who has made a big difference in her community. Her sound advice comes through many years of experience. This should be a must read for every parent."
—Orlean Koehle, Author of "Common Core, a Trojan Horse for Education Reform" and "The Hidden C's of Common Core"

"Rosie Avila is a respected school board member. Her book does not just talk about education through her stories she takes us inside. She is a pioneer and a mentor for many of us who entered politics."
—Dr. Ken Williams, Physician and Surgeon, Orange County Department of Education Board Member, 20 years

"Compelling! I need three copies for our leadership team."
—David Holland, Inner City school teacher, Speaker, Author of "Island of Nowhere," Business Owner

"Rosie's passion, convictions and heart for the community comes through. It is heart-warming. Very inspiring!"
—Viola Floth, Founder of Parents Who Care

"*America Needs A Superhero* took me down memory lane. I want my grandchildren to grow up with the values and freedom I enjoyed. This book is a wake-up call to America! Read it and pass it on while there is still time."
—Cynthia Martinez, Spirit of Hope Award winner (Bob Hope award) and Governors Award recipient, Author, and founder of Words of Comfort, Hope and Promise, a non-profit serving men and women who serve in the military

DEDICATION

This book is dedicated to my husband, Jim,
who lived through these events with me.
Thank you for listening to me, advising me, and
giving me your common sense when I needed it.

And to my father,
who held us close to his vest and
gave us a love for America and a passion for freedom.

FOREWORD

Going over these life experiences has been exhilarating and exhausting. I trust you will enjoy reading about these adventures. But most importantly, I hope you will be inspired by what I have learned along the way.

Sometimes I would just like to retire with my husband, Jim, and watch reruns of *Bonanza, Magnum PI,* and *NCIS.* But there are still political battles to fight. There are young, angry men who need mentors, bruised people who need encouragement, and those caught in addictions who need to be set free. It is not time to sit down. America is in trouble, and she needs our help.

Here is the winning plan! I am convinced it is what will save America. Together, united, we can restore America. We can reclaim her goodness and her greatness. Some are called to politics and must answer the call. Others are called to make a difference in their communities. We know how to wonderfully transform individual lives. And that is the Good News! It was love for a rejected child, in the movie, *The Giver,* that changed the world. It was unconditional love in the book, *A Wrinkle in Time,* that removed the darkness that was covering the earth. And in the Bible it was love that turned the world upside down!

Love never fails. The good news of God's love is what will save America. The fatherless are waiting, and the single moms need a visit.

As I finish this manuscript, the Santa Ana winds are blowing. Through my living room windows, I can see the trees swaying violently back and forth. Everything that can be shaken off the trees is falling down—dead, dry branches, loose leaves, and old shriveled berries. The wind howls as it swirls around the house. The local newspaper says the winds are 78 mph, and we are advised not to travel. While danger surrounds, somehow, we still need to go!

When the wind blows, we can count on warmer weather. It is also said that the Santa Ana winds often are what cause our Orange County fires. May the winds start here in Santa Ana and in your hometown and blow across our land, bringing instead a different kind of fire, one that purifies us and unites us with a love we so desperately need! And may this book be but a spark that starts the fire!

All of the stories in this book are true. Some names and identifying details have been changed to protect the privacy of individuals.

TABLE OF CONTENTS

Part I
What We Need

America Needs a Superhero

"Faster than a speeding bullet! More powerful than a loco-motive! Able to leap tall buildings at a single bound!"

"Look! Up in the sky!"

"It's a bird!"

"It's a plane!"

"It's Superman!"

"Yes, it's Superman—strange visitor from another planet who came to Earth with powers and abilities far beyond those of mortal men. Superman—defender of law and order. Champion of equal rights, valiant, courageous fighter against the forces of hate and prejudice, who disguised as Clark Kent, mild-mannered reporter for a great metropolitan newspaper, fights a never-ending battle for truth, justice, and the American way."

Chapter 1
America Needs A Superhero

It was the 1950s, and television was a recent invention. We all watched *Ozzie and Harriett, I Love Lucy, Leave It to Beaver,* and, of course, *Father Knows Best.* And in the '50s, fathers did know best.

Women stayed home, wore housedresses and pearl necklaces, and made dessert just so they could take it away from their children at dinnertime when they misbehaved. The suburbs grew with new cookie-cutter homes, picket fences, and tree-lined streets, and everyone wanted to "keep up with the Joneses."

I was just turning six.

On December 8, 1953, on a cold winter morning, our propeller airplane left Guatemala and flew to America. As we descended into the Los Angeles airport late that night, I looked out the airplane window at the patchwork blanket of twinkling lights. I was in awe. Los Angeles looked like shimmering jewels.

My older sister, Veronica, was wearing the same outfit I was: a blue skirt and white blouse with blue suspenders embroidered with bright flowers, made for this special trip by my aunt Ericka. My older brother Fred was nine and a great help for mom and dad as they had little Richard, then one year old, on their laps.

My father was happy to be bringing his family of six to this great country, a land of promise, America, the land of the free—a land where he could speak out in safety.

It was two days before I was to turn six, and I did not know what it meant to be put on a blacklist, a government list of people identified as troublemakers. I did not really understand freedom. Little did I know that this concept of liberty or freedom was to become one of my life's guiding passions.

The night we landed, we visited a grocery store. Amazing! It was incredible — all kinds of food in one place. How blessed America was! I looked out on an abundance of food available with so much variety. The food was organized on shelves, not in baskets on the floor. Dad bought us our first milkshake. I can still remember how good it tasted.

We slept in a hotel off of Century Blvd near the airport. And when I got up and walked out in the morning, I saw it. A great big donut was overhead. I mean huge. It was cement. It is a Los Angeles landmark now, but for me then, it was a "Fievel" moment, when the cartoon character, a little mouse, came to America and cried out, "Big Cats in America!" when he faced the animals in danger. For me, however, it was a joyful thought of "Big Donuts in America!" It wasn't until later that we, too, would face the dangerous fat cats. But growing up, it was "big donuts": sweetness, blessings, and abundance in America.

Yes, America was a land of great prosperity. Most people in America could eat donuts, ice cream, and other sweet delights every day. Such variety abounded, all kinds of material goods were set before you. Young families were purchasing their own homes, buying cars and getting the latest gadgets.

On my sixth birthday, I was given five dollars and taken to a toy store to pick out a toy. It was incredible. With so many choices, I had a hard time picking out one toy, but I settled on a beautiful little girl's tea set. Back in third-world countries like Guatemala, this is only a dream — a small part of the American Dream.

I was in junior high when I had a big "Ah-hah" moment. You know, one of those moments when you get it — a new discovery. My sixth grade teacher, Mrs. McCloud, said, "When you take your shower every day…." That was all I heard. A shower every day! I looked around. Do my friends in the class take a shower every day? Am I supposed to take a shower every day, too? At our house we had the Saturday night bath. And each of us took the bath in the same bath water. I think it was the two girls first. But I remember the dingy bathtub ring by the time the three boys were finished.

Even water was in abundance in America. As we adapted to American life we bathed more frequently. Later while in college, I traveled for two months in Europe and spent twelve days with a German family. I had taken a bath on Saturday, and now it was Wednesday. I asked the mother of the house if I could take a bath again. She said she would ask her husband. A big argument ensued. My German was limited, to say the least, but I knew it was about my request for a second bath.

I was able to have the bath, but I realized it was a sacrifice for the family. I used as little water as I could. How blessed we have been, enjoying an abundance of water, piped directly to us, in almost every room of the house. Today in my own two-story house, I can get water out of twelve faucets or showers!

America was exceptional. It was a land of opportunity. You could be anything you wanted to be in America! There was a ladder that could take you to the top. They called it upward mobility. People were compassionate and would help you along the way, like with the scholarships I received for college. If you worked hard, you were rewarded. It was indeed the land of the free. People were treated with dignity, and you could pursue your own happiness.

Of course, Dad was glad to be in America. I can still see him as he rubbed his hands together in glee upon our arrival. But this nine-hour flight was, I am sure, not without worry. First, Dad had been the only survivor of a small plane crash years earlier when he was a steward for Pan Am. The small craft had only the crew aboard as it flew over the city of Guatemala. The plane crashed into a jungle mountainside and caught on fire.

Fortunately, my dad managed to get out. Barely seeing, he was led by a young boy to a farmhouse. Because the plane carried gold bullion, Pan Am was very motivated to find the plane, and soon my dad was whisked away for emergency care. Now years later, traveling with his precious family, it was the first time Dad was back on a plane. While he may have preferred a boat, he wanted to leave Guatemala as soon as he could.

Secondly, I am sure other thoughts ran through his mind on that nine-hour flight, such as how he was going to provide for his big family in this new land. He looked around and saw that the airplane needed to be cleaned. This was perhaps especially true after this family with four wiggly children was on the plane for nine hours. Dad's first job in America was cleaning out airplanes. I remember that because he once brought home a beautiful purple sweet-smelling Hawaiian lei that someone had left on the plane. Being an airplane cleaner did have its perks, at least for this six-year-old girl.

But this job was not as great as Dad's next job, where he drove around the streets in an ice cream truck, selling ice cream. Now that is every kid's fantasy. Dad also drove a Helm's Bakery truck delivering donuts and other baked goods right to people's doors. Like I said, for me there were many donuts in America, and we got our fair share.

This was a courageous move for my dad, not just him getting on a plane but starting a new life in a new country—a country that epitomized everything my dad stood for.

My dad, who was born in Czechoslovakia, was well aware of the Communist aggression in Eastern Europe and its ruthless takeover of Czechoslovakia. This was just after World War II from 1945 to 1953, just prior to our coming to America. He understood the freedoms people lost under a government-controlled society. During those same years, Guatemala was becoming Communist. My brother shared with my parents how he was told in the schools that there was no God. The children in his class were asked to pray for bread. They closed their eyes and prayed. They were then told to open their eyes and see if there was bread on their desk. "See, there is no God," the teacher said.

My father recognized the atheistic propaganda and spoke out. He did not want his four children raised in government schools learning the socialist philosophy. He did not want us to develop a Marxist victim mentality, a belief that government should provide for everything, and a philosophy that would divide the classes between the rich and the poor. Dad spoke up in Guatemala and later heard that his name was on a blacklist, a list of people who opposed the government. Being a new Christian he wanted his children to grow up knowing God and understanding freedom. He decided it was time to leave.

Back in 1953, before the immigration laws were changed to make it easier to come to the United States, each person entering America was required to bring with them $1,500. My dad had to have $9,000 in cash for the family to enter America. He also had to know a trade that was currently needed in America. After high school my dad had learned to be a machinist while working with his uncle, and, yes, the United States was looking for machinists.

My dad had to sell everything he had in Guatemala — his truck, his small house, and a gas station. In 1953, $9,000 was a lot of money. The US government did not take the money; the government only required it so that we would not become dependent in our new country. We were expected to be able to take care of ourselves. With the money, Dad had enough for a down payment on a house and for a car to drive to and from work. Basically, to come to America, we had to burn our bridges behind us.

Dad worked at different jobs, took drafting and machinist classes at night, and soon found a job as a machinist. After coming to America, Dad and Mom had their fifth child one year later, and we were all so proud of our baby brother, who we called our little "gringo," our American baby.

Mom stayed home to care for us five children. I am not sure if she wore pearls like Mrs. Cleaver on TV, but she did wear housedresses and was very busy at home. She provided day care for many neighborhood children. With so many personalities, life was never boring. I remember one child in particular that the children called "Puddlehead" because he was always wetting his pants. Back then we used cloth diapers instead of absorbent disposable diapers. This certainly kept Mom busy. Mom also took in ironing from these working parents.

Mom's earnings allowed us to go to church camp and other fun outings. But we kids all learned early on how to sell door-to-door. Homemade looped potholders, handmade silk flower corsages, and Christmas gifts like pen sets and tablecloths, as well as Christmas cards were among the items we sold to pitch in for the family. We knew all of the neighbors. Our oldest brother, Fred, mowed lawns, had a paper route, and later worked at McDonald's. He used his money to fix an old car in the garage so that he could drive himself to work. Dad was glad when Fred could drive us to some of our church and school activities.

Fred built a large pigeon coop in the backyard where he raised pigeons. We could not afford toys, so we dug a big hole in the backyard — a deep six-foot hole. We put a little ladder down one side and sat at a table at the bottom where we shared one Dr. Pepper with tiny cups and cut up a candy bar into six pieces. This was our clubhouse. Another time, we collected cardboard boxes from the grocery store and made tunnels all over the backyard. With flashlights we crawled for hours, imagining we were in a large cave.

Later when we moved from Inglewood to Manhattan Beach, we used a toy loan that was next to the public library. Each week we would check out a toy, take it home, and play with it. If we brought it back clean and in good condition, we would get a star on our chart, and with ten stars we could choose a new toy that we could keep as our own.

My sister had her eye on a beautiful black doll. Finally, the day came when she got to take her doll home. It was a wonderful day. And it was a great way to develop the habit of using a library, and taking care of things. It was a good habit that helped us later on in life.

At Christmastime, our mom let us collect the Christmas trees from all of the neighbors' trash. The backyard was filled with trees, a wonderful forest. We had a lot of fun running in and out between the trees playing tag. We played school in the garage and had wonderful dancing and singing performances on the front porch. We watched TV shows about cowboys and Indians and played like we were Indians passing one of the tests to become a warrior. Indians had to run for miles keeping water in their mouth. If, at the end of the run, they could spit up a mouthful of water, they were considered worthy to become a warrior because they exhibited self-control conserving the water. My brother, sister, and I would walk for hours with water in our mouths walking around and around the classrooms at the nearby school. We would mark down how many times we could go around the building before we swallowed the water. By having to use our imagination, resourcefulness, and creativity, we were never bored.

As I remember, there were three things that made my father mad: when we left the lights on after leaving a room, when we talked on the phone too long, and when we used hairspray in the bathroom. Back then, you had to pay for each minute of phone time, and with five teenagers, that added up. He would always say, "Phones aren't for talking; they are just for your business." And when you had to share one bathroom with seven people, he hated having to smell and feel the sticky mist of the hairspray when he had to use the bathroom. We had to remember to go to the back porch to use the hairspray. We learned to be frugal, conserve resources, and be considerate of others.

Every school had a school nurse. My mom found out from the nurse where we could find a low-cost dentist. I hated going to the dentist. They had to give me a sedative, a nasty-tasting liquid, before I went. My mother never drove a car, so she took us on a bus to the dentist along with our two younger brothers who were not in school yet.

At night we would lie in our beds and tell stories to each other of how we would torture the dentist, throw him down a cliff onto a patch of cactus, shoot him out of a cannon, or blow him up. I think it was because we watched Daffy Duck and Porky Pig cartoons. Now, years later as an adult, I must admit that I love going to the dentist, particularly as I raised my own five children. It was the only time that I got to really relax and rest during the day. And on those wonderfully comfortable reclining dental chairs and with a little sleeping medication, it felt so gooood!

And of course we watched Mighty Mouse cartoons on Saturday morning. The beautiful damsel was tied to a log that was going down a conveyor belt at a saw mill. Time and again, Mighty Mouse would save the damsel, just in time, before she reached the blade and was sawn in half. "Here He Comes to Save the Day" was the theme song. Watching our black-and-white television was a privilege after we got our Saturday chores done.

Today many of us worry about America and the American Dream. We are not sure that our children will be able to afford those cookie-cutter houses in the suburbs. We are not confident in our public schools, and we worry that America is spending too much and has run out of money. We also worry that we will no longer be able to "keep up with the Joneses."

Maybe, more than fifty years later, I am still affected by Mighty Mouse, hoping that somehow, someone will come to save the day for America. Maybe someone will fly in and remove us from that conveyer belt that is moving us into impending danger.

America is divided. Perhaps someone will come and keep us,

like the damsel, from being sawn in half.

At meeting after meeting, I hear people say, "We know America is in trouble. I just wish someone would tell us what to do." America is looking for leadership, someone to unite us, someone to come, like Mighty Mouse, and save the day!

Chapter 2
A Good Offense

It was the 1950s. When we came to America, the political slogan was "I like Ike." General Dwight D. (Ike) Eisenhower, a war hero, was elected president. The United States had just come out of World War II. We knew there were real enemies in the world, such as Adolf Hitler, and that the cost of war was high. It was also a time called the Cold War. The Soviet Union, or Russia, who was showing signs of aggression, was our new enemy. There was a distrust between our nations, everyone feared conflict, but no one wanted another war. The threat of an atomic bomb loomed like a large mushroom cloud over our generation. We were also in a race to create nuclear arms and conquer the new frontier of space travel.

The deployment of "Sputnik," a Russian unmanned satellite, shocked America, as the Russians got ahead of us in space exploration. This also created the awareness that we could be spied on from a satellite in space.

While we were looking out into space, Russia was expanding its reach on the planet through its Communist International, or "Comintern." Country after country around the world fell to Communist domination. First, Russia took the Baltic nations and became the USSR, the Union of Soviet Socialist Republics. Then China fell to Communism. Afterward, it spread to African nations. And then Communism reached our hemisphere, capturing Cuba, just off our Florida coast. It was called the domino effect—one nation helped to topple the next. Now Cuba could be used to bring Central and South America into the fold.

Communism was spreading, the nuclear bomb was tested, and we all lived under a cloud of fear. People started to build underground bomb shelters, and at school we had regular air raid drills. The eerie sirens would sound, and then we would all duck for cover under our school desks, making sure that our faces were down and that our hands protected our necks. For the first time, young people had a sense that our whole nation could be annihilated. We knew the president had a special red phone with him at all times, where he could order retaliation immediately if we were attacked by the Soviet Union.

Space exploration and the threat of an atomic bomb meant America had to keep our scientific superiority. Science became king. This was a matter of national survival.

In the '50s when we arrived in the United States, many wanted to know what Communism was all about. Communist study groups were formed. Why were Cuba and China becoming Communist? What was this ideology that was spreading across the world from Eastern Europe to Africa and Asia? Now the Communists were in our own hemisphere, in Cuba, in Guatemala, Nicaragua, El Salvador, and other southern neighbors!

Russian spies, such as Alger Hiss, were also discovered in our own government. It seemed the Communists were everywhere, even in our nation's capital. In a famous case, Julius Rosenberg, an engineer, and his wife Ethel were put to death in the electric chair for conspiring to commit espionage. Julius headed a spy ring that passed top-secret information concerning the atomic bomb to the Soviet Union. Others whom Rosenberg recruited spent 10, 15, and 18 years in prison. The Rosenbergs were accused by the President of immeasurably increasing the chances of Atomic war and the possible deaths of tens of millions. As a youth, Julius Rosenberg was the leader in the Young Communist League while attending Seward Park High School. In 1939, Congress set up a committee to uncover citizens with

Nazi ties. Now in the '50's the House Committee on Un-American Activities was used to investigate those with Communist ties.

The Communist philosophy was attractive and quickly spreading. Many were deeply concerned. Some were watchful. It was said that people were now "looking for a communist under every bed." Senator Joe McCarthy, an outspoken critic of Communist sympathizers, was demonized. While many thought of him as an alarmist, he was certainly aware of the dangers of Communism, and its tendency to metastasize like a fast-growing cancer.

After all of the real scare, and what some called hysteria, of the '50s, strangely, now many years later, our children do not know about Communism, the hold it had on our nation, and the terrible toll it took on Central American nations and other countries in our hemisphere. We have been intimidated. No one wants to be associated with "McCarthyism." The mere mention of the word Communism is cause for ridicule. This intimidation has kept us from talking about Communism and from sharing our real history with our children.

America went to war in Vietnam, a long strange strip of land, thousands of miles away in Asia, on the other side of the world. South Vietnam had been our friend. We had a military station in their country and an agreement to protect them. When Communist North Vietnam threatened South Vietnam, one of our ships was attacked, and we decided to help them. We also wanted to take a stand against the spread of Communism. Enough was enough! We wanted to show Russia and China that they could not take South Vietnam, our little friend.

The Vietnam War took a great toll on our nation. Fifty-eight thousand American lives were lost in Vietnam. How could a great nation like America lose a war? We were devastated. What went wrong?

Presidential candidate Ron Paul has pointed out that Congress never really declared war in Vietnam. Breaking with the Constitution, which requires Congress to declare war, we did not consult the American people and allowed Democrat Presidents John Kennedy and Lyndon Johnson to take us into war.

America, along with other nations, formed the North Atlantic Treaty Organization (NATO) to protect Europe and the Southeast Asian Treaty Organization, (SEATO) to protect Asia from Communist aggression. Both were subsidiaries of and reported to the United Nations. Some feel that it was America's involvement in this international organization that prompted us to go to war in Vietnam, and more importantly our entanglement with other nations also tied our hands as to what we could do. Tragically, we consulted with other nations, some which did not have our best interests in mind. Rather, we should have received a consensus from the American people and a Congressional Declaration of War, as required by the US Constitution.

We should have listened to George Washington, our first president, who warned us in his Farewell Address, "peace, commerce, and honest friendship with all nations, entangling alliances with none."

There was a lot of support for the war from those who understood the tyranny of Communism. We felt helpless watching more and more nations fall to Communism. We recognized the danger within. Now we could finally do something!

Our nation also had plenty of anti-war demonstrations, too. Many of the demonstrators were young people who had not lived through WWII and did not understand the evils of tyranny. In previous wars, particularly WWII, everyone got behind the war effort; the people understood we had a real threat with Hitler and his fast-expanding, aggressive, and brutal regime. When Japan bombed Pearl Harbor, enraged Americans retaliated. In contrast with World War II, during the Vietnam War, young people, such as Hillary Rodham and Bill Clinton, led demonstrations against the war. Many young men refused to serve in the military and went AWOL to Canada rather than be drafted into the conflict. Rather than uniting around the war we were divided. Adding to anti-war sentiment, for the first time we could see the casualties and brutality of war each night in our living rooms on national television.

Jane Fonda, an actress, was a traitor. To many, she is called "Hanoi Jane." She went to Vietnam and visited the Viet Cong, our enemies. She smiled and took pictures with the Viet Cong sitting in their tanks, laughing with them. To our brave servicemen, this was a slap in the face. The Communists took her to see a Prisoner of War camp. Afterward she spoke openly at rallies and on television, stating that our prisoners were being well cared for by the Communists, lying for our enemies. To many, this was treason, and they never forgot.

Henry Mark Holzer's 2002 book, *Aid and Comfort*, made the case that Jane Fonda should have been tried and convicted of treason for her activities. In April 2005, the Houston Chronicle reported that Vietnam Veteran, Michael Smith, stood in line for ninety minutes at Fonda's autobiography book signing, and when he approached her, spat tobacco juice on her.

Another notable name during this time was Angela Davis. She was wanted by the FBI and ran for vice president of the United States as a member of the Communist Party USA in 1980 and 1984. Jane Fonda, Angela Davis, and other Communist sympathizers were allowed to speak on college campuses. To many, this was an outrage and a sign that something was terribly wrong with our country. While our sons were dying in the killing fields, our universities were rapidly becoming hotbeds of Marxist propaganda. Angela Davis taught for many years at the University of Santa Cruz and San Francisco University in feminist studies promoting gender equity and "social justice."

It was said of President Clinton that he started his political career by dodging the draft and paid a visit to Moscow instead. Soon he was found leading anti-war demonstrations in the streets of England as well as the United States. He married his fellow demonstrator Hillary Rodham, became governor of Arkansas, and then the president of the United States. Interestingly, on his last trip in public office as president, Clinton traveled to Vietnam with a huge entourage accompanying him. It seemed his purpose was to commend the president of Communist South Vietnam for the fine job he was doing. Clinton had come full circle, starting and ending on the wrong side of freedom.

According to an article, "Road to Moscow: Bill Clinton's Activism from Fulbright to Moscow" by Fedora, August 22, 2007 (http://www.freerepublic.com/focus/f-news/1884984/posts), Bill Clinton traveled to Moscow over winter vacation in 1969 to 1970 and had connections to KGB agents. David Maraniss is quoted, "Over the summer vacation that year, Clinton returned to the United States, dividing his time between taking steps to avoid the draft and organizing antiwar activities."

After serving two terms as president, Clinton visited South Vietnam. In a November 2000 article by Vu Kim Chung, "US President Clinton Makes Historic Visit to Vietnam" (http://www.oocities.org/hoan_kiem/12-2000/VN-suthamclinton.html), it was reported that Bill Clinton was warmly received in Vietnam, commended the president of Vietnam for his economic progress, and promised money to help Vietnam as they normalized diplomatic relations and built new business relationships.

Vietnam was a war that should not have been fought. Not because it was not a just cause, but because we did not go there to win and we did not make the case to the American people. We did not have a winning strategy. We were only there to contain the enemy, not defeat him. We did not make the case to the American people, uniting the nation behind the effort. We also did not evaluate the strength of the enemy, particularly the threat of China and others joining the war to help the North, who sent in an endless supply of men and arms. After ten years of fighting and huge losses, Congress grew weary of the war and ultimately withdrew funding.

Although it probably was time to quit due to the

micromanaging of the war by an international organization and Washington, who limited our actions; sadly the withdrawal of funding further tied the hands of our military and put our brave men in even greater danger. Many also were bitter because they believed that, after so much bloodshed, we were close to victory. Without America's aid, Saigon fell, officially ending the war two years after we left.

In a recently released movie, *Ride the Thunder*, a Vietnamese and American commander on the ground are angered that America will not let them fight and take the war to the North, stopping the war at its source. They called it an unwinnable war because there were no goals and no strategy for victory. The men are just dumped in the jungles to fight a confusing battle while being greatly outnumbered. The movie ends with the question, "Was it worth it?" It shows a Vietnamese man who suffered greatly in the Communist re-education camps, but was later allowed to come and live in America. He says, "Yes, it was worth it because two million got out alive to enjoy freedom in America."

My boyfriend served in Vietnam. My brothers served in the navy and in the air force. A friend from church died in Vietnam. I still remember his casket entering the church draped in the American flag. Most of us were not untouched by the war.

Many have asked, "Why go to war, if we do not intend to win?" Before going to battle, we have to decide what victory looks like; we have to consider our enemy and evaluate if we have the means to win. We also need to consider the potential costs in lives and dollars. We have to ask ourselves, "What are our goals? Do we have the will to win?" Then we have to articulate the cause to the American people, get their consent through Congress, and as a united nation, fight for nothing less than total victory.

Our leaders, directed by other nations, did not intend for us to utterly destroy the enemy; they wanted us only to contain them. We surrendered the blood of our precious young men just for containment. Containment means they will rise again to fight another day. Fifty-eight thousand American lives and more than one million Vietnamese lives were lost. The cost was too high.

In the Old Testament, the Israelites—God's chosen people—were instructed for particular battles to destroy their enemies. If they did not destroy the enemy, then they would have to fight them again and again.

It cannot be said strongly enough. War demands a resolve to win.

This is a great lesson to learn in the political arena as well. We cannot merely contain those that work politically to destroy America, its freedom, and its values. We need to defeat them. We need to have a game plan to win—an effective offensive strategy.

We cannot be content to just fight defensively, taking on each battle that our enemies throw our way. There are too many battles to fight, too many emails to send, and too many petitions to sign. When wars drag on, precious resources are depleted and soldiers get weary. We cannot continue to fight our enemies again and again.

We cannot be content to beat them back two steps when they are taking three steps forward. Gradually, step-by-step, they are taking ground. Occasionally we may win a battle, but then have to fight that same battle again. Aren't we tired of playing defense? In war, defense is not enough. Today, more than ever, we need a resolve to win, a winning strategy, and a goal that is nothing less than victory! We need a good offense.

Chapter 3
A Winning Plan

As a school board member, I would often visit classrooms, see what the teachers were teaching, and speak with the children. One day a copy of the *Weekly Reader* caught my eye. The *Weekly Reader* is a four-page mini newspaper written for grade school children. It enables the children to get used to reading a newspaper, and the teachers are able to discuss some of the issues of the day.

There was an article on the Vietnam War and one on North Korea. I asked if I could take a copy of the *Weekly Reader* home. According to this little newspaper, the Vietnam War was a civil war, and we helped the South. Period. That was it. There was no mention of our effort to contain Communism. No mention of the great cost of 58,000 American lives. The article on North Korea simply stated that the people in North Korea were starving, and the wonderful United Nations is shipping them food. Where was the explanation that in Communist countries, many people starve due to food shortages and rationing? I know a small newspaper cannot explain everything, but it could have put in a few simple statements that told the true story.

I was alarmed. I wrote the Vietnamese leaders in my community, to explain this travesty. Concerned at this censorship or revision of history, I asked them to help me set the record straight on Vietnam. "Please help me teach this generation about tyranny and freedom," I wrote.

I feel a kindred spirit with the Vietnamese people in America.

The older Vietnamese community, too, worries that their young people do not understand their passion for freedom and their hatred for Communism and tyranny. They lost their homeland and millions of their people, and we lost 58,000 of our best young men. And all of this was for a mere "civil war"?

One day I turned on the television and heard former Secretary of Defense Robert McNamara, who is considered the architect of the Vietnam War. He also concluded that the Vietnam War a mere civil war. I began to see that it was not only the children's newspaper, but also our leaders who were revising history. The question is, *Why?* Was it that we never had a plan to win, but only to contain Communism? Was the war fought only to help a friendly nation who had given us an airfield?

Was McNamara intimidated by the liberal media? Or perhaps he never really understood the evils of Communism. Perhaps McNamara did not want to leave the impression that we should continue to fight Communist aggression, with its Socialist system, and its world domination dream.

For most Americans, who understood freedom and the threat of Communism, the Vietnam War was our attempt to *stop* the spread of tyranny and oppression. It was our need to protect America by slowing down communist expansion and a concern for our friends that took us there.

While McNamara may have conveniently forgotten his own history, the Communists have learned some lessons along the way. Today, those seeking a new world order, desiring to bring every nation under state rule and a global regime, have moved from Marxism, with its violent overthrow philosophy, to Fabian Socialism, which advocates a slow transition from within, in a "boiling frog" scenario. The poor frog is slowly boiled to death but he is unaware because the temperature goes up very slowly.

When nations, such as China and North Korea, have succumbed to communist rule, starvation and death have followed. It is hard, if not impossible, to feed the people with a totally state-owned economy. I remember watching television programs where people in Russia were seen standing in long lines, waiting for a half-pound of butter or a half-pound of meat– their government rations. The people also had to wait for months to get their government-assigned apartment or car. Land ownership and business ownership was frowned upon. The state owns everything and doles out or distributes goods or resources to the people. Without the pride of ownership and the benefit of labor, there is no incentive to work hard. Many have learned the hard way that Communism, or Socialism, in its pure form cannot support its people.

China is one example. China is still a Communist state, run through extensive central planning and committee governance. People are oppressed and controlled through personal files which determine an individual's state in life, the intimation of neighborhood informants, and many human rights violations. But today in Communist China we see tremendous economic growth due to the opening of its markets under President Richard Nixon. Republican President Nixon hoped that we could win them over to our philosophy of freedom by showing the people how Capitalism and the Free Enterprise System worked. But instead China has used their new economic power unfairly against us by manipulating the currency, not having the same expensive environmental standards, and other unfair practices. They have become wealthy by using a different playing field. Rather than adopting a free enterprise system and a new form of government, they have adapted a new kind of Fascism, allowing the people to own some businesses and share in profits. But in essence these businesses are still owned by the state, as they are heavily regulated by the government.

It is nearly impossible for totalitarian regimes to support the physical needs of their people. Under state-run governments, personal incentive is taken away, and there are no competitive markets to spur on the economy. According to Scott Manning

in an article called "Communist Body Count," (http://www.
scottmanning.com/content/communist-body-count/) more
than 149,469,610 (almost 150 million) have died or starved
to death by their own communist governments. The disclaimer
was, "These numbers are mid estimates and do not include those
that died in war." The Vietnam War alone would have added
another two million people to that count.

Recently I attended a "Thank You America Day" luncheon
in the Vietnamese community. The wonderful seven-course
dinner brought plate after plate mounted with wonderful tasty
Vietnamese food. In Orange County, California where I live,
we have a large population of Vietnamese people; the largest
group outside of Vietnam resides here in "Little Saigon." The
Vietnamese are so grateful to us for helping them in their battle
against the Communists. The community wanted to express their
gratitude for America with this special event. Even though I was
no longer running for Congress, I wanted to go to reconnect
with the wonderful Vietnamese community. While they were
seeking to express thanks to America, I was the one who came
to say thank you to them. I stood at the podium, greeted them,
and stated, "The Vietnamese community is God's gift to the
United States because they are here to remind us of the amazing
gift of freedom and its high cost."

Young people today have no reason to fear totalitarian governments, because many have little knowledge of their oppressive and
violent past. History has been revised, and the liberal media still
intimidates anyone who tries to tell the truth. In college classrooms,
students are told that Karl Marx was the good guy. "Marx had
wonderful dreams for society," sociology textbooks explain. Colleges,
even Christian universities, now have social justice majors. Young
people are asked to join in a battle against oppression, and this
includes political action. They are urged to encourage governments
to bring in a new "just" world through the redistribution of goods
and resources, creating a "just" and equal society.

The older generation has no idea just how limited the knowledge of our young people is. Today's young people have been taught social studies (formally called history) in our public schools starting in kindergarten using politically correct thematic units. Children, through selective censorship, learn that U.S. history is the story of the oppressed and oppressors. My daughter's third grade history textbook was one tragedy after another. First, Christopher Columbus killed the indigenous people, California mission priests beat the Indians, Whites enslaved the blacks, and the Japanese were sent to internment camps. Today Hispanics are being discriminated against, and the poor are taken advantage of by the rich. What a sad, oppressive history to give our young eight-year-olds!

Selective censorship, collaborative learning (group work), and critical thinking schemes all distract from the learning of real history and are methods of indoctrination. Is it any wonder that our children do not know what really happened in the past?

Our children's teachers are taught that the answer to these historical injustices is diversity (multiculturalism) training and social justice. Diversity treats all cultures as equal, and minimizes the greatness of American values. Social justice education is the study of the oppressed and the oppressor, and calls for government redistribution of wealth, or socialism. Thus the new teaching strategies and textbooks are preparing our young people to be socialist global citizens, not freedom loving Americans. Many young people hate America, yet need a country to belong to, a place to call home. They lack an understanding of socialism and what it does to a nation, but they seek a new philosophy and a new world. They are restless and unhappy. We saw some of their frustration in the Occupy Wall Street demonstrations.

We forget that today's young people never used vinyl records, eight-track tapes, and have no idea what a real hair dryer (with a plastic headcap) looked like. It is easy to forget how different our culture is today. I have five children, and one day I realized that the younger two children never went to Sea World! Because I had that memory of enjoying the amazing ocean animals with my children, I assumed all of them had the same experience. Education too has changed. We expect that today's children are learning what we learned in school.

The world is changing at a rapid pace. While this is true, the concept of "a changing world" is used not only as a means to understand change, but also as a rational for bringing in change. At every educational conference for teachers or board members, we are all reminded that the world is changing, moving from an agricultural age, to an industrial society, and now ushering us into the information age. With all of these changes, they claim the schools have to prepare the students for the future, a new age. Some even claim that the past is no longer relevant.

The irony is that knowledge of the past prepares young people for the future. But in schools, the key word is *imagine*. "Image a world where..." Children are told to imagine a better world, a utopian society, a "just" world. The concept of the future is an imaginary utopian society. But, of course, what all of these changes show us is that we really do not know what the future will be like. Who could have imagined the Internet, flying across the skies, or walking on the moon? But never mind reality. The dreamers, social planners, and educational elites have a perfect utopian, man-managed society planned for our future.

Not only is the past no longer relevant (they say), but enduring values like *freedom* and *truth* can mean what you want them to mean. Everything is relative and young people are asked to construct their own new meanings. *Relativism* means that truth is whatever you want it to be. But relativistic thinking is only a transition, a way to get people to let go of their firmly held beliefs. *Change Agents* in conferences describe the "Change Process" as moving from traditional, to transitional, to transformational. But in reality, they are moving us from truth, to no truth, to "our" truth.

The final goal in the change process is to have everyone think the same as prescribed by the social planners or the global state. In this new world, freedom is redefined. Just look at how President Franklin D. Roosevelt redefined freedom with his four freedoms speech where he included "the freedom from want." Based on this idea, we will be free when the government can make sure all of our needs are met.

When talking about these concepts, using the word *Communism* is taboo. It will bring ridicule every time! To avoid the ridicule, we use words like *statism*, *socialist policies*, the *New World Order*, *tyranny*, *government control*, and *totalitarianism*. We try to find ways to talk about slavery to the state without using the word *Communism*. The fear of being linked to McCarthyism is still silencing those who do.

When I grew up, it was normal to talk of Communism. Socialist countries were called Communist countries. Technically, Communism, or "world peace," is attained only when the whole world is living under socialism. That is why they are so aggressive in gobbling up other countries. The social planners want a peaceful world. And in the end, the utopian society dream justifies all of their brutality and lies. The end justifies the means. Communists talk about world peace, but they are not talking about peace for today. To them, world peace will be realized only when the whole world is under a one-world socialistic system.

In talking about Communism, I do not want to be marginalized, but I will not be intimidated either. The benefits of using the word Communism for a man-made, totally government-controlled system is that there are examples in the world that have used the word: Communist Russia, Communist Cuba, Communist China, and Communist Vietnam, so we can point to real-life examples.

Liberals are constantly redefining themselves when one word or organization becomes suspect; they just redefine themselves, form another organization, and take on another name. Could it be that the American people in the '50s successfully exposed Communism, only to force it to go underground, rename and reinvent itself?

For example, in education, Mastery Learning reinvented itself and became Outcome-Based Education. The discredited Modern Math of the '80s came out as the new "New" New Math of the '90s or integrated math of the 2000s. When Comprehensive Sex Education—with its SIECUS Guidelines that promoted mastur-bation, anal sex, and same-sex experiences as ways to reduce birth rates—was criticized, it was then marketed as Abstinence Plus. Once people caught on to the Hitler-like eugenics with its targeting of minorities and disabled people, Margaret Sanger's population-con-trol organization just renamed itself to Planned Parenthood and created a new marketing campaign. Even today, as community organizers such as ACORN are exposed for their corruption, they just rename themselves and hang out their new shingle.

So how do we talk about totalitarian regimes, social engineer-ing schemes, global planning, tyranny, state control, and slavery? The old utopian dream of yesterday was Communism; the new utopian dream of today is what former President George H. W. Bush, Sr., and wealthy entrepreneur George Soros call the New World Order. But if freedom lovers use the word "New World Order," it is no longer called "McCarthyism" but instead "a con-spiracy." The new name for redistribution of goods, or socialism, is "social justice." It just sounds so good. Who would not want a just society? And doesn't the Bible speak of justice? Social justice, like Karl Marx's philosophy, also pits "the oppressed against the oppressor, the rich against the poor" creating "class-warfare," as a means of overthrowing our present system.

In America, we have always had a tension between freedom and tyranny. That is because each generation has to fight to stay free. The concept of more government control is nothing new. In the '40s, we fought Hitler and his Nazi (National Socialism) expansion. In the '50s, we fought the Cold War with Soviet

Russia; in the '60s, we fought the War on Poverty, in the '70s and '80s, we fought Communist expansion in our Hemisphere in Cuba, El Salvador, and Nicaragua. In the '90s, we fought the eight national education goals, Goals 2000, with its concept called "Life Long Learning." In the 2000s, after the terrorist attack on New York's Twin Towers that killed more than three thousand people, we fought a War on Terror. Since 2010, we have had to fight the "Affordable Care Act" (Obamacare), which is the nationalization of health care, lowering the quality of care and increasing overall costs. We've also had to fight the "Wall Street Reform and Consumer Protection Act" (Dodd-Frank Act), with its numerous new government agencies that control banking, credit cards, insurance, trading, derivatives, credit rating, and other aspects of our economy through excessive government regulation of businesses. While claiming to prevent another 2008 financial crisis, critics claim these new regulations will further hurt business and the economy.

Today those of us who cherish freedom fight the new "Common Core" educational standards that remove education control from parents and local communities. Common Core, which was secretly pushed on state governors, violates three federal laws that forbid the establishment of a federal education system. Another struggle is our battle against the deceptiveness of "social justice," with its "just society" rhetoric and socialistic dreams that are creeping into our churches and Christian universities. This is perhaps a greater fight because it includes some of our own brothers and sisters, not just the atheists of the past. The fight continues, and only the names change.

It is the ageless battle between good and evil. Truth always produces freedom. And lies and deception always produce captivity. Is it any wonder why our legislators are being kept in the dark, being asked to vote for massive new laws that have great-sounding names without first being given enough time to read them?

At least in the past, Americans recognized our enemy, and tried coexistence and détente, with its "live and let live" or "let's just get along together" philosophy. Today with all of the deceptive terms, Americans are confused. President Ronald Reagan tried to set us straight by exposing the enemy, calling Russia, the USSR (Union of Soviet Socialist Republics), "the evil empire." And he also challenged Russian Prime Minister Gorbachev to "Tear down this wall!" The Berlin Wall kept men imprisoned in East Berlin, Germany. President Reagan understood that tyranny is aggressive and, like cancer, it keeps coming back. It will never rest until the world is under its control. It is a never-ending battle to stay free.

Senator Jim DeMint, in his book, *Rescuing America*, tells how just a few years after the writing of the Constitution, the federal government was already planning to take more control. It is natural for men to want more control. That is why our nation needs the restraints of the Constitution.

The Scriptures talk about the political systems of the world. The Old Testament book of Daniel describes a large statue with a head of gold, chest and arms of silver, stomach and hips made of bronze, its legs of iron and feet, which are part clay and part iron. Each of the parts represents a different kingdom or political power. But then at the end, a big rock not made by human hands rolls in and crushes all of the political kingdoms. It shows us that God is in control and in the end, He, the Rock, will destroy the kingdoms of this world and come to reign.

In the book of Genesis, the ancient people built the Tower of Babel, a tower that would reach the heavens. After Noah's flood, God told the people to inhabit and fill the earth. In rebellion, the people wanted to keep everyone together, to unite and build a powerful kingdom. While they wanted to build a tower to the heavens, in a sense they wanted to be God, and bring heaven to earth to create a better society. According to Genesis, if the people actually united and became one, "a collective seamless society," nothing would be impossible for them. God understood the power in unity. They wanted to build a new kingdom, a kingdom independent of Him, so He decided to separate them. Using the divide-and-conquer technique, God gave them different languages and confused them. This caused them to scatter. Even back then, God knew how to confuse these one-world system dreamers and destroy their arrogant plans to bring fame to themselves and live apart from God's plans.

With schools and leaders revising our history, intimidation like "McCarthyism" keeping the truth about our struggles for freedom from being told, and little children imagining rather than learning, it is no wonder we are again being led astray by the enemies of freedom. But God, as in the story of the Tower of Babel, knows just how to confuse the plans of those who would make us one, under a controlled, utopian society where all are enslaved. God has a plan. And that is good news!

This book is about that plan.

Chapter 4
An Understanding of Our Enemies

God confused the people at the Tower of Babel with language, and the Devil must have learned something. Today he is using the same tactic, confusing our language. While God knows how to confuse evil plans, our enemy also knows how to confuse the people. This happens through "doublespeak." It is interesting that when we speak out plainly about what we see happening, we are ridiculed. But when the enemies of freedom speak, they seem to have legitimacy. These global planners have figured out a way to speak freely and move their agenda forward. They use deceptive words for the same old concepts. Most people think they are saying one thing, while they are saying something else. Actually it is very smart. It's a little like when Jesus spoke in parables. The people would hear his words yet not fully understand what he was really talking about. Only his disciples, or the true believers, would know what he meant.

The doublespeak we have today must be a kind of wartime secret code. There are those who really understand the social planner's global schemes, and there are those who use the same language and ascribe to it a different meaning. And when the next step takes effect, the language and its real meaning is accepted.

Take, for instance, words like *lifelong learning* and *participatory democracy*; both sound so good.

Republican presidential candidate Newt Gingrich, in his book, *Renewing America*, discussed education using the words "lifelong learning" as a positive thing. I do not think Newt Gingrich, a very knowledgeable man, understood that "lifelong learning" is a bad thing. It sounds like a good thing. He did not know it is a plan to re-educate Americans and keep them in line. Not only Newt Gingrich but also most educators like the concept of lifelong learning, continually learning throughout one's life. Later you will see that lifelong learning is not about individuals growing in knowledge, but rather government-prescribed and electronically monitored lifelong learning.

President Bill Clinton used the words *participatory democracy* a lot. Most people thought Clinton liked freedom or what many think of when they think of democracy. But Clinton was talking about a new governance model called Shared Governance. It is not government by the people through respected elected representatives but rather government by a powerful elite central committee. They create the central plan and appoint local committee members who are charged with implementing the plan.

Communist nations use committee governance. The Communist Party rules with their central committee. Most of us are familiar with the name Chairman Mao, Mao Zedong, or Mao Tse-tung, a ruthless Chinese leader. He was the father of the People's Republic of China and is called Chairman Mao because he was the chairman of the central committee of the communist party.

The Chinese people were organized into local committees in order to implement the central plan. They were all asked, or we could say required, to "participate" in fulfilling the goals of the Chairman and his committee. All opposition was ruthlessly suppressed. Dissenters were eliminated or sent to re-education camps. Mao's 1958 agricultural reforms, *The Great Leap Forward*, failed and millions died of starvation. In 1966, when he was losing popularity, he led a new "cultural revolution" to purge the country of "impure elements" (people); millions more died.

The United Nations promotes *"participatory democracy,"* or *"shared governance,"* and it is presently used in many of our educational institutions. It masquerades as decentralization but it is in fact a centralization of power.

I believe that President Bill Clinton knew what he was talking about when he used the term, "participatory democracy," but of course he would not have called it communist tyranny. Most of our universities use participatory democracy or shared governance; in fact, in 1988, California AB1725 mandated that community colleges use shared governance and have faculty senates. Naturally most think it is a good idea "to share" the governance of the institution so that more people can participate. They do not understand that committee governance, while seeming to decentralize power, always leads to "control by a powerful central committee," or executive committee, who controls the agenda and carefully selects who sits at the table of the other committees in order to ensure a preconceived outcome.

In education with these socialistic tactics, carefully selected participants such as teachers are usually intimated, coerced or rewarded with pay to sit on these committees to go along with the central plans. In the end, using the Delphi method, committee members are manipulated to vote for the pre-planned agenda. In the political sphere, "Shared Governance" takes the power away from elected officials who represent the people and gives it to an elite few. In the case of a university, "Shared Governance" gives control to the executive committee and takes the power away from appointed university trustees who were selected for their character and entrusted with the mission of the institution.

With so much doublespeak and manipulation, it can be confusing unless you understand freedom.

My dad taught us well at our kitchen table. He explained, "This is what a Communist, a totalitarian tyrannical system, looks like, and this is what a free society looks like." In Central America, he became alarmed upon seeing the Communist land reform programs and socialist propaganda in the Guatemalan schools. As a steward for Pan Am, my father traveled back and forth to the United States where he fell in love with America and its freedom, not to mention the beautiful Texas women.

In a Communist, central-controlled, managed utopian society, the government wants to control the thoughts, philosophy, and actions of its people. Freedom of speech is not tolerated; everyone has to speak the "company line." The whole system depends on everyone cooperating. You have to watch your back because citizens of the state, your very neighbors, are asked to tell on you and identify you to the authorities. Russia had the KGB, and the Nazis had the Gestapo, a secret state police. If you are suspect, by saying or doing the wrong thing, you will face increased surveillance and imprisonment. And if you are lucky, you will receive re-education and asked to show your new thinking through journaling. Many are killed or sent to concentration camps to do hard labor in unimaginable conditions. Everything you say and do is kept in your file, and you receive promotions or demotions depending on what is in your file. Your job and health care are provided by the government, so you have to be very careful to cooperate so as not to lose your job or medical care. Control is everything.

Today's socialists, called Progressives, want to be managed by man, not directed and led by God and his principles. In contrast, in America, our founding fathers shouted, "No king but King Jesus!" They left the rule of King George III in England and hated his continued desire to control them and tax them without representation. The Declaration of Independence lists twenty-seven grievances against King George and makes the case why America should be free. The colonists knew men could be ruthless and oppressive, and they understood that God was loving, good, and wise. Man's government brings brutality and slavery, while God's principles of government produce freedom and peace. And America has proved it.

Thomas Paine, in *Common Sense*, a very popular pamphlet written just before America's War for Independence, argued against the tyranny of a king, where laws came from above, from the crown, where people's lives could be controlled at the whims of a mere man. Paine wanted us to be a people of laws that were created by a moral and religious people who relied on God's guidance. It was better to have the laws come from the people who had to live by them rather than a king who was above the law. Thomas Paine stated that, in America, the people's law would be king. The "People's Law is the Ruler's Law," he declared. We were all to be equal under the law. Thomas Paine's writings were very important because they helped to create the American consensus to go to war against Great Britain. General George Washington, who led the soldiers into battle during the American Revolutionary War, read Paine's *Common Sense* to his troops.

After the war, the thirteen colonies had a convention and sent representatives who discussed the type of government they wanted and wrote the United States Constitution. In America, we created a system of government called a "Constitutional Republic" that was "for the people and by the people." The laws would be made by the people through their chosen representatives. The *rule of law* insured that everyone had to live by the law. No one was above the law, not even the president or congress. We created a government with three branches: the presidency to lead the people and set the agenda, the Congress who represented the people to make the laws, and the Supreme Court to make sure the laws followed the Constitution. These three different *branches of government* ensure our laws are constitutional and represent the will of the people. It is called *checks and balances*. It was a way to guard against tyranny, where a few make the rules behind closed doors.

In contrast, a Communist socialist society creates a government for the "little people" by the "elites." Only a few, the chairman or the powerful central committee and its members, or party leaders, know what really is good for the people. Socialism is based on atheism—the people are not a self-governed moral people who follow God's principles. The assumption is the people need to be controlled externally by force not internally by a moral conscience or God.

In 1954, President Eisenhower had "under God," inserted in our Pledge of Allegiance during his administration. And in 1956, "In God We Trust" was officially made our national motto and mandated to be printed on our paper bills. The first bills came out in July of 1957. Previously we had "In God We Trust" imprinted on some of our coins, starting during the Civil War. But the words first appeared much earlier in 1814 in the fourth stanza of the Star Spangled Banner, our national anthem, "For this is our motto – In God is our trust."

On Facebook, someone sent a video of how the "Star Spangled Banner" was written. I wished I would have kept it. It was so special. Francis Scott Key, in 1814, boarded a ship to negotiate the release of a prisoner and was detained. Several prisoners were locked up underneath the hull of the ship. A few miles away was Fort McHenry which had a big American flag proudly waving in the wind. A large fleet of British ships arrived. The British demanded that the American flag must come down. If not, they threatened, they would bomb the fort.

The flag was not lowered and the British bombed the fort all night long from their ships. Actually they bombed the fort for twenty-five hours. Naturally the prisoners were scared with all of the noise. Francis ran down to tell the men what was going on. The prisoners asked, "Is the flag still up?" "Yes," he answered. Francis ran up again to see what was happening and then come back down to report to the prisoners. Again, they asked, "Is our flag still flying?" When the light from the bombs that were "bursting in air," shined Francis could see that the flag was still there waving. He wrote, "O say can you see…does the Star Spangled Banner yet wave?…over the land of the brave and the home of the free."

Representative Charles E. Bennett, a World War II veteran and a twenty-two-term member of the House of Representatives, introduced the Resolution to have "In God We Trust" on our money. "Nothing can be more certain than that our country was founded in a spiritual atmosphere and with a firm trust in God," he proclaimed on the House floor. "While the sentiment of trust in God is universal and timeless, these particular four words 'In God We Trust' are indigenous to our country." Further Bennett invoked the Cold War struggle in arguing for the measure. "In these days when imperialistic and materialistic Communism seeks to attack and destroy freedom, we should continually look for ways to strengthen the foundations of our freedom," he said. Another representative, Charles Oakman from Michigan, further explained, "One of the most fundamental differences between us and the Communists is our belief in God." The resolution passed and "In God We Trust" was inscribed on our money.

On June 14, 1954, Flag Day, President Eisenhower signed the bill to put the words "under God" into our Pledge of Allegiance with these words: "In this way we are reaffirming the transcendence of religious faith in America's heritage and future; in this way we shall constantly strengthen those spiritual weapons which forever will be our country's most powerful resource in peace and in war" (see *The American Presidency Project*, June 14, 1954, http://www.presidency.ucsb.edu/ws/?pid=9920.)

President Eisenhower, whose campaign slogan was "I like Ike," wanted the world to understand where our foundation lay. Our founders trusted in the Providence of God. The Declaration of Independence, our national mission statement, says that we are endowed by our "Creator" with certain unalienable rights: the rights of life, liberty, and the pursuit of happiness. They knew it was the purpose of government to protect our God-given rights.

Before becoming president, Dwight D. Eisenhower was the commander who led our troops to defeat Adolph Hitler. During the Cold War against Russia (USSR or Soviet Union), President Eisenhower wanted to show the world that we were not like the ungodly atheistic Communists. We trusted in God and looked to him for wisdom. It was not that our trust in God was something new, it was just that prior to this time our faith in God was assumed, perhaps self-evident, and part of our public fabric. President Eisenhower also understood the power of prayer, and in 1953, we had our first National Prayer Breakfast.

No wonder the American people liked Ike!

Six months after our family left Guatemala, in July of 1954, the United States, concerned about the spread of Communism in our hemisphere, helped Guatemala overthrow the socialist-leaning president Jacobo Arbenz. My father's cousin had property in Guatemala near the border of Honduras. He was accused of allowing the American-trained Guatemalan troops to pass through his land. The Communists captured him, cut out his tongue, and he was shot in a firing squad. From my youth, I understood that these Communists were ungodly, evil men, trained in terror, who tortured their victims and then brutally disposed of them.

Without the restraint of religion and morality and with no fear of God, people and governments can abuse their power and become very oppressive. As Communism expanded, millions were tortured, mutilated, and murdered, and millions starved to death.

History has shown that Communists rule with terror, intimidation, and cruelty. Do they think of themselves as cruel and oppressive? They do not. They think of themselves as good because they want a beautiful, just society where the poor and disenfranchised will be cared for. These progressives have a utopian dream that blinds them from seeing the reality of their evil ways. They feel so strongly that world Communism, "social justice," or a New World Order is the only way to have world peace—that the end justifies the means.

In some ways, we can understand. Promoters of social justice are yearning for a "just" society, the Kingdom of God on earth, for a time when "...they shall beat their swords into plowshares, and their spears into pruning hooks: nation shall not lift up sword against nation, neither shall they learn war any more." (Isaiah 2:4). What they are saying in their hearts is, "The kingdom come!"

They may be saying, "The kingdom come," but they are not saying, "*Thy* kingdom come." The problem is, they do not want to say, "Thy will be done." They want a man-managed society, not a society based on religion and morality. They want the kingdom without the King.

They hate America. As our founders shouted, in America, we have no King but King Jesus! Men hate God and love lawlessness. They want to do their own thing.

Because I was taught to understand political systems as a young girl, I have had an advantage. I can see what others sometimes do not see. It is said that unless you know what a real twenty-dollar bill looks like, you cannot recognize the counterfeit.

God too has given us truth so that we would recognize deception, or the counterfeit. He has given us directions and rules to live by, rules that protect us and give us peace. He did not make us and leave us alone to construct our own meaning. He left us a guidebook so that we would understand our purpose. "You will know the truth and the truth will set you free" (John 8:32). It is truth that sets us free.

In the fight for freedom, we first need strong leadership, a superhero, a good offensive strategy, a winning plan, and an understanding of our enemy. When you know how to look at the world and understand the tactics of the enemy, you will not fall for the deception. You will understand its doublespeak and know how to decode it. Once you can decode it, you can defeat it. In every battle we need to understand the enemy's nature, his weapons, and his strength. Once we understand the enemy, we can have confidence in our winning plan.

As in the '50s television program, *Father Knows Best*, my father did know best; he taught us, and he brought us to the greatest country on earth—a nation that respected God, tried to live by God's principles, and experienced the most amazing prosperity and blessings the world has ever known.

Part II
What Went Wrong?

The Hippies Tried to Tell Us

"America is great because America is good. If America ceases to be good, America will cease to be great." —*Alexis de Tocqueville*

"Children are not a distraction from more important work. They are the most important work." —*C. S. Lewis*

Chapter 5

Where America Went Wrong

When our family came to America in the '50s, we had the great American Dream. Now there is fear in the air...a consciousness that all is not well. Reality is setting in that we are losing America, losing our remarkable way of life, our personal freedoms and our blessings.

A Frenchman named Alexis de Tocqueville visited America in the early 1800s. He wanted to see what everyone was talking about. In Europe, there was great interest in America. He was looking for what made America great and wrote:

"I sought for the greatness and genius of America in her commodious harbors and her ample rivers, and it was not there. In the fertile fields and boundless prairies, and it was not there. In her rich mines and her vast world commerce, and it was not there. Not until I went into the churches of America and heard her pulpits, aflame with righteousness, did I understand the secret of her genius and power."

"America is great because she is good..." he observed.

One thing that surprised Tocqueville was that there was such a huge middle class in America. This stood out in sharp contrast to Europe. In Europe, there was a sea of poverty, the masses lived in very poor conditions, and only a small number of people, the aristocrats, could enjoy the privileges of wealth. In America, everyone could rise to enjoy the pleasures of the rich. And most did.

This large middle class in the United States has amazed my relatives in

Central America. They are surprised that my brother who did not have a college degree could earn a good wage in sales. In America, almost everyone could own a nice-sized home, own a car, and take great vacations. In third-world countries like Guatemala, only the elite, the professionals with degrees, and owners of successful businesses could rise to enjoy a lifestyle that is common for most American families. In Latin America and other third-world nations, like 1800s Europe, there are masses living in poverty and only the privileged few who live well.

In the United States, there was not a large chasm between the rich and the poor. And if we were poor, we knew it was only temporary because we had big dreams. We were working toward the American Dream. Maybe we were on the first rung, but we were climbing up the ladder of opportunity.

In the last thirty or forty years the American Dream has faded. In Los Angeles and other urban areas, city after city there are now more and more "barrios," or low-income areas. It is looking more like a third-world nation than the America we knew in the '50s, with the well-kept homes and tree-lined streets. Wrought-iron fences with sharp points and bars on windows have replaced the picketed fences, and green lawns are now cemented to allow for more cars. And in some places clotheslines are hung across yards while food trucks honk their horns. These food trucks come to the neighborhood to sell because many residents cannot drive or do not own a car. Paint is chipped, window shutters hang down, and old, broken items fill the yards. Poverty has increased in America.

Due to a moral decline and a soaring divorce rate, many women are now single and trying to raise their families alone. Most women lose more than half of their income after a divorce. And men who remarry struggle to help support two or even three families.

In the '60s, there were some people living in poverty. This has always been a great concern for Democrats. President Lyndon

Johnson sought to reduce the plight of the poor and declared a war on poverty. A new welfare system was created. Government checks were issued so that people had just enough to sustain themselves. But now forty years later and billions of dollars spent, the verdict is in. We did not eradicate poverty. It seems we only increased it. How could this be?

Not only do we have welfare recipients, but their children have become accustomed to a government paycheck as well. Poverty has become a way of life, not a temporary condition. Sadly, these government programs have demoralized the poor, destroyed initiative, and robbed many of their dignity. There is great despair over lost opportunity, and hope is gone. Rather than ending poverty, we have created generations of dependency.

There was one thing America forgot. Although President Johnson may have been well-intended, he did not follow the biblical admonition that "if you do not work, you should not eat." In fact it was this precept that saved the early American colonists. Settlement after settlement ended in starvation. First the new settlers tried to work as a commune. But in 1608, when Captain John Smith, the president of the colony, saw that the rich English aristocrats were not willing to work like the others, he laid down the law: "If you do not work, you shall not eat." Soon the pilgrims were producing enough food and established the first permanent colony, at Jamestown, Virginia.

As more Americans depended on the government for their paycheck, or their "daily bread," they no longer had to work at menial jobs. Why work when you can make the same amount staying home?

When people stopped working, low-income jobs became abundant. Our Mexican neighbors to the south peeked over the fence and said, "I can do that." So they came over. They came in vast numbers, and they continue to come. In the last twenty years, we have had a deluge of unskilled workers enter our country, legally and illegally. Our immigration system, border security, and corporations have encouraged them by looking away while our laws were violated. Who else would mow our lawns, take care of our children, wash our cars, pick our grapes, clean our offices, or work in our factories?

Many of these new immigrants are trying to raise large families on minimum-wage jobs that were never meant to support a family. These entry-level jobs—washing cars, cutting lawns, working in fast-food restaurants, and cleaning offices—were meant for high school and college students who were living at home. These jobs were meant to be temporary, while people could get further education and learn a trade.

As more and more cheap labor became available, wages have been suppressed. My daughter's father-in-law provided for his family as a meat cutter. Butchers used to make $20 an hour, enough to raise a family. But with more cheap labor competing for the jobs, wages came down to $17, then $14, and $12 an hour, making it more and more difficult to make a decent living cutting meat—much less raise a growing family. Today he would not be able to raise his family of six with the same standard of living doing the same work. New immigrants are living with low wages, but also our own sons and daughters are having a harder time finding work with a decent income to provide for their families.

Young teens have a hard time getting valuable work experience because young and older immigrants have come to take these jobs. Thus many youth lack the confidence, experience, and incentive they need to move forward to higher-paying jobs, college, or further training. Some young people are not challenged, not expected to work, and end up floating around wasting their youth, perpetually in a state of adolescence. Low-wage jobs are necessary for young people to get work experience and have the incentive to go to school and find training to get better-paying jobs. Rightly, many worry that the uncontrolled influx of illegal aliens suppresses wages. And low wages are destroying the America we once knew.

Additionally, immorality has also taken its toll on society. Many of our children are born out of wedlock. Single mothers struggle, and more and more children are growing up without their fathers. Young, able-bodied men, without the direction of a father, are turning to street gangs looking for a place to belong. Rather than finding work, they are joining ethnic gangs, supremacy groups, and dropping out not only from school but also out of society due to drug abuse and its cycle of crime and violence. And many are in prison.

The high divorce rate has left many men without a loving wife and satisfying physical relations. Some men have been demoralized by aggressive women, the cost of supporting previous families and have lost hope in marrying again. Some have turned to evil practices to meet their physical needs. Pornography has become a billion-dollar industry in the nation, eating at our souls, destroying marriage, and breaking down our very foundations. And some men caught up in these vile addictions have sought after innocent children, molesting young boys, or creating an industry of rape, the sex trafficking of young girls.

Everywhere sexual acts are commonplace: on television, in movies, on the Internet, and at parties. Needless to say, we have been ravaged by a moral decay. With the "free love" sexual revolution of the '60s and the development of contraceptives, we created the notion of unwanted babies. Consequently, since 1973, we have killed 57 million of our offspring through legalized abortion.

We have sunk to a new low, even allowing the gruesome practice of partial-birth abortion. Partial-birth abortion, the killing of a full-term, beautiful baby, is done by holding the baby in the womb at birth, brutally stabbing the baby in the back of the neck with scissors, and sucking its brains out. And incredibly, it is the mothers that have sought these procedures out! How barbaric we have become, killing our own fully formed, precious babies! As Scriptures predicted, "The love of many has [certainly] grown cold!" (Matt. 24:12).

Many forces have negatively affected our youth. Drug abuse is rampant, drinking is popular, and promiscuity is acceptable. As urban cities have grown, gang involvement has increased. Gangs terrorize neighborhoods and lure more and more young people into a life of violence and crime. Hard-working parents, single motherhood, or absent or incarcerated fathers have created a void in many children's lives. And character-crippling government programs have encouraged more out-of-wedlock children and removed the incentive to work.

Middle- or upper-class parents are busy also, supporting their upper-class life styles, climbing the corporate ladder, or just struggling to keep up. They work hard and long hours and are distracted with many activities, often leaving their "latchkey" children to fend for themselves.

Teens today, caught up in self-loathing, cut themselves, no longer feeling and yet they still cry for help. Anorexia or bulimia, the names of often-deadly eating disorders, are new words for our age.

Schools tell teens, "We know you are going to have sex, so here is where to get your condoms. Have sex, but do it responsibly." Planned Parenthood invades our schools: "Let us supply your condoms and when they do not work, let us pay for your abortions." Yes, Planned Parenthood gets richer while teens and their parents are left raising fatherless children and dealing with rejected, emotionally hurt daughters. And young men are put under horrendous burdens, supporting babies they never planned to raise. Under the guise of preventing sexually transmitted diseases, these invaders undercut parents' values and encourage young people to be sexually active. They care nothing of the ruined lives, heavy burdens, scars, and guilt they leave behind!

A national speaker for abstinence, Luis Galdamez, who tries to point young people in the right direction, once shared with me, "After I speak, sometimes the girls come up and say, 'I thought I had to have sex with the boys. Thank you for telling me that I don't have to.'" Many teens think sex is required of them. No one has told them differently.

Bristol Palin was thrown into the limelight when her mother, Sarah, ran for vice president of the United States. Bristol, being pregnant prior to being married, became a national symbol for teenage motherhood. Honorably, she wanted to use her experience to help others and became a national spokesperson for abstinence. But Bristol was caught off guard during an interview and said, "Abstinence is not always realistic." She was condemned as being hypocritical. But she was exactly right. Abstinence is the right path to take if you are looking forward to a good marriage, a life free of guilt, no disease, and children growing up with their fathers. But Bristol is right, as it is not a reasonable expectation in today's world with our present sex-crazed media and culture. And with comprehensive sex education in schools, the assumption is that most will have sex outside of marriage.

And, sadly, the assumption is probably right. According to David T. Moore in his small booklet, *America, You Are Too Young to Die,* in 1960, a survey showed that 53 percent of America's teenagers had never kissed, 57 percent had never "made out," and 92 percent of our teenagers were virgins. In 1990, just thirty years later, 75 percent of teens were sexually active by age eighteen. One in five loses her virginity before her thirteenth birthday. And 19 percent of America's teenagers have had more than four sexual partners before graduation from high school.

As teens try to naturally separate from their parents and check out other values, peer pressure and media messages can be overwhelming.

I had a neighbor who rented the house next door come to me and ask, "Can I just sit on the couch and watch? I want to see how you raise your kids." She had a five-year-old, an eight-year-old, and a stepdaughter who was sixteen-year-old. She said casually, "I just went and bought her some condoms—after all, it is the '90s, right?" Even a board member of our local YMCA told me her husband was buying condoms for their son. If parents, community leaders, and teachers do not believe in our children, why should our young people believe they can stay pure? And without God's supernatural help, it is very hard, if not impossible.

Churches do little in the way of sex education, leaving it up to the God-less public schools and tired, overworked parents, who themselves may have been or are promiscuous. Bristol Palin is right. Sexual purity is unrealistic when schools continue to lie to children, redefine words such as fetus and intimacy, provide condoms, and sneak young girls out for abortions. School sex education programs do little to promote a healthy respect for marriage. Cultural forces make it harder and harder for teens to plan ahead, set goals, finish school, get a decent job, and build a secure family.

Abstinence speaker Luis Galdamez brought a dozen teens to speak on behalf of Abstinence Sex Education to our public school board meeting. Thankful young people shared, "Finally, someone has told us how we can have a good marriage and a good future. I now have hope." Another shared, "My mother was divorced four times, and it hurt." One more told us, "My uncle has AIDS, and I was afraid. Now I know what to do." Teens who have experienced the consequences of our sex-crazed culture are grateful to learn of a way out. Many want to start over and live right. But where is the encouragement?

As vice-presidential candidate Sarah Palin and many other parents know, life does not always turn out as we hope or as we have taught our children. Sometimes the culture and peer pressure is too much for teens who are normally trying to separate from their parents and become more independent. We all fail and make mistakes, but when we fall, we do not need to stay and wallow in the mud; we can get up, clean ourselves off with God's forgiveness, and keep on going in the right direction, being confident that God can use even our mistakes and turn all things together for good.

England's former Prime Minister Margaret Thatcher spoke in Anaheim at a national school board conference, and I was fortunate enough to hear her. She talked about education and about the importance of giving kids a moral compass. She said they sometimes get lost, but if they have the moral compass, they can find their way home again. So many of our children do not have a compass, much less a moral compass!

As I have raised my five children in a nice middle-class neighborhood in Orange County, I have learned that there are certain questions that you should not ask your teen's friends. Never ask, "How many children are in your family?" Pain and confusion move across the teens' faces. After a pause, they say, "Well, counting my father's family in New York and my stepdad's other family, I think we have nine children. But I am not sure." Another question to be avoided is, "What do your parents do for a living?" Again confusion arises, "Which parents do you want to know about?" Life has become very complicated and very painful!

And while the Frenchman, Alexis de Tocqueville, observed in the 1800's that *America is great because she is good,* it is also true that if *America ever ceases to be good, she will cease to be great.*

Somehow we seem to have lost that greatness.

Chapter 6
The Devastation of Our Youth

While many of these cultural forces have devastated the lives of our youth in the suburbs, it has risen to catastrophic proportions in the inner cities. Welfare policies discourage marriage, discourage work, and place young children under unbearable situations.

Over-crowded high-rise apartments are common. Many families have to share one home. A teacher reported that a girl in her classroom could count twenty-one people who lived in her house. And often, whole families of four or more share one room. According to a nonprofit newsletter from Kid Works, one young girl complained to a mentor that with so many people living in the house, she could never get in to use the bathroom. Her mentor showed her how she could go to the bathroom in a diaper.

These close quarters leave children with no place to do their homework, no freedom to be themselves, and no lawns to run and play in.

Even our schools struggle to give children grass to play in. Often school playgrounds are worn out because many soccer teams, both youth and adult, use the playfields during after-school hours, and there is no time to reseed. Finally, after great discussion and public opinion, our school board decided to close some of the fields and allow the grass to grow.

We took some children from our after-school clubs on an outing at a park, and a few children were in awe. They were impressed to see so much green grass. The same thing happens when we take these children to the beach. Santa Ana is about thirteen miles from the ocean, but many children have never seen the ocean. Some children have been surprised by freeways because they have never been on them before. Parents work six days a week and need to clean house and rest on Sunday after Mass. Many parents do not drive or cannot afford cars.

In such crowded living spaces, often children are exposed to sexual activities at an early age and are vulnerable to sexual abuse from other renters as well as family members. Drug abuse and alcoholism is prevalent, which often leads to sexual and verbal abuse or domestic violence.

Sadly, many young children also find themselves trying to raise their drug- or alcohol-addicted parents. One of the boys in our boxing club lives above the old street boxing gym in a small room with both of his alcoholic parents. Once we started our boxing club tutoring program, adding donated computers and more caring mentors, this young thirteen-year-old boy soared.

We took him to a community meeting to share his story. There he stood a little nervous, dark haired, light skinned with a few freckles, in a white shirt and tie. "I used to get bad grades all the time, I mean F's, and I am in a continuation school for bad behavior, but since I have been in the tutoring program, I am now getting A's and B's. They just said I could go to regular school again."

The injustices of life, particularly verbal, emotional, and phys-ical abuse in the barrios, create angry young men. One judge, Judge Hudson, had enough. He began speaking to groups, "Who will come and mentor my angry young men?" He passionately pleaded. Life is not fair—young boys are supposed to grow up playing marbles and baseball and resting under a tree dreaming of a happy future. But instead these vulnerable youth are verbally and physically abused by alcoholic or drug-crazed parents.

When I was waiting outside the boxing club talking to some

boys, an intoxicated mother came out and started laying into her son. I do not know if she saw me or if it just did not matter. She called him some of the vilest names and accused him of sending her boyfriend away. I was so disturbed, it took me days to recover from the verbal abuse, and it wasn't even directed at me. I had never heard such language and rage. I was stunned! I never heard people talk that way, much less to their own child. It pierced my heart, and I know it hurt his. How could someone live, much less succeed, with vile condemnation day after day? Her poison spilled out, defiling his soul.

Every year we take inner-city children for a week of camp in the mountains. At camp, we had a young girl who always closed her fist while saying, "So you want me to beat you up?" Our counselor made it a joke and closed her fists too and said, "So you want me to beat you up?" It became the saying all week: "It is time for breakfast, we need to go, or 'do you want me to beat you up?'" "It is bed time, you need to get in your sleeping bags, or do you want me to beat you up?" They joked.

But it was no joke. As the week went by, the young girl opened up. She shared her story. Her father would become enraged when he knew his wife had visited friends. He would take a knife to his wife's blouse and threaten to rip it off of her with the knife. After many such threats, the girl could not take it anymore, and she ran to the neighbor, and they called the police.

The police came and took her dad away. But as he left, he glared at her and yelled, "I will kill you for this!" She and her family lived in fear, dreading the day he would get out of jail. The day arrived; her father came to the door knocking wildly. A family member heard the commotion, came out, and shot the father, killing him right there on the front porch.

This young girl was no longer scared but she was scarred. She had lived with fear and now, rather than relief, she is left with guilt and deep sorrow. After hearing her story and providing some hugs, the counselor asked her if she was still afraid, "What are you most afraid of?" She replied, "When I get older and marry, I am afraid my husband will threaten to tear off my clothes with a knife."

Children see unimaginable things: their mothers beat up, or threatened with fists, guns, or knives. Many live in fear and anger. Going to and from school is also frightening—they have to watch their backs, as someone might want their lunch money or want to retaliate for some gesture or look that was made. Every day many students in America are shot or killed on their way to, from, or at school. Children should not be walking in fear.

Just outside one of our high schools, right after school, in front of young people walking home from school, a boy was shot down. It moved the community, articles were written, and prayer vigils sprang up, but what can they do? Another boy is shot, another boy goes to jail, and another mother cries herself to sleep.

When I served on the city's anti-gang commission, EPIC (Early Prevention and Intervention Commission), we received monthly reports of where the shootings occurred and how many died the following weeks. The police sergeant told me that there used to be reasons when a boy was shot—they used to know each other—but now it is random and senseless.

My friend's nephew, who lived in northern California, was stopped by a gang member with a gun. "Who do you claim?" the gang member demanded, meaning, "What is your gang affiliation?" The boy was not part of any gang. He froze and did not know what to say. "Who do you claim?" the gang member demanded. "I am an American," he blurted out. And the gangster pulled the trigger and shot him dead.

When I speak to groups of young people in our inner city, sometimes they will line up and ask for prayer. Their number one prayer request is for their father, their brother, their uncle, or their mom who is in prison. Second, the teens ask for prayer to finish school. With life in such chaos, overcrowded conditions, with no place to do homework, and language barriers to overcome, these wounded spirits hope to barely make it through school. At graduation ceremonies, one of my favorite parts of being a school board member is getting to shake the hands of those that made it. But of course, there are many others that don't graduate, often 30 to 50 percent.

A thirteen-year-old White junior higher from a local church rode his one-wheel bike into Santa Ana. He came to talk and do magic tricks with the kids on the street. He was unprepared for what he would learn. As he prayed with them, a reoccurring request was that there would be dinner that night. Besides praying for family members in prison and school that was hard, they just wanted to have dinner. Many of us have never had to wonder if there will be dinner at night. Kate, one of our elementary club leaders, also reported some of the children in her after-school club were not eating dinner. Yes, here in Orange County, the richest place on the planet, children are going to bed hungry. I said, "Forget the cookies! Let's make sandwiches" for our after-school club snacks.

According to Big Data Partners, a marketing website, Santa Ana is the sixth most Spanish-speaking city in the United States, with 69.7 percent Spanish-speaking households. And for many new immigrants, Santa Ana is the gateway to the United States. Many immigrants come to the United States via Santa Ana. Some stay, but many also move away to other cities once they get accustomed to this new way of life. While it is hard to know, half of the people in Santa Ana are said to be illegally here.

In the '90s, California Governor Pete Wilson proposed a ballot initiative, Proposition 187, that would deny social services and free public education to children who are here illegally. ABC television news anchor Jim Avila came to televise a program from Century High School. It is still fresh in my memory. During the debate, a student shouted, "How would you like it if you grew up illegal?"

It was something I had not contemplated. For some, this is their identity. This is a heavy weight on a young person struggling to find his place in the world. Where do I belong? And doesn't your identity affect what you do? If you already broke the law and are illegal, isn't it harder to respect the law?

Parents are deported and children are left with aunts, uncles, brothers, sisters, and grandmas. Also, when parents are incarcerated for stealing, domestic violence, or selling drugs, the children have to move to live with grandma.

A boy from one of our school character clubs saw it happen. His father who had left came back home and shot his mother right in front of his eyes. Can you imagine the pain and horror? No mother, and now a father in jail. Who will raise him and his brothers and sister? Our elementary club leaders attended the funeral and gave support to the boy.

Many teachers complain, "How can I teach the children when half of the class is not there at the end of the year and new ones are coming in all the time?" A student asked our after-school club leader, "I have to move to a different school, but can I still come to your after-school club, even if I am in a different school?" "Yes, of course" was the answer.

Another tragedy is the abandonment of children by their own fathers. Once people settle in, the communities are tight; people know who each other are. Many grow up their entire lives in one neighborhood. A boy shared his aching heart with a counselor. "I walk down the sidewalk, and I see this guy walking on the other side of the street. I know he is my dad, but he never says anything. I wish he would say, 'Hi, Son.' If he would only say, 'Hi, Son,'" he lamented in great anguish. "I wish he would just say, 'Hi, Son.'" Being abandoned is very sad, and being rejected is really tough, but not even being acknowledged certainly brings despair.

So many children grow up without their fathers. One such man, a coworker now in his forties, asked me a strange question.

"I did not grow up with a father. I do not even know what a father does. What is a man? What does a man do?"

No one had ever asked me that before. I paused. Then something came out of my mouth. "A man mows the lawn." "Now that was profound!" I scolded myself. "Why did I say that?" How would that help this man-boy?

Then I got it. "A man owns something—a car, a house, a family, and he is responsible for it, and he takes care of it. A man works to own or build something, perhaps a business or family, and has to nurture it."

Did that mean this forty-five-year-old had to give up riding his bike, going to Magic Mountain, or buying boom boxes for the back of his car? Many older men in the inner city are caught in a time warp, never growing up, never assuming the responsibilities of a man. It is not that they are irresponsible; it is just that home ownership seems out of reach, marriage is not expected, and having out-of-wedlock children is commonplace. Gangs, drugs, crime, and prison terms steal their youth. It is just that they never learned how to become a man. No one was there to show them.

Working in our organization, he had proved he could take care of a program and be responsible for young people. When interest rates were low, I encouraged him to buy a house. We had been steadily paying him for ten years, and we expected to continue. "Instead of you renting a room in someone else's house, why don't you be the one that rents rooms to others, and maybe you can pay the house off by the time you are ready to retire," I suggested. Now he owns a house and, yes, he mows the lawn!

While no one is there to teach our young boys how to be responsible men, ironically, the schools are there to teach our young boys how to have sex and create more fatherless children.

Another female coworker who came from Mexico, and I hear it is true in Guatemala also, shared that it was a cultural practice to take boys when they turned sixteen to a prostitute to have him prove he is a man. This actually happened to a Hispanic friend of mine, and now he has three children living with three different mothers in Los Angeles, San Diego, and Riverside. Each weekend he drives in all directions to pick up his kids for the weekend. He works very hard to provide a house and individual bedrooms for his children. And before he spends any of the money he makes, he has to pay $1200 a month in child support! No wonder he now believes in abstinence.

While Latin Americans have their strange rituals, here in America we allow deceivers such as Planned Parenthood, who disguise themselves as Camp Fire Girls (or Latino Health Access), to enter our schools to promote the SIECUS Guidelines (Sexuality Information and Education Council of the United States), which tell our children to be responsible for their sexual pleasure and disregard their parents' old-fashioned views.

With the SIECUS Guidelines, teens are taught "to be in charge of their sexual pleasure." While discouraging intercourse, they encourage teens to have sex in other ways, through masturbation, oral sex, anal sex, and same-sex experiences. While this advice may seem shocking to parents, to those who want to limit population and reduce birthrates, this is a rational utilitarian solution to young hormones and an over-crowded world.

Our elected school board members who vote for programs that follow the SEICUS Guidelines for Comprehensive Sexuality Education lead teens into unhealthy, deviant sexual practices. The SEICUS Guidelines actually suggest our sons and daughters take showers with their boyfriends and use erotic videos. The goal is pleasure—not caring committed families and beautiful babies.

Teens are told to use condoms. Local community clinics are recommended by school sex-education programs. And, of course, these clinics are ready to provide the condoms free of charge, as promotional tools, knowing full well the teens will return for a free (taxpayer paid) abortion when they fail or are not used. These con artists and traitors run to the bank with bags full of money, not caring that it is the parents and teenage girls who are truly left holding the bag!

Many Hispanics are pro-life and choose to let their baby live, much to the chagrin of the abortion mills. Some boys step up to the plate and father the child. But when they don't, young girls are left raising yet another fatherless child.

I was at a California School Board Association conference in San Diego, attending a presentation on the new mental health law passed by the voters, when I heard a startling statistic. One out of five Latina girls considers suicide, and a large number actually attempt it. According to a 2012 report from the Center for Disease Control and Prevention, 13.5 percent of Hispanic female students, grades 9 through 12, admitted attempting suicide—significantly higher than blacks (8.8 percent) and non-Hispanics (7.9 percent). Overall it is thought that 17 percent of Latino girls actually consider suicide and are twice as likely to attempt suicide. In some areas like New York or the Bronx, 21 percent of Latina girls have attempted suicide, and it is attributed to a "clash of cultures within the Latino immigrant community" (http://www.nydailynews.com/life-style/health/suicide-rates-latina-teens-skyrockets-new-heights-immigrant-moms-daughters-weigh-article-1.125351).

Young girls in our Hispanic communities have a lot of pressure. They have the regular pressures of life in the inner city and face difficulties at school due to cultural and language barriers, but they also are bombarded by conflicting messages. Grandparents want them to get married early, single parents need them at home to take care of siblings, and the American culture tells them to get a college education and put their career goals first.

These girls with Catholic pro-life values are pressured by their peers, the culture, and school sex-education programs to have sex or to have an abortion. Sex Education programs, promoted by Planned Parenthood, tell teens their parents' values are old-fashioned. And when the girls get pregnant, if they keep their baby, the teen mothers feel that they will never be successful, have a career, or go to college. And when the boyfriend leaves, they feel rejected and alone. Often grandmas are called upon to raise their grandchildren. And on the other hand, those that do abort their babies face emotional trauma, guilt, and later remorse. Additionally, many teens enter adolescence with inner trauma, as sexual abuse is common.

I was sitting on the stage dressed in my red suit, with a beautiful gold corsage on my lapel. I looked at the high school auditorium filled with graduating junior high school students. The girls' dark hair was curled or put up and accented with fancy hair barrettes. The boys' neckties, neatly tied, stuck out beneath their graduating gowns. I knew for many that this was their last graduation ceremony. With high dropout rates, a little more than half would be there four years later to walk across the field.

I wanted to encourage those who were struggling. I gave my regular "God Allows for U-Turns" speech. I loved to use the story of the famous neurosurgeon Dr. Benjamin Carson who turned his life around. When he was in fifth grade, he was failing in every subject and getting into trouble. And he and his mother were often called to the principal's office.

His mother, a simple washwoman who scrubbed floors for a living, said, "Ben, we have to do something about this. From now on, you have to go every week to the library, find a book, and read it. On Friday you will need to turn in a written book report to me." Ben first got books with just pictures in them. When he ran out of those books, he read books that had just a few words under the pictures, and then he read books with short paragraphs and a few pictures. Once those were all read, he read books without pictures.

Soon he became interested in what his teachers were saying. To his teachers' surprise, he was the one that was always raising his hand in class to answer the questions. When he graduated from high school, he had full paid scholarships to every Ivy-League school in the nation. He could not decide which one to go to, so he said, "Whichever school wins the College Bowl this Sunday, that is where I am going to go." College Bowl is a television program that featured college teams competing academically. Yale won that Sunday, so that is where he went to school.

Every week, his mother took the book report, looked it over carefully, and told him she was proud of him. Only later did he come to realize that his mother could not read. I hoped parents with low education levels in the auditorium would be empowered to hold their sons and daughters accountable. And perhaps on this graduation day, some of the graduates would decide to do something different, change course, and apply themselves to their studies.

Then our young school board member, a beautiful thirty-three-year-old, came up to speak. I cannot quite remember what she said, but it went something like this: "All of you should be like me; I am a successful lawyer. I have gone to college and achieved my dreams." I looked at the crowd filled with proud parents, grandparents, and many extended family members. I recalled someone sharing with me that grandmas in these immigrant communities, many who live with their children, tell their young granddaughters, who are fourteen, fifteen, or sixteen, to put on lipstick. They say, "You need to find a man to provide for you and take care of you." They were married at sixteen, and so were their daughters. Now it was time for their granddaughters. What were they thinking as they listened to this lovely school board member? I also knew many young girls just wanted to be mothers.

I was a mother of five, actually pregnant with my fifth, when I was elected to the school board. During my first election campaign, I would say, "I have a baby in diapers, someone in elementary school, one in junior high, and another one in high school, and one on the way." I loved being a mother, and I knew just what this unmarried thirty-three-year-old was missing...the love and kisses of young children. "Can women really have it all?" I wondered.

At election time, because the press covered our debate on sex education, this young school board member inferred that she supported an abstinence sex education program. Yet rumors were flying that this young, liberal school board member was working behind the scenes with the fifteen teenagers who were recruited to bring in the abominable SIECUS Guidelines for Comprehensive Sexuality Education. She, like most Progressives, misrepresented herself to the parents and voters. Campaign fundraising fliers were also circulated that she strongly supported the gay agenda.

It is a tragedy that innocent young people are blatantly used and manipulated to bring in the World Center for Populations Options agenda of population control. The fifteen teenagers recruited by "Camp Fire USA (Camp Fire Boys and Girls) Speak Out Program" and funded by the California Wellness Foundation did not fully comprehend what they were asking for when they walked in with the destructive SIECUS Guidelines under their arms. This deceitful effort in Santa Ana was but one of a dozen such initiatives in California promoting policies and education.

A few years later, our Latina role model school board member was pregnant and subsequently married the state official who fathered the child. Her wedding was two months before her due date, and she invited many friends and influential people from the community.

Previously, I had been unhappy that she had tried to hide the success of the fundamental schools by changing the method of acceptance from "first come, first served" to a lottery. Fundamental schools did all the right things: they taught the kids in English, taught reading with intensive phonics instruction, and insisted the children memorize all of the math facts. And their test scores were high, in the seventieth and eightieth percentile, while most of our schools were scoring in the eleventh to thirtieth percentile. These schools also had a patriotic emphasis.

Parents who were aware of the schools camped out for a week in advance to make sure their children were able to attend these high-scoring schools. The fundamental schools were called schools of choice, but the problem was that it was a well-kept secret. I asked that a letter describing the schools be given out at each of our schools. Unfortunately, the district made twenty-five copies for each school and put them behind the counter and gave them only to parents who asked for the flyers. I had raised my children and lived between a neighborhood school and a fundamental school, but I did not know the difference until I came on the school board. Because of the camping out, the newspapers gave these excellent schools much publicity, which caused more parents to demand this kind of education for their children and in the end pushed the district into creating more fundamental schools. When I first was elected to the school board, there were three fundamental schools. When I left, there were nine.

I could never understand why the schools did not copy the success they had in the district. When we finally, after huge battles, implemented English instruction, phonics reading, and traditional math, as was used in the fundamental schools, all of the schools' test scores went up.

We have always stressed that parent involvement is important and that parents need to advocate for their children. Camping out for a good education was a way for the parents to vote with their feet. Now this young Latina board member who supported all of the new failing teaching methods wanted to make getting a good education only a chance, a crap shoot by using a lottery system, rather than first come, first serve.

She was so happy that she had gone to Sacramento, our state's capitol, to get the legal opinion to support the lottery system, as a means to get accepted at a fundamental school. It seems liberals will go to extraordinary lengths to destroy good education.

Counting the days back from her due date, it appeared she was crawling in bed with the very elected official who gave her the legal opinion on the lottery!

Years later, she ran for a county elective office with her husband's campaign money. It was reported that she was addicted to drugs. She was disgraced when sex tapes came out showing her under the influence of drugs while having sex with her drug pusher. It became obvious she did not believe in abstinence, as her campaign statement indicated.

This is not to single out this board member's lack of honesty or her desire to deceive the voters. I have observed that most liberal board members have to misrepresent themselves on their ballot statements. It is the only way they can get elected. They understand that their positions are contrary to the will of the people.

This sad saga is included to show how much God cares about the children. He will expose those who try to destroy them and their futures.

How long will we tolerate the devastation of our youth? How long will we tolerate elected officials that deceive the voters? How long will we vote time and time again in the name of kindness to continue to fund devastating welfare schemes and deceivers like Planned Parenthood?

I am asking, "How long?" How long will our children cry from sexual, physical, and verbal abuse? How long will it be before we comfort the crying mothers and encourage young girls in their despair? How long before men will show young boys how to be caring responsible men?

God is a father to the fatherless and ministers through his people. When will we start caring for those who cannot care for themselves?

Chapter 7

The Hippies Tried to Tell Us

It was November 22, 1963. I was a teenager in high school when President John Kennedy died. We all remember where we were; I was a cheerleader waiting excitedly in my classroom for the bell to ring so we could hop in cars and carpool to Santa Maria, five hours away, to a CIF football game. Then the announcement came over the loudspeaker: "The president has been shot." It changed the whole mood. What did this mean?

Maybe it was an outward sign that something had died in America...something important.

Growing up as a teenager in the '60s, I had long hair, wore the long skirts in earthen colors, loose blouses, and dangling beads. I also had large, brightly colored flower earrings to go with the neon clothing. We wore bell-bottom pants. For my eighth-grade graduation, I ratted my hair and wore a beehive, a very high, poufy hairdo with a kind of French roll.

We walked through the hippie colonies, with beads hanging in the doorways, candles and incense burning. The dudes sitting on the floor smiled strangely and gave us two open fingers, the peace symbol. We often picked up hitchhikers and took them as far as we could. One boy in our church named Jack hitchhiked and never came back. It was eerie that a popular song sang, "Hit the road, Jack, and don't you come back no more...no more."

We had a close-knit family. Dad always told us, "When you have children, keep them close to your vest." Our family went to church together; we even prayed and read the Bible together at home. Dad would teach us magic tricks, and mom would teach us gymnastics in our living room. We had the greatest family vacations traveling through Mexico to Guatemala, or traveling up the California coast, camping out. I remember when we slept in a large Indian tepee. I remember my brother playing his harmonica as we sang, "Tie me kangaroo, ye sport. Tie me kangaroo sport." And driving with seven people crammed in one car was not always easy. Dad would slap one of us once-in-a-while, telling us to settle down in the back seat. But he always made our trips fun. Dad had been a tour guide in Guatemala, so we seldom missed anything on our trips. He took us to museums in downtown L.A. And on weekends, we enjoyed drives along the beautiful California coastline.

We went to church camps with our age group at Cedar Crest and Forest Home and sometimes rented cabins with our family at Hume Lake in the Sequoias. In high school, I was involved in student government, was a flag twirler on the cheer squad, and a homecoming princess. My dad always said with great enthusiasm that we girls looked like "mangoes." I think he loved mangoes.

As a history/social science major in college, at first I thought that the '60s, with its counterculture revolution, the hippie movement and sexual revolution, had destroyed the family. But now I have changed my mind. One night during my run for Congress, I spoke at a CRA political meeting in a home. I decided not to use notes that night, and as I talked about America's decline, I realized it was Rosie's fault! Since my name is Rosie, and I used the famous Rosie the Riveter "We can do it!" poster in my congressional campaign, this realization was intriguing. As I addressed national issues and their solutions, I began to see more clearly the problems our nation faces today.

I have always listened to the news and enjoyed discussing politics, but before running for Congress, I had been busy looking after my five children and my local community; serving as an elected official on the school board; and worrying about the children who could not read, do math, or speak English. We also started a nonprofit organization and were busy providing after-school tutoring programs for inner-city at-risk children and teens. At the local level, in the public schools and out in our communities, I was seeing firsthand how our social fabric was falling apart.

But the question now was, How did this exceptional country, the land of opportunity, with its unusual greatness, get to this low point?

World War II was different from other wars like the Vietnam War or the Korean War. This was a world war; many nations were involved. Everyone at home got involved, too. The American people stood behind the war effort. Some sold war bonds. Others planned USO entertainment events for the troops. The theme was "United we stand." All the magazines were asked to do covers with the theme. People were energized, united, and ready to work together for the cause.

The media was different back then. People gathered around their radios to hear the news. It was personal because many local boys went to war. It affected almost every family.

The men left, and the women kept the economy going by working in factories. They not only took the jobs the men left behind but also made bombs, guns, ammunition, airplanes, and tanks for the war. There was a lot to do, and everyone did his or her part to pitch in. Women stepped up to the plate. This was a good thing.

Rosie the Riveter became the symbol of war support. The poster of Rosie, with her scarf around her head, her blue overalls, and her sleeves rolled up for work, was used to recruit more women into the workforce. The sign said, "We can do it!" All of the "Rosies" rolled up their sleeves and went off to work. And, like the sign said, they did it!

The war ended in victory, and the men came home. And you know what that means? Yes, indeed. Babies, babies…lots of babies were born. It was called a baby boom. Today, many of us older people born in the late 1940s are called baby boomers.

The men were back, and the babies were here. It was time for Rosie to come home and raise the children. But Rosie liked working; it gave her a sense of accomplishment. And if she stayed at work while her husband worked, too, they could afford a bigger house. And, of course, with all of these children, they needed a bigger house.

Dad went one way to work and mother another, so now they needed a second car. And soon they needed a nicer-looking car. That is, if they wanted to "keep up with the Joneses."

It soon became evident that they were both rushing off to work in the morning with not enough time for a relaxing breakfast. The kids had to get to school, and mom and dad had different times that they had to leave. Now they really needed a toaster, a blender, a washing machine, and other gadgets to make their lives more convenient and expedient. Mom did not have time to use that old wringer washing machine, ice boxes needed to be bigger and more efficient, and those new steam irons were essential. The larger family income fueled the demand for new and better products, à la the Disneyland ride in Tomorrowland called the "Carousel of Progress."

Soon Americans were in love with their homes, their cars, and their gadgets, and although they saved time, these all took more work to maintain. Both parents worked, had more responsibilities at home, more rooms to decorate, more cars to wash, and more pools to clean. Parents worked hard, were tired…too tired for sex, or was that a headache? And yes, they were both too tired to spend much time with their kids. They tried to fool themselves. "It isn't the quantity; it is the quality of the time we spend with the kids that counts." "If I have less kids, I will have more to give each child." "Kids cost a lot, especially with all of those daycare costs, dance lessons, and college costs, and we now have the house and the pool and the cars and the gadgets."

Soon everyone was having two children, maybe three if you did not get a boy and a girl. In many cases, raising kids was no longer the center of the marriage relationship; there was more time to pursue personal interests, take yoga classes, golf with the guys, and make travel plans. Soon parents were sidetracked from the key responsibility of raising kids. Young children were ushered off to day care, and then later became latchkey children who went home to an empty house. No longer were there mothers like Mrs. Cleaver or Harriett Nelson, with the cookies and milk to greet you as you came home from school.

There were big changes in America. Now American homes also had become war zones, a war that "Rosie" could not fix. The roles of fathers and mothers were challenged and then blurred. Mom had no time to wear pearls and make a dessert just to take it away from their children when they misbehaved. Husbands no longer came home to a glass of iced tea, slippers, a newspaper, and a clean house, much less a kiss from his awaiting wife. And if mother had to work and then cook dinner, why couldn't Dad also cook sometimes? Or at least he could do the dishes. And why did Mom have to do the laundry all of the time? And who will bathe the kids? There were bitter words exchanged as men and women tried to find new roles and divide up the responsibilities. Homes had become like the popular 1989 movie, *The War of the Roses*. The movie illustrated the difficulties of these new relationships, the option of divorce, and a couple's battle over material possessions and custody of the kids.

In fact, the movie had such a cultural impact that in Germany they coined a new word, "Rosenkrieg," taken from *The War of the Roses* to describe the often vicious and painful process of dividing up material possessions and custody of the kids.

As children were shuffled off to day care, some of those children came to our house to be babysat by my mom. Diapers were now changed by strangers. Where were the little kisses? Somehow the children did not get as many kisses as they needed.

The children were also tired and cranky, worn out from being away from their parents all day.

I once heard a hippie say, "I don't want to be like my dad, have a briefcase, and work ten to thirteen hours a day." Sons and daughters watched as their parents tried to keep up with the Joneses. But somehow the Joneses kept getting bigger houses and fancier cars. "I don't want to keep up with the Joneses!" the hippie said. So what were they to do? They did not want their parents' lifestyle. They felt something was missing. So they took off.

All they wanted was a little *peace* and some *love*. They longed for a simpler life. "I do not need the gadgets, the fancy houses, the cars. Just give me love and peace." The grass always looks greener on the other side. And the flower children took off hitchhiking in search of peace and love. And they certainly found "the grass."

The parents scratched their heads, "We worked so hard for them, giving them this beautiful house, all of these great toys, and now look at how ungrateful they are? And that beard and those clothes! How are they going to get a good job looking like that!?" "You have to grow up and cut your hair. Shave that beard, too! I do not want you in this house looking like that." And their response was, "OK, I'll leave." And they did.

They left home. They set out hitchhiking, went to Haight-Ashbury in San Francisco, and found some love. It was called "free love." They joined love communes and found some drugs to ease their pain. Some went south, and kept on hitchhiking and walked all over Central America and into South America. They were now fatherless and motherless to some extent. We all tried to figure it out. What were the hippies all about? What were they trying to say? I don't think we got it.

They left home and not only rejected their parents' lifestyle but also their parents' values. They rejected the materialism. But far more serious than the rejection of their parents was the rejection of their Christian heritage. With no values, no rudder to steer their boats, they soon lost their conscience and lost their way. But they found each other in communes, and some fell prey to cults. The Charles Mansons or Jim Jones' of this world had become the new father figures.

The invention of contraceptives did not help the situation, giving a false security. Sometimes they failed or were not used, then "free love" led to the notion of "unwanted babies," and the solution became abortion.

Now without a home and parents to support them, and without values, these hippie "kids" sank deeper and deeper into guilt and depression. They had cut the cord at home. Basically, they were homeless and hopeless. "Here, try this grass, you will feel better." For a while, they could forget what they lost at home: a mom, a dad, a sister, or a brother, and all the material goods. Their hearts still longed for love and peace. And that was stronger.

Soon grass, marijuana, was not enough; they turned to harder drugs to anesthetize their guilt and sadness. All they wanted was a loving home, a refuge from the world, and a caring mom and dad that loved each other, but now they were called "potheads."

Sadly, now many years after the "peace children" grew up, many are still "potheads." I heard a statistic that there are more drug addicts today who are in their fifties and sixties than the younger generation. As the hippies turned to harder drugs, their life further deteriorated. Some were able to pick themselves up and return home. And while some got off the drugs, others could not kick the habit and today continue to lean on government Methadone clinics for their daily fix while working as lawyers and doctors.

Others escaped the hippie "counterculture revolution" and the drug culture, and continued to try to keep up with the Joneses. We did not get the message; we missed what the hippies were saying, so we stayed on the treadmill in "the rat race." We just did not know how to get off. So we ran and ran, and we continue to run. We still require the latest car, the latest CD, the latest iPhone or iPad. And even if it we could not afford them, that's OK. We have a pocket full of plastic. "Let's see, should we use Discovery, B of A, or Chase? Is it Visa or MasterCard?" Being $20,000, 40,000, or more in debt has become commonplace. The rats, sadly, have been buried under a mountain of debt. They run slower, but they still run.

True to form, our government has reflected what we have become. It spends and prints and spends and prints. Not only personal debt was mounting but also government debt has sky-rocketed, and with increased taxes that pay for ever-increasing entitlements, we have to run and run some more.

At first, working was an option for women. Most home mort-gages required one income. But as our homes got bigger, working became mandatory because now home mortgages required two incomes. Even after the kids grew up and left, mothers stayed on the job.

Women were no longer pampered homemakers working at home, preparing a warm dinner, and waiting for the kids to arrive. Marriage lost its glow. With the increased tension of way-ward children, the adjustment to new roles, and the pressures of a career, marriage was strained until it broke. And divorce hurt.

And if they were divorced, many women spiraled into poverty, losing 40 to 70 percent of their income, and now they struggled to raise and support their families alone. Working was no longer a choice but a necessity. It was very difficult trying to be a mother and a father to their children. Dealing with the emotions of both their children and a past spouse also was stressful. And it was tough, with their own emotional, physical, and material needs going unmet. Many lost hope in traditional marriage. It was just a painful dream. The mere mention of marriage with its dashed hopes brought pain. This seems to be the real war on women.

Contrast this to an observation by Alexis de Tocqueville who wrote about the state of women in America in the early 1900s: "I have no hesitation in saying that although the American woman never leaves her domestic sphere and is in some respects very dependent within it, nowhere does she enjoy a higher station. And if anyone asks me what I think the chief cause of the extraordinary prosperity and growing power of this nation, I should answer that it is due to the superiority of their women."

In today's world, the question is, can women have it all? And my answer is, yes! It is just that we need to prioritize and understand our calling as women. It is obvious that women have children, and they start there in their tummies. I always say, "Our small babies come out of the womb and move into our hearts." They need us. And frankly, we need them. Their demanding care makes us less self-centered, more caring, and stronger individuals. So when it is time to have children, it is time to have children. It is not time for anything else. It is not time for demanding careers or full-time college. We are "mothers," and we have been given the greatest title in the world.

As our children grow up and enter school, our community needs us. Even while raising children, we can be reading about the needs around us, writing letters to legislators, volunteering at our local school, at after-school clubs, or feeding the homeless and supporting other needy families. We can take our children with us as we volunteer, teaching them also to care for others. All of my five children have developed caring hearts.

Because they have been exposed to the needs of others they have taught autistic children, adopted both older and younger orphans, created an organization to address homelessness and volunteered at our non-profit workplace training boutiques. They have also helped at soup kitchens and senior centers. My son led a weekly after school club when he was sixteen and put on many youth entertainment events. These activities have helped them discover their strengths. And in the process they have developed great leadership skills.

As we volunteer for nonprofit causes, we have great

opportunities to develop our own gifts and talents. Assisting in a nonprofit office doing the accounting, coordinating fund-raising events, creating craft projects for after school programs, teaching character lessons, coaching a sport, making cookies or volunteering at a non-profit thrift store help us develop our own passions and skills. There are endless ways to help make our communities better places, and our kids can do it right along with us.

After we have strengthened and encouraged our husband, raised our children, and reached out to your community, it may be time to start a business or work part time. Your husband, with your support, perhaps has been able to put away some savings. These funds can be starting capital for your own catering business, craft shop, or sports gear store. Perhaps your husband is ready to launch out and start his own business, and you can assist him. Or maybe it is now time to work in the corporate world, creating more retirement income. To everything there is a season. Proverbs 31 paints a beautiful picture of a woman who has it all! The virtuous woman makes sure her home is well taken care of, as well as caring for her children and her community. She reaches out to the poor and needy, and she buys and sells items and purchases property.

While raising my children, we heard that they were discussing sex education in the school district. A couple of friends and I started to attend the school board meetings. We had learned about a wonderful sex-education program that was being used by public schools in San Diego. It was called Sex Respect. It taught respect for marriage, self-control, and cautioned teens to wait. It had been used in San Diego County with much success. After a year of creating reports and speaking to the board at public meetings, the verdict was in. Sex Respect was accepted! My friends and I were so happy when it passed the board vote and became a program in the schools.

Several years later when my son was in junior high, I attended a sex education orientation for parents and asked about the Sex Respect program that was on the list. I noticed that the program was now scaled back to two days instead of the five days. "Oh, that program," the teacher said. "We threw that out years ago! When I got a divorce and had to be a mother and a father to my children, I realized that there is no such thing as a role for a mother or a father." Roles had become so confused. In her brokenness and pain, she threw out the idea of the family, a mother and a father joined by commitment, raising children. Instead of teaching wholeness, we were now teaching brokenness.

The smoke fills the air. The hippie's guitar plays and the singer sings, "Where have all the flowers gone?" It is as if they are playing, "Where have all the mothers gone?" "Where have all the mothers gone, long time passing?" It is very sad, and it seemed it was Rosie's fault.

Chapter 8
The Culture of Death

The drug culture of the '60s became the drug epidemic of the '90s and the international economy of the twenty-first century. In the news, we hear about the bloody drug cartel wars in Mexico. Each night, trucks loaded with cocaine are smuggled across our borders. In the dark of night, trucks arrive behind the old, run-down, crowded apartment buildings near downtown Santa Ana.

During the day, children watch out the windows as older youth and men make a deal. They see the dealers shove wads of twenty-dollar bills into their pockets. It isn't just the poor that come for the high. It is also the rich, in their fancy cars, who drive up, get their stash, and whisk off into the night.

Tommy Cota, now a Calvary Chapel Pastor, tells how at sixteen he purchased a Lincoln Continental with his drug-dealing money. He would also tell thirteen of his friends, "Come on, let's all go to Disneyland; I will pay." So off they went. After an hour or so, "That's enough. Let's go." And they left. They had no concept of money and no concept of real work.

In the '50s, there was little drug use in America. In the early '60s, I remember hearing about a few kids who would take drugs, but they were a very small fringe. Our high school presented the play, *West Side Story*. I loved it. The dancing gang members were exciting! And one of the main stars was called Rosie (my name), and the song she sang even mentioned where I was born—Chichicastenango (a remote Indian village in Guatemala). In church, we saw the film, *The Cross and the Switchblade*. Drugs and gangs seemed so foreign or something that only happened in New York, in the Bronx.

But by the end of the '60s, we saw the hippies strung out on drugs. And it seems we have not been able to get rid of drugs since. Drugs have almost become institutionalized. Young people in both the suburbs and urban communities battle drug addiction. Even the rich have to have their Prozac, Zoloft, or another anti-depression medication to make it through the day.

Drugs keep coming into America. And we keep buying them. Our appetite for drugs enriches Columbia, Mexico, Guatemala, and many other nations. We tried a drug czar to help us win the War on Drugs. First Lady Nancy Reagan made it her cause to urge young people to "Just say no!" TV ads tell parents, "Talk to your kids about drugs." Hundreds of teens are kicked out of school each year because of drugs, and our prisons are filled with drug offenders. The cost is astronomical, and the cost in lives and productivity is indeed a national tragedy.

We continue to pay for methadone clinics; lawyers and businessmen drive up regularly to get their federally paid fix and drive away. The homeless too live near methadone clinics, so they can get their daily heroin substitute. And now marijuana is legal in four states: Colorado, Oregon, Alaska, and Washington, but the Colorado Governor John Hickenlooper has warned other governors to wait "before legalizing marijuana as Colorado continues to navigate an unknown, nonexisting federal regulatory landscape for the industry" (http://www.msn.com/en-us/news/politics/colorado-governor-legalizing-pot-was-bad-idea/ar-AA8vHAC?ocid=u227dhp). We cannot fully know the consequences this will have on the future of our nation.

When I ran for Congress, I walked precincts in tough neighborhoods. A group of young men were laid back, sitting in their front yard, enjoying a beer and perhaps a smoke with their friends. They gave me their advice on winning the election. "First," they said, "go buy a T-shirt that says Fullerton on it, and wear it when you walk around. Here in Fullerton we just have one gang, not like in Santa Ana that has so many. Then tell everyone that you will legalize marijuana or give it out. Marijuana mellows us out. Then we will only smoke pot and have barbeques. You won't have to put us in prison for doing bad things." "Really," I said, "I just don't look good in T-shirts."

When my congressional campaign ended, a remnant from our campaign team decided to stay and rent our campaign office on historical Main Street in Garden Grove. It is a beautiful, quaint, tree-lined bricked street that has several interesting restaurants and once was filled with antique shops. About ten of us chipped in to pay the rent, and we turned our campaign headquarters into a high-class thrift consignment store, a vintage boutique, so we could learn how to start a small business.

Soon it dawned on me that we, with our nonprofit organization, had never developed a workplace training program for older youth. It seemed God had given me a new team to fulfill our mission. It was a great location. Friday nights on Main Street there were classic car shows, and one of the restaurants featured Elvis Presley with his concert videos and memorabilia. In fact, twice a year, on the month Elvis was born and on the month he died, the street was filled with Elvis impersonators. It was a perfect business (with donated items) to train inner-city young people how to work, be successful employees, and start and run small businesses.

A partially homeless man hangs out on historical Main Street. He came every day to our store and soon started volunteering for us. He shared that two of his children, both who were homeless, even the one who is in and out of jail, had no problem getting a medical marijuana card. "They just paid $150 for the card from their welfare check. They were never asked to show medical records."

A few years ago, I looked out my window at my home in a very nice middle-class neighborhood and saw a police squad kick down the door of our neighbor's house and arrest a young man. Several young renters were growing marijuana in all the bedrooms and family room. It was quite an elaborate operation with coolers and other equipment. I never noticed the cameras on the roof. Marijuana has become quite a business! And it was in my neighborhood.

Inner-city gangs center on the drug traffic. Gangs are often run as businesses by older adults. It has become a generational thing. Adults recruit their children, cousins, and younger teens to do their dirty work of selling drugs, keeping watch, and doing random drive-by shootings to keep the neighbors in fear. Often young people, as young as nine years old, are asked to join the gangs. Some join for protection, and others join because of peer pressure or intimidation and just because it is the thing to do. It becomes a way of life, a part of the culture.

The gangs mark their territories. "This is our territory where we sell drugs." When I flew a girl from Santa Ana across the country to a reform school, she shared with me how she would sell drugs to the kids in school. She explained that when gang members run out of drugs and another drug dealer wants to sell, they rent their territory for a cut of the profits. That is how they retain their profits, ownership of the hood, and their respect. They want to be recognized as owners of their territories. They put their business sign—graffiti—on the walls for all to see. They stand guard to see if anyone enters the territory that might be selling drugs to their clients, stealing their profits. The word gets out, and teens generally know there are areas you must avoid and places you just do not enter.

Young boys watch television and see nice homes and nice cars. They see the drug dealers drive up in their fancy cars. As they grow up, they find out school is hard due to living in poor conditions and language and cultural barriers. When they can get a work permit at fourteen, some find out that they do not have a social security number and cannot work. They now learn that they are illegal. They feel betrayed. "Why did they tell me in school I could be anything I wanted? I can't go to college. I cannot even work; what can I do?"

If you do not have a father at home, and there is not enough money for food, there is great pressure. "How can I help my mother feed the children? My mother needs me to work. What will I do?" They break the law and work when they can, and if they cannot find a job, they are ripe for the gangs and drug pushers. They will be tempted to sell drugs, steal, or engage in other illegal activity. And even when they find steady work, they are now in hiding, using fake ID's, feeling guilty and estranged. They lose their conscience and begin to lose their self-respect.

When I first joined the school board, I attended a parent meeting on how to keep your kids out of gangs. The speaker walked back and forth and asked several questions. "How many of you are Mexican?" Hands went up. "How many of you are Chicanos?" Many of the same hands went up. "How many of you are Latinos?" Hands went up. "How many of you are American?" Hands went up. But now the parents were confused. The speaker said, "Well, if all of you are confused, how do you think your kids feel?"

As a side note, later I saw some teens doing a play that helped explain some of the confusing terms. A boy came out wearing a big sombrero, a large belt buckle on his belt, and cowboy boots.

"This is a Mexican," they explained. "Chances are, he just came from Mexico. And if you are a hardworking man of Mexican descent, wearing work clothes, providing for your family, and trying to make your way in this country, you are a Chicano," they continued. "But if you wear a suit, perhaps come from different Latin American countries, and earn more than $30,000 a year, you are a Hispanic. If you are politically active and vote then you are a Latino. And perhaps if you are a United States citizen and speak English, you are an American." I do not know if this is exactly true, but their little vignette helped me make sense of the terms and showed me when to use them.

Nevertheless, new immigrants are acclimating and learning to live in a new country, and sometimes it is very confusing to try to fit in. This is particularly true for young people. Just when all young people are going through their own identity crisis—"Am I good looking?" "Will the girls like me?" "Am I smart or am I dumb?"—immigrant young people often ask themselves, "Am I American or Mexican?" "Where do I belong?" Am I legal or illegal?" "And if I am illegal and have broken the law, is that really bad? "If I am already illegal, why not do illegal things?" "Isn't survival and the love of my family important?" "And if that means joining a gang and selling drugs, so be it."

Alcoholism and drug abuse is rampant in low-income communities. And so is domestic violence. It goes hand-in-hand. Alcohol can make a person mean, and drugs can change a personality too. Verbal abuse begins, and then domestic violence ensues. Physical and verbal abuse takes its toll, filling young men with rage, and rightfully so.

Gang members want respect. They will fight when they feel disrespected. They want to be respected by their peers. When teens struggle in school and cannot read, they feel dumb. A friend of mine, who founded ABC Learn, Inc., in Los Angeles, teaches teens inside the juvenile facilities how to read. She says, "The teens try to cover the fact that they cannot read. And they act out to hide their inabilities. They would rather be in front of a judge that says, 'You are a bad boy,' than to be in front of their peers and be called 'stupid.'"

A gang can give you the respect you so desperately need. You can be a tough guy. You can show you are not afraid to pull the trigger in a drive-by shooting. You can fight as good as the rest of them. Now you have a family who respects you, your "homies"; you have a place, a turf, to call your own; you have protection; and most importantly, you have respect!

When we started the after-school club at Garfield Elementary, we told the principal and teachers we were teaching eight character traits: responsibility, integrity, initiative, respect.... They said, "Stop! Teach respect first!"

After a year of having our after-school club at Garfield Elementary, the vice principal approached our after-school club leader, Mike Hoover. "You know, ten-year-old Miguel, in your club? We were going to expel him. He joined the Loper Gang and was teaching the kids the gang signals. He had very vulgar language. And he was sharing with the kids how he got 'jumped in' [initiated] into the gang. But since he has been coming to your club, he has really changed. Keep doing what you are doing. We are not going to expel him."

A federal government program called "Weed and Seed" identified an area in Santa Ana for its high rate of gang involvement. Their strategy was to use police raids to weed out the gang leaders; many were arrested. Their thought was that if you remove the leaders, you weaken or destroy the gangs. But as the leaders went off to prison, those in the gangs competed for the leadership, and new leaders rose up to take their place. Problems arose when former gang leaders were released from prison. Also, other gangs tried to take over gang territories. If seemed that the violence escalated. This is what we saw in Mexico when the government tried to be tough on the drug cartels. Other cartel members rose up to take the place of those who were imprisoned or shot.

For a while, the Weed and Seed program had rounded up the troublemakers. An article in *The Orange County Register* newspaper said to the effect, "The police have 'weeded' out the gang leaders, weakening the gangs, but they have no 'seed.' No one is coming in to give the kids an alternative and lead them in the right direction." I remember reading the article, setting the newspaper down, getting off my couch and yelling, "I have the seed! I will seed the territory!"

It was the beginnings of my yearning to provide good programs and caring mentors who would bring hope and purpose to these youth. After all, as an elected school board member, I was charged with overseeing their education. There are some things that the schools are not doing. I felt the young people needed a spiritual dimension to their lives.

Old graffiti is painted over on the wall, and a new business sign, new graffiti, goes up in its place. It is a never-ending battle. In the darkness of the night, graffiti "tagging crews," groups of young boys, roam the streets, placing their names on the walls. It becomes a status symbol to see your name, your "gang moniker," up on buildings, fences, and on freeway overpasses. Now everyone will know they are somebody. It is a way for them to mark their territories and alert others not to sell drugs there.

For the adult gang members, it is about money and drugs. For older boys, it is about respect. If you look at a gang member in a wrong way, they call it "mad-dogging." And that can provoke violence. They want respect in the hood, and respect from their fellow "homies." For younger recruits, it is about protection. They know they have to watch their backs as they walk to and from school. But if they have a gang, they will be protected. Once in a gang, you are trapped. It is difficult to get out. If you are young, you can sometimes get out of the gangs by allowing other members to beat you up. But if you are older, frankly you know too much, and you may be hunted down and killed. In some neighborhoods, the sounds of gunshots at night are commonplace. And even those of us on the south side of town in nicer neighborhoods can hear the ringing of the shots.

At a mentoring meeting at Templo Calvario, a local church, a youth worker shared his experience. He overhead two boys talking, "When I get to the 'big house,' I will do this and that." The boys talked about going to jail as if it was expected, a way of life. Not something to be avoided but something inevitable. Many of their relatives are in prison, so why wouldn't they go? And when your father is a drug dealer, and your brother is a gang member, the expectation is that you too will join the gang or go to prison.

I arrived at our nonprofit after-school boxing club, a historical street "Rocky-type" boxing gym. It was about 4:30 in the afternoon and the gym was filled with teens and activity. Teens were jumping rope, punching bags, lifting weights, and dodging punches in the ring. Lou, a dedicated coach, was training a young boxer. Bam! Bam! Bam! The gloves hit the trainer's mitt. The music played, and the bells rang. You could smell the sweat. It was alive in there!

I had brought a guest to see the boxing club. But then I saw them: three girls. They carried a small box with a picture of a fourteen-year-old boy. They approached us and asked, "Can you help? Our friend just died, and the parents do not have money to bury him. We are collecting money to help them." "How did he die?" I asked. "He was shot on the street a few blocks from here." "How old was he?" "Fourteen." "What was he like?" my friend asked. "He was so funny; he was full of life," they smiled. "We will miss him," they said with a tear in their eyes. "That is very sad." They nodded. "Yes, we would like to help. Here is some money." We placed some bills in the box. And a mother placed her son in a bigger box.

For some, it seems a way of life, but the pain is real. The community seems helpless. The community rises up from time to time, has a candlelight vigil, then another mother's son dies. It seems there is nothing they can do.

How can people kill other people? It is just not right. In America, life has been devalued by adults and lawmakers, not just our youth. Abortion is legal. Even our own Santa Ana Congresswoman Loretta Sanchez, supports abortion on demand and thinks nothing of voting three times to continue the gruesome partial-birth abortion procedure, the brutal killing of a healthy full-term baby by stabbing the baby in the back of the neck and sucking out his brains, during the last half of the pregnancy. Many have called it infanticide, and even

President Clinton, dubbed the "abortion president" by Congress, acknowledged that it "seems inhumane." It is the culture of death.

With adult leaders who set examples like this, can we expect anything else from our youth? Babies are killed in the womb. Life has so little value. Older boys are killed in the streets. And again life has such little value. In the movie trailer for *Noah*, Noah goes out to see the wickedness of the people. As he walks out of the town, he lifts his feet one at a time, and blood drips down. Our streets and our homes too are running with the blood of our children. What has happened to us?

Chapter 9
Caught Between Two Countries

I came to realize that gangs are like countries. The "homies" draw up boundaries, claim territories, create rules, and elect leaders. And they are willing to die for their "homeboys." Sometimes as a school board member, we are given books of the students' poems. One poem caught my eye. "Caught between Two Countries" expressed the confusion that a lot of immigrant children feel. Due to the close proximity, many students go back-and-forth between Mexico and the United States.

Everyone needs someplace to belong to, values to share, a place to call their own, and a family to support them. The "homies" need homes. I do not believe teens always join gangs because their home life is bad. Many good kids from good homes join gangs. There are many wonderful families in our inner cities, where parents are attentive, involved, and caring. Children have large extended families with grandmas living at home and a cousin on every block. Sometimes it is just the culture, the peer pressure, the normal need to separate from mom and dad that draws them. Some need protection. Others are curious. And some kids just want to do the wrong thing; it is in their nature. And we all know teens and maybe some adults that just have to learn the hard way.

As a school board member, I attended many festivals, student presentations, plays, and programs in the schools. The contrast was clear. In our "fundamental schools" on the north and southern borders of Santa Ana, the children are taught in

English, learn to read with phonics reading methods, and had regular patriotic assemblies. Fundamental school scored the highest in the district, above the eightieth percentile. Though these schools of choice once had mainly Anglo children, now with a school population of 96 percent Hispanics, they are at about 90 percent Latino. At a patriotic assembly, the children sang with all of their hearts, "I am a Yankee Doodle Dandy, Born on the Fourth of July." The children ran out with big letters and pictures, the ABC's of America: apple pie, baseball, and cowboys. Johnny Appleseed came out, planting the apple trees everywhere, and Casey in his baseball uniform was up to bat, while dancing cowboys and cowgirls with cowboy hats and red scarves ruled the day! They shouted out the names of the fifty states.

The next day, at an inner-city school program, boys and girls entertained the parents with the typical Mexican Folkloric dancing. The boys in their sombreros tapped their shoes, and the girls with their ribbon woven hair held out their colorful dresses for all to see. The children stood in rows in their school uniforms and calmly sang, "We are the world. We are the rainbow." They were the new world citizens, "No home here, in America, for us," they seemed to say. "We are but a part, a color of the rainbow of cultures in the world." It grieved my heart.

America is not a country like any other. To be Chinese, you need to be Chinese. To be Japanese, you need to be Japanese. But America is different. America is a set of values we share, not an ethnic culture. Anyone can be American! American values are for all who will embrace them. How will these children know about America, the beautiful and the free?

England's Prime Minister Margaret Thatcher stated that America was different than European nations who were built on history. America was built on "an idea, the idea of Liberty." Once in a while, I would hear a patriotic song or program in the inner-city schools, but there was a strange feeling, a sense of heaviness in the air. It was as though the song was insulting some of the children. It was strange. There are many parents who come here to the United States just to get a few dollars saved so they can go back to Mexico or Guatemala to start a store, a transportation company, or a restaurant. They come to work to make $5,000 or more and then go back. I have met them in Guatemala. They still see themselves as Guatemalan or Mexican.

The majority of parents and children who come here to stay, however, want to know about America. They want to know what made this country so prosperous. They are eager to become American, but our schools will not let them. Sadly, they will not learn what it is to be an American in the schools. When I came to the United States in the '50s, we learned about America, and we learned to love America, her freedom, her personal liberties, abundant opportunities, and her sense of justice and respect for law.

Often these young people do not feel like they belong in either country, Mexico or the United States. And it isn't just illegal children; instead of teaching the students about America and its great values, inner-city young people are given a devastating multiculturalism, or relativism, that says no one's values are better than others. They call it *diversity*. "Everyone's values need to be respected. We need to be sensitive. We need to be tolerant. Don't promote your own values." The end result of this philosophy is that our children are growing up without values.

There is Hispanic Heritage Month, Black History Month, Asian-Pacific Heritage Month, and Women's History Month. I do not know why, but I hated these months. Shouldn't we appreciate Black history all year round? Shouldn't we teach black or Asian history regularly when we teach history in our classrooms? And if we treat women with respect and give them the freedom to pursue their own happiness, why do we need a special month set aside to do that? I grew up respecting great female heroes such as Israel's Prime Minister Golda Meir, England's Prime Minister Margaret Thatcher, and Deborah the judge and warrior in the

Bible who led her people into victory. There are injustices to women all over the world, but the solutions have to come from a foundational belief that all men, and that includes women, are equal in God's eyes.

Overall, throughout our history, America has elevated women. This is because of our Judeo-Christian roots. Men grew up honoring women, opening doors for them, appreciating their uniqueness, and pampering them. Men saw themselves as protectors and providers. In fact, years ago when I saw a *Time* magazine cover that showed the women working in the Soviet Union, I felt sorry for the women who had to go out, drive big trucks, and clean streets. It is no wonder that atheistic Russia celebrates annually "Workforce Day" rather than "Mother's Day."

The evidence is in: the women's liberation movement did not help women. It belittled men, destroyed marriage, took fathers out of the home, created latch key kids, and threw millions of women into poverty through divorce. The tragedy of the movement is that it has caused women, children, and men untold heartache, isolation, and loneliness. This is the true war on women.

In the past thirty years, television sitcoms have usually portrayed men as weak. Where are all of the strong father figures we used to have in the '50s? Where are Mr. Anderson, Mr. Cleaver, and good old Ozzie? Actually, we have had *Little House on the Prairie*, *The Waltons*, and *Bonanza* series, but they were, of course, dressed in old-fashioned clothing, certainly from another time. We still celebrate Women's History Month in our schools, but after women's lib, it seems the men now, more than ever, need their own month.

Ironically, with the rise of multiculturalism, or *diversity*, we are being asked to appreciate other cultures even if they treat women terribly, cut off people's hands when they steal, and sometimes burn widows when their husbands die. But if we appreciate our own American culture, which for many years put women on a pedestal, cared for the innocent and elderly, gave us an amazingly fair judicial system, and produced incredible individual freedom, we are ridiculed as being old fashioned, arrogant, and insensitive.

Many of us have been uncomfortable with the concept of diversity, but have not known why. In *Diversity: The Invention of a Concept*, Robert Wood, a former associate provost at Boston University and a current professor of anthropology, shares that we have always studied how people with differences try to get along. On the book cover, it is said that "Wood argues in his book that the new *diversity* does not mean variety and multiplicity; but rather, means *a new kind of regimentation* that fixes people into artificial categories and dispenses rewards in proportion to the size and political muscle of social groups. Real diversity, he proposes, is far different from this imposter *diversity*. Wood demonstrates that the *diversity* principle…is at odds with America's older ideals of liberty and equality."

In wanting to categorize everyone and attribute social power to groups, diversity pits everyone against each other. This new diversity ideology misses the whole point. Because America is about ideas of liberty and equality, *everyone* can be American; we do not need to be divided by our ethnicity or our cultural roots. Multiculturalism and diversity is killing our children, and it is killing our nation, dividing us rather than uniting us.

I appreciate my Guatemalan roots. I enjoy visiting my birthplace, Chichicastenango. I am in awe of beautiful Lake Atitlan, with its majestic volcanoes. I am in Guatemala several times a year. I go back-and-forth frequently, visiting relatives. I appreciate the beautiful countryside, the incredible refried black beans and fried platanos, the amazing colorful weaving, the marimba music, and the colorful paintings. But I *love* America, I live under its rules, under the Constitution, and I enjoy its blessings. Just because I was born in Guatemala does not mean that I cannot be an

American and embrace its values. We are a nation of immigrants.

America is not perfect. And neither is Guatemala. Currently, Guatemala is considered one of the most dangerous places in the world, with its murders, kidnappings, and corruption. The United States has become a great nation because America was good, but the further we get from our founding values based on a belief in God, the more crime, greed, and corruption we have in America.

I have embraced the values of hard work, self-initiative, and self-government that made us a great and prosperous nation. Cruelly, diversity training and multiculturalism and failed government programs are denying these new immigrant children a home here in America. Alienated, they are looking for a country to belong to, and when the schools do not share the great values and first principles of our country, these vulnerable young people have to look elsewhere. They have to look for someplace where they can hang their hat, a place to belong, a country to protect. And they find it here in the 'hood, with their homies.

Chapter 10
Bringing Hope

Steven Woods, living in a beautiful neighborhood in south Orange County, was attacked by a gang member who shoved a rod through his head. The gang epidemic of our inner cities finally got the county's attention when an upper-class boy was killed by gang members. This was the '90s, and gang violence was at an all-time high. Due to the outcry, Harriett Wieder, a member of the county board of supervisors, called a meeting at the Disneyland Hotel to discuss and find solutions for the escalating gang violence.

A concerned mother, a thin beautiful blonde, whose daughter had joined a gang, called me to attend a meeting on gang violence at the elegant South Coast Westin Hotel. She had talked the hotel into giving her use of a conference room for several months and had assembled community leaders for a panel discussion. Debbie, tall and sophisticated, pranced around the room with her microphone and asked, "What we were going to do about this terrible problem?" Debbie was persuasive. She was desperate for answers, and she was a mover.

Debbie and I talked, and if you knew Debbie, it was for hours on end. She wanted to create a non-profit organization to get teens out of gangs. "I talked to lots of gang members," she said. "I went out and asked them what they needed. They need jobs," she concluded. "They need hope." I agreed. With her urging, I found myself on panel discussions, cable television programs, and radio interviews discussing gang involvement.

After months of dialog, she called me, "Rosie, I can't do this! I do not know how to create an organization! You have to do it." And then she was gone.

That was it. It fell on my lap, but it was also now in my heart.

In 1996, I had four focus groups to make sure my ideas were supported. In 1997, I gathered a small group of people who also had a heart for our youth. An intermediate grade teacher and outreach consultant, an adoption lawyer, a sports director, a character education trainer, a gang rehabilitation director, an elected school board member, and a few others together formed a nonprofit organization. We met in the adoption lawyer's boardroom, formed a board of directors, and created our mission statement, vision, goals, and objectives. We had a big dream.

Our vision was to mobilize thousands of people to come and mentor inner-city youth. I read articles on how to recruit, manage, mentor, and retain volunteers. The vision grew bigger and bigger. We saw thousands coming. We wondered, "Where will we train and serve so many volunteers?" We dreamed of using a beautiful, historical building in downtown Santa Ana for a mentoring center.

In my mind, I could see the mentors coming, I felt an urgency; we had to get ready!

We were filled with passion and ready to take on the world. After meeting weekly for several months developing our mission statement, vision, and goals, we realized we needed to start small. "All we need is one mentor and one child, and we can begin," I told the group.

It was my twenty-fifth wedding anniversary, and Jim and I were going on a tour of Israel with the pastor who married us, Pastor Chuck Smith, from Calvary Chapel of Costa Mesa. "Let's take a break," I encouraged the team. We had spent a lot of time meeting together. We were now united in our purpose. "When I get back from my trip to Israel, we will look for somewhere to start." I had no idea what lay ahead for us in Israel.

In Jerusalem, at the Hyatt, with 450 people in our group, a couple sat at our table. The man was a hard-nosed New York–type cop, and his wife was a beautiful blonde. As the cop looked up, I asked, "What do you do?"

He said, "I am a police sergeant in Santa Ana." I got excited. "I am a school board member in Santa Ana." We had something in common. I had been giving presentations on the eight national education goals, so was always eager to share my startling discovery. I continued, "I have been studying the national education goals. Maybe sometime we can get together, and I will share with you what I have learned. It involves the police. And it seems that the government is trying to take away so much of the role of the parents." His beautiful wife jumped into the conversation: "I think they should take the children away from the parents." I was set back, "I do not think this lady has my family values!" I thought to myself.

"Why do you say that?" I asked. She told us her story. "I grew up in the Bronx of New York. I would come home each day from school and stand at my doorway trembling and would run and hide under the covers in my bed. I never knew if I was going to have dinner that night or if I was going to get beat up. My parents were alcoholics and into Satanism. I would pray and pray that someone would come and take me away from my parents."

"W-o-w." I said slowly. "That is sad." I paused. Then I continued. "You look wonderful, and you are dressed so well. No one would think that would be your story. How did you get from there to here—to the Hyatt, on this beautiful tour of Israel? What made the difference in your life?" I asked.

"It was two things," she immediately responded. "Two teachers took notice of me. They knew my name and asked me questions. They showed an interest in me. I felt like someone cared and knew me. Second, we moved to a nicer neighborhood, and I wanted to look good when I went to school. We got a box of used clothes, and I found a jumper I liked. It was a little too big for me, so I took safety pins and pinned it up on both sides with lots of pins. I thought I looked great, but when I got to school, the kids all laughed at me. I ran home, got on my bed, and cried and cried. I said, 'This is never going to happen to me again. When I get older, I am going to become rich!' And so I did. I own a shopping center and two businesses."

What an illustration for the mission statement that we had just written! "…to bring hope and purpose to the children and youth in the inner city." Hope and Purpose is what the kids need. Having an adult spend time with you, asking questions, listening, showing an interest in your life brings hope, hope that perhaps you are really somebody, that you count. Additionally, through our programs we want to have the young people purpose in their hearts to do something with their lives—perhaps decide to get their homework done, to pass the next test, to graduate, to become a nurse, a teacher, or to just become rich. But most of all, we want them to determine that they will be good people and do the right thing.

There is a youth minister named Greg Johnson at a church called The Rock, in Anaheim, California. He started a program called J12. He asks, "Where was Jesus at age twelve?" The answer is, "He was at the temple talking to the church leaders." "What did he say?" Jesus said, "I must be about my father's business." The kids in his group wear t-shirts that say, "I must…" "If we can get kids to purpose to follow God and do the right thing," Greg says, "we will never hear about them during their teen years, not in newspaper headlines, in prison, or in trouble until they are ready to fulfill their purpose, and walking into their calling." I thought that was very cool! No kids in trouble, just kids with a purpose.

We realized we had to get to the children before age twelve. When I was on the city's Early Prevention and Intervention Gang Commission (EPIC), they came to the same conclusion. We have to work with kids when they are young. We cannot wait until they are in their teens. As I drove, a speaker on the radio confirmed the need: "Children's values are formed from five to ten years of age."

Young children need to be in a safe place with caring mentors. They need to be hearing and discussing good things, encouraging them to purpose in their hearts to do the right thing. Some of our first programs were after-school character clubs at local elementary and intermediate schools. We offered structured sports, academic tutoring, and character development lessons based on the stories of biblical and historical heroes.

There in Jerusalem, at the Hyatt, I shared with the tough cop and his lovely wife about the organization that we had just started and our vision and our hearts for the kids. Police Sergeant Rich Murg said, "I know a friend who has a boxing gym in Santa Ana. Since Frank's brother, who started the gym, died, it has been vacant for five years. I will see if Frank, who owns the boxing gym, will let you use it."

Two days after we got home from Israel, I got a call. Rich said in his gruff cop voice, "I talked to Frank, and he said you can use the boxing club." "Yeah!" Just think—I had to go to Jerusalem to find a place to start in Santa Ana. God did say in Acts 2 of the Bible, to start in Jerusalem. And so we did!

What was I going to do with a boxing club? I do not know anything about boxing. I do not even like boxing. I was not sure it was the right thing to do in a tough neighborhood, an area surrounded by two active gangs and next to a bar.

I thought I might just have an elementary club for younger children at the gym and call it a kid's clubhouse. I was an elementary school teacher. And the boxing club was across the street from an elementary school. I realized it would be easier, and the parents would feel safer to have their young children stay at the school. We decided to have a children's club at the elementary school. One of our board members wanted desperately to have an after-school club at her intermediate school. So we opened up one there as well.

The question remained: what were we going to do with a boxing club? The more I learned about the boxing club that had opened in the '70s, the more I realized it had a rich heritage. So many young men had wonderful memories of working out there. Even when I walked precincts in Garden Grove for my congressional race, I ran into a man who looked at my campaign flier and said, "Wait a moment!" He left me at the door and brought back a framed award he had won years ago at the Santa Ana gym.

Soon I set off trying to find a boxing coach. I tried a few, but one disappeared one day without explanation. He was a professional appearing on HBO, coaching boxing. Another coach had political ambitions and was just there long enough to receive city recognition. Once he got the award, he was gone.

One day I was at our skateboard competition event. About a hundred attended. The young children and teens from our new skateboard club were competing for trophies. Professional skaters judged the students' five-minute routines. We had a band, and my son-in-law came out and made balloon animals and crazy balloon hats for the kids.

Then I saw him! He was riding his bike and stopped by our skateboard club competition event. I asked him what he did. "I mentor kids," He told me. He had invited several boys to his house to pray every morning and to learn to box. Soon eleven boys were showing up, and there was not enough room to work out. He continued, "So I am practicing with the boys outside on the lawn at Santa Ana High School." "I gave them a T-shirt with the initials FBI on the shirts." "What does that mean?" I asked. "Forming Boys of Integrity," he replied. I knew I had found the man! "Come to my office, and we will talk. Maybe we can do something together. You have some boys and a club, and I have a boxing gym."

In my office, Joe shared that he had spent time in prison. Now he wants to change lives.

Down at the boxing club, every day you will find fifty to sixty kids fighting it out, not on the streets, but in the gym. Our teen sport program at a historic street "Rocky" type boxing club has been operating for twelve years. When we celebrated a $50,000 grant from Northgate Gonzales Markets, a sixteen-year-old David told some visitors, "I have been coming here for three years, and these have been the best years of my life!"

Beside the weekly workouts, the boxers attend boxing competitions, and many are winning and bringing home big, gold boxing belts and trophies. One of the boys lost thirty pounds with all of that great exercise! On weekends when the teens are not at tournaments, they go on field trips or engage in community service projects. You might see them painting out graffiti, cleaning parks, collecting items for relief efforts, or heading to Magic Mountain for a day of fun or sliding down a hill in the snow-covered mountains of San Bernardino.

They have a safe place. For a few hours each day, they do not have to watch their backs. They do not have to be that tough guy; they can be themselves. They are loved, and they know we care. For them, this is family. Often you will hear them say, "Here, we are somebody!" Yes, indeed! They are.

One afternoon at the gym, our boxing club director heard a ruckus outside the gym. He looked out the door to see what was happening. A boy from the club yelled at him, "Joe, get back in the gym!" Joe ducked back in, but another boy was darting out the door. "No! Don't go out there," Joe instructed. "But I want to go out and do something good." "No, Stay here!" Joe insisted. Soon the boy who was outside walked into the gym, bleeding and bruised. "Joe, I just got out of the gang," he said. "But I had to get beat up." Joe put his arm around him and said, "I am so proud of you! You chose to do what was right even though you knew it would cost you something."

"See, Joe," said the other boy, "I wanted to go out and get beat up so I could leave the gang, too. I guess I will have to get beat up tomorrow." They can get out of the gangs, but sometimes the cost is very high. And when they are older and are part of the drug trade, they cannot get beat up and leave; they know too much. The cost then may be their lives.

Part III
Making a Difference

Five Angry Women

"In politics if you want anything said, ask a man. If you want anything done, ask a woman." —*Margaret Thatcher*

"If you set out to be liked, you will accomplish nothing."
—*Margaret Thatcher*

Chapter 11
School-Based Clinics

I hurried out of class, walking through the halls of our high school out to the parking lot. There was Mike, who was four years older, waiting for me in his black and white '56 Chevy. I felt so special, only sixteen, going out with this handsome, older fraternity guy, the fraternity president, no less. I had his fraternity pin on my maroon cashmere sweater.

I met Mike just before I was sixteen. I was almost "sweet sixteen and never been kissed." He came to visit our church, peeked over at me, and told my brother's friend, Jim that he wanted to date me. I was unaware, but my older brother had told Mike that he could not date me. Fred, my brother, approached me and said, "If Mike asks you out, tell him I said you cannot date him. He is a wild fraternity guy."

I wasn't even sure who Mike was. After a few months, my brother came back and said, "You can now date Mike. He got saved at church, and he has really changed." I quickly called my girlfriend Patti and told her that my brother had changed his mind and said it was OK to date Mike. She told Jim, Mike's friend, and Mike asked me out.

I had hardly dated, except to a church Valentine dinner, a trip to the beach in junior high with a boy I had met at a youth group, and at summer camp outings. Now I was with this older college man who used to be a wild fraternity guy. Mike was romantic; he saved his money and took me out to eat at expensive restaurants like waterfront Ports O'Call in Long Beach. I enjoyed dressing up and eating daintily in the candlelit restaurant hoping to impress this guy with my sophistication. And yes, he gave me my first kiss. He came to the football games and watched me cheer as a flag twirler. He was a lot of fun. We went on picnics, to concerts, to the beach, and to movies. He even danced with me on the pier in the evening fog after we watched Mary Poppins.

Four years later, Mike and I stood outside of my college dorm. It was dark outside, but the area was well lit with the lights from my dorm, Delta Chi. I was attending Biola College (now University), and Mike was ready to graduate from Westmont, a college in Santa Barbara. Once again we were discussing our future.

When Mike went to Vietnam he wrote and asked me to meet him in Hawaii to get married during his R&R (Rest and Relaxation). I was not ready.

Now twenty-one, here we were once more talking about marriage. Mike began. "I don't feel like I am who you are supposed to marry," he said. "It seems like you should marry a missionary or a pastor. And I cannot be that." "I never said that," I replied. "I know," he said. "You just are that way; you want to change the world. I am older now, and all I want to do is settle down, use my business degree, buy a two-story house with shag rug carpet, and have some kids." "Really, Mike, I would like that, too," I reassured him. "I just want to know that I am marrying the right guy, the one God wants me to marry. I would marry a mechanic if that is what God wanted me to do."

We went our separate ways. Ironically, Mike ended up as a missionary to Russia with Campus Crusade for Christ, using his business skills, and I, well, I married the mechanic, bought the two-story house with gold shag rug carpet, and had five children.

When I married Jim, we were told we would not be able to have children. As I was contemplating what that would mean, I heard a story of a couple that desperately wanted a child, believed a Bible verse, and soon conceived. I found a great verse in the

Bible: "God will make the barren woman a contented mother of children." That verse was for me. And it was not long afterward that I started having children, and more children. Soon Jim asked, "How do you stop this?"

We had five miracles! And I was truly a contented mother of children. I loved being pregnant, and I loved raising my children. I worked as an elementary school teacher until a month before I had my first child. Then I was blessed to be able to stay home and raise the kids while Jim worked as a jet aircraft mechanic for TWA, Trans World Airlines.

Jim went to college for two years, at Mount SAC, San Antonio College, and learned Airframe and Powerplant mechanics, and with that jet mechanic training was able to feed, clothe, and put a roof over the seven of us. He worked for TWA, and when American Airlines bought out TWA, he worked for American Airlines, first as a jet mechanic and then as an inspector of the mechanical work, signing off on the airplanes. His career also gave us free air travel—a nice benefit!

Jim did not think it was feminine for me to talk about politics all the time. So he asked me to quit taking the newspaper for three years. When I was growing up, we always watched the news and talked about politics at home. It seemed hard, but I did it. While I was not very involved in national news during this time, I did know everything that was going on in Huntington Beach as I read the community paper that came to the house. Looking back, it was the best thing. I submitted to Jim, focused on my family and home. Later when I went into politics, Jim was my best supporter.

Our second child, Debbie, was born with cerebral palsy. As a baby, she did not roll over, sit up, or respond like other children, and we were referred to a neurologist. He simply told us, "Take her home and give her good mothering." I thought that was strange advice. For a year, I cried, grieved the loss of my dreams for her, and soon was depressed, laying on the couch a lot, crying. One day my sister came over and said, "That is enough! Here is a broom; I want you to kick the Devil and his depression out." I got up, took the broom, waived it wildly in the room, and proceeded to walk the Devil out. And I kicked him out the door, waving the broom at him. And that was that. The depression left.

A few days after the neurologist told us Debbie had cerebral palsy; there was a cerebral palsy thrift store truck in front of my car as I drove down the freeway. I took down the number and called and discovered their developmental center was a few blocks from my house. I was invited to attend the classes. Debbie was featured in their promotional video clip. She was a movie star! She was our star for sure. She became my great buddy and friend and showed me that I could live a full life while I brought someone else along. Her story will be saved for another book.

Jim and I had four girls. I really wanted a boy when we were having our third baby. Just before I gave birth, I read in the paper that a rabbi was having his twelfth child. The twelfth one was a boy and when he was born, the eleven other girls were screaming with joy. Now that was encouraging!

My next-door neighbor, who had two boys, had her third child at the same time. Our babies were two weeks apart. We had always joked that if we both got the same sex, we would trade over the backyard fence. When we had our third girl and she had her third boy, the deal was off. Once we saw beautiful Cindy Praise, there was no way we would trade her, not even for a boy.

When I was expecting my fifth child, we were prepared for Princess Stephanie, a fifth girl. The bassinet was covered in white, fluffy, gathered dotted-Swiss material. The bassinet was decorated with little artificial red and pink roses all around the edges. To our surprise, Jordan, our boy, was born. I called home and told the four girls, "Get the flowers off the bassinet! We are bringing home a baby boy!"

I remember when the four girls came to the hospital to see their baby brother. They looked through the glass. I held him up so proudly. Their faces fell. OK, so he was a little wrinkled and looked like an old man. But you should see him today. He is a handsome young man. Actually, the earth shook the day he was born. We had a mild earthquake in the hospital that night. My sister-in-law still calls him "Jordan Shaker." I knew in my mother's heart that he would someday shake this world up and do amazing things.

The kids grew and attended public school with the exception of a few years when we had our girls in private schools. Little did I know I needed to understand both private and public schools! I also homeschooled for several years and was glad I had earned an elementary teaching credential in college. My credential enabled me to oversee twenty-five homeschool families, with forty-one children. I also became a Stanford Testing Administrator who tested and analyzed the children's learning needs. This experience, teaching multiple grade levels, evaluating curriculum, and analyzing test results, along with my experience in special education with my daughter gave me a broad view of current educational curriculum and teaching methods. As a substitute teacher in both public and private schools, I was able to go into hundreds of different classrooms, observing different styles of teaching and classroom organization.

When the AIDS epidemic hit, in the late '80s, there was a national awareness, a bit of hysteria, and perhaps rightly so. It was sad to hear about the many who were dying of AIDS at such young ages. Friends of those who were dying made quilts to commemorate the lives lost.

The AIDS epidemic in Africa also caused fear. People were concerned about it spreading through contact with blood, saliva, and same-sex sexual practices. California passed a law that all schools had to teach the children about HIV or AIDS. "But at what age?" some of us mothers asked. A few of us mothers were interested in how sex education would be taught, so we became involved at the local public school district. We advocated for a successful abstinence program that was being used in San Diego, called Sex Respect. It taught a respect for marriage, responsibility, and commitment. It was reported that the program also improved student's responsible behavior in other areas.

It took two years of actively speaking at school board meetings, bringing in experts, and providing statistics and case studies before the elected school board finally accepted the program for eighth graders. We were very happy. But the day the board passed the sex education program we wanted, the board announced they were going to bring in school-based clinics. The clinics would be funded by a Healthy Start grant voted by the State Legislature as SB620 in 1991. During the last two years advocating for "Sex Respect," we had learned a lot. We had learned a lot about school-based clinics. We looked at each other and thought, "Oh, no, not another battle!"

We knew school-based clinics were supported by the Support Center for School Based Clinics at the World Center for Population Options, and they had population control as their goal. We soon learned that an administrator from the organization California Tomorrow opened an office at the school district. We were aware that he was instrumental in opening up school clinics up and down the state. "Why did California Tomorrow have an office at the district?" we wondered. The board had not even discussed having school-based clinics, much less voted on it. This was evidently an important program or movement.

I decided to join the parents' committee on school-based clinics. The clinics sounded so good: free health care for all students and conveniently accessible right there at the local school. How wonderful! It was a poor parent's dream come true. What caring people. "America is amazing! More than we expected," these immigrant mothers rejoiced.

A friend called one afternoon and blurted out, "You'll never guess what I found at the Cal State Fullerton Library!" "OK, what is it?" I asked. "I found the California Tomorrow Plan. It was written in 1970!" We looked at it and could not believe our eyes.

It called for zero population growth by the year 2000. On the top of every page it stated, "The problem: Too many people." Across on the opposite page it read, "Zero population growth by the year 2000." The way to control the population growth in California was to tax or punish families who had more children and to bring in school-based clinics to encourage the population to limit their families. The plan contrasted two Californias—one without population control, Plan A, where the "land use" could not support the population. It also discussed a California, Plan B, with population control, which made for a better California in the future. "Land use" was a key word in the document. The land could not sustain a large population.

One afternoon, after the parents' committee on school-based clinics, I waited for the person from California Tomorrow who was leading the meeting to walk out of the meeting room. I asked him, "Tell me. I know you are working for California Tomorrow. What is California Tomorrow, and what does it do?" He thought for a moment and answered. "It is about land use and ethnic balance."

I was surprised at his honesty. Having read his organization's California Tomorrow plan, I understood what he meant. But why did he never mention "land use" or "ethnic balance" or "population control" or "limiting families" in the parents' meeting?

"Ethnic balance," of course, coincided with Planned Parenthood's history, as its founder Margaret Sanger was an admirer of Hitler's eugenics, the creation of a superior class of people by intervening in their genetic structure. Sanger started her organization with the expressed goal of reducing the population of poor minorities and retarded people, whom she felt were inferior.

The night the school board members voted for school-based

clinics, the public crowded into the school auditorium. A larger room than the regular school district boardroom was needed. Hundreds came to address the Board of Education. The board meeting lasted until two in the morning. The room was packed as speakers lined up to talk. Soon the room was filled to capacity as Hispanic parents not only took seats but also stood in large numbers along the back of the room.

My friend stood by the door and saw the buses coming. The new arrivals were told where to go as they stepped off the buses. All of them spoke Spanish. My friend, who knew Spanish, listened. "I do not know why he always takes us to these things," they muttered in Spanish. "We do not even know what they are talking about in there." Nativo Lopez, the local Latino activist and community organizer, had just brought in a busload from his English and Citizenship classes. Most were new immigrants and had no idea why they were there. They were given armbands to show their solidarity in support of school-based clinics.

The whole process from start to finish was full of deceit. It was difficult to explain what was really going on, as no one would believe that the schools were deceiving the people into limiting their families under the disguise of giving health care.

The board voted to bring in school-based clinics. But they added our five conditions. Two of our conditions included: "No clinics at school sites, only medical vans." That way we could get rid of the vans if they violated the conditions. "Only K–5th grade so they would not use the clinics to give out condoms and take teens to Planned Parenthood clinics for abortions." But later we learned they broke the condition by adding preschoolers. It appeared this gave them access to child-bearing parents so they could get them to tie their tubes and limit their families. Often this was done through intimidating stakeholder meetings, which included social workers, clinic personnel, district attorney representatives, and other professionals and experts who coerced these low-income women to violate their Catholic religious views and limit their families.

We knew the population control people were happy to get their foot in the door. Those in the district who were deceived and wanted health care for the poor felt they won. And by adding the conditions, board members felt conservatives would be happy. It was a win-win for the elected board. As usual, school board members were happy to avoid taking a stand and be able to vote to please everyone.

The social planners, elitists, and population control change agents are patient and know change has to come gradually.

We did not stop the clinics, but with the five conditions, we raised some awareness and put some stumbling blocks in their path, delaying their full implementation. But knowing the determination of the population control forces, we knew we would have to fight another day.

It did not take long. On April 15, 2010, First Lady Michelle Obama came to San Diego to inaugurate the "Building Healthy Communities" initiative, funded by The California Endowment. In its first year, the Endowment spent one hundred million dollars toward creating community advocates for school-based clinics and other programs. Santa Ana was promised ten million dollars for community programs within the next ten years.

After the school board voted for school-based clinics, the question remained, "How could we trust the district to keep the conditions? Where do we go from here?" Soon we knew what to do. My friends said, "Rosie, you have to run for school board to make sure they keep their promise and abide by the conditions." That was the start of a great adventure.

Chapter 12
A Mini Revolution

You can imagine my surprise when I opened the newspaper the day after the election. My picture was on the front page; the caption read, "Back to Basics School Board Member Wins in Santa Ana." The article basically stated, "This lady just got elected. Surprisingly, she beat out the three incumbents! She wants to get the schools back to academic basics and is against bilingual education."

Inside the opinion pages, the editorials read, "The election of the spunky Rosie Avila to the Santa Ana School Board is the start of a mini revolution." And it was.

In 1991, the year I was elected to the school board, the mission statement for the Santa Ana school district read, "Creating a global citizen in a changing world." I hated it!

The rational was: Globalization is here, and since the world has changed from an agricultural society to an industrial society to an information age, we now need to become global citizens. "Our society is changing; everything else has to change, too." This was always the mantra.

We are American schools, and I thought we should create good American citizens. After all, we all live under the US Constitution. We enjoy the blessings and the protection of our country, and are supposed to live by its rules. I was not sure it was the job of the school district to make a new kind of citizen.

When I left the school board seventeen years later, the district mission statement read, "The Santa Ana Unified School District is dedicated to high academic achievement, in a scholarly and nurturing environment, in order that the students can fulfill their goals in life." Yes, things had changed. The schools had returned to effectively teaching children how to read, write, and master math. And most children were learning in English. It was not easy, and there is no other way to describe it: it was a mini revolution!

A few days after my election to the school board, my husband gave me a gift. It was a picture of a cup of coffee in a dainty flowered tea cup with a saucer. Next to the tea cup on the beautiful tablecloth was a cut rose bud on top of a small calendar planner and a rolled-up newspaper with a pair of glasses. The top read, "Some Leaders are Born Women"…and on the bottom, it read, "Behind every successful woman is a man who is surprised." Was he trying to say he was now glad I was reading the newspaper?

I was thankful that I could use my teaching experience in both private and public schools in my new role overseeing the education of inner-city young people. The destruction of the family, the growth of our inner cities, and the increase in violence had certainly taken its toll. But in the end, nothing has a greater impact on society than the education of its youth.

Tragically, our public schools are hell-bent on teaching evolution as fact when it is merely a theory. And scientific knowledge today lines up perfectly with the Big Bang theory that illustrates the creation story. "God said, and it was!" Instead of giving our children hope and purpose, our schools have removed hope and purpose. It borders on child abuse to tell precious young boys and girls that they were once some oozy slime that came together by chance over billions of years. How can we educate young people for greatness when we start out with such a hopeless, purposeless, dismal foundation?

The children need to know they were created by a loving Creator for a high and important purpose. They need to learn about all theories, including creation because it is in fact what most of the people in our local community believe!

Creation is also declared and established in our national mission statement, The Declaration of Independence, "that all men are created equal, that they are endowed by their Creator with certain unalienable Rights, that among these are Life, Liberty and the pursuit of Happiness."

God has no place at school, they said. Yet they teach another religion. The children are told to believe in themselves. They are taught to believe in man. A humanist agenda is taught, plain and simple. Man is the center of the universe, not God. They can look only to government or themselves for help.

I hope I never have to hear another graduation speech again that tells the excited and apprehensive graduation class, "Goodbye. Believe in yourself." Why does that anger me so much? For seventeen years, I have had to hear that message over and over and over again. And it is very depressing to think that we have only ourselves to look up to. While some eyebrows raised, I continued to send the graduating class off with the words to a popular saying and song, "Vaya con Dios"—Go with God.

Today's young people do not need to believe in themselves; they just need to know that someone believes in them, in their worth…someone as important and all-knowing as God!

The notion of evolution permeates the school system and our society. Everything is evolving. We live in a changing world. The fact that we live in a changing world is used to justify any change they want to make. Nothing is permanent. Everything is relative. There is no truth.

First society puts the children down by saying they are only a product of random chance. Then the schools try to build the identity of the child up by bringing in self-esteem programs. And the taxpayers pay for both. Is it any wonder the children are themselves confused?

Another way they try to build children up is by respecting and honoring their past culture or ethnicity. But in their zeal to teach multicultural pride and acceptance, the schools neglect to teach the children great principles such as our national values of liberty, justice, and equality. This further estranges them from the American culture, for in the end they feel they have to fight for their national pride, the rights of their ethnic people, amidst an array of cultures.

Sadly, immigrant children do not feel they have a place in this country. Children no longer understand our first principles and amazing history. Yet they are now living in America. The longer they are here, they begin to lose their roots in their country of origin, and without knowing what America is about, they have no identity in America.

It appears that this is intentional and is part of the making of a global citizen. The end result is that all nations, or "nation states" as they call them, will be under new world governance. But first, national pride and national values need to be minimized. For without a strong national identity, people will now be ready to accept the notion of a global citizen.

On our coins we read "*E Pluribus Unum*," which means "one from many." This motto was written to express the new unity of the colonies that came together to form one new nation. Over the years, it has come to mean the concept of the "melting pot" which describes many people with different cultures coming together as Americans, sharing the same values.

But today, rather than a melting pot, multiculturalism has destroyed our national unity. It has Balkanized us, divided us. We only need to look at countries like Bosnia, Ireland, and particularly Iraq where Sunnis, Kurds, and Shiites fight one another for power. Do we want our nation to splinter with ethnic groups within our borders, jockeying for respect and privilege? Look at Los Angeles where Black gangs, Hispanic gangs, and Asian gangs fight for the same turf. With the new influx of Muslims, conflict is rising in some areas, as sharia law is now competing with our own local laws.

Have we completely lost respect for American values? Are they not good enough to pass on to our children and share with newcomers?

Before I ran for the school board, I walked around from classroom to classroom and saw that most of the children were learning in Spanish. This just seems wrong. The schools state that their goal is to educate and prepare children for higher learning in colleges and universities. Yet the children were not being prepared to learn in English.

It seemed strange. They called the teaching methods bilingual education. But for the most part, bilingual education methods did not make children bilingual. Instead they created young people who were not proficient in either Spanish or English. These failed bilingual teaching methods first taught children in their primary language. In Santa Ana, which has a 96 percent Hispanic student population, Spanish was, of course, used. Once the children are proficient in Spanish, they can go on to learn in English. Most of the children studied in Spanish until about the fourth grade. Then they were transitioned into English. This meant children, even if they were born in the United States, entered Junior High with a second grade English vocabulary.

For years our schools have taught with these failed bilingual education methods, neglecting to give the children a mastery of the English language. A study by University of California, Riverside, (UCR), commissioned by the school district showed that more than half of our children were still in Spanish or English Language Development, ELD, classes by ninth grade, and many never became proficient in English by the time they graduated. How could they succeed in college or in the workplace?

One teacher told me she was substituting in a fifth grade class. A first-grade teacher said, "Why don't you have your fifth-grade students come in to our class and read with my first-grade children? They are both reading out of the same English reading textbook." She was stunned. "There is no way that I will let the fifth graders be humiliated like that!" Yes, it was not uncommon for students to read at a first-grade level in fifth grade. No wonder all of the intermediate teachers complained. "How can we get these students ready for high school work?"

It was abusive! They were asking the children to run in a race, but first they chopped off their feet. How cruel we have been to the children! What is wrong with us? How could we have held these children back for so many years? And they spent billions of our own tax money doing it!

How can our inner-city students qualify for well-paying jobs without mastering English? I hammered away, "English is the language of success." "If they want to be doctors, lawyers, businessmen, they need English! My relatives in Guatemala know that! That is why they send their children to schools where they can learn in English. Everyone around the world knows that you cannot be an airline pilot or an eye doctor without learning to read in English."

And how can these new immigrants learn how to vote intelligently without knowing or reading in English? Without English, they miss out on hearing the public discourse and are easily manipulated by community organizers like Acorn, La Raza, LULAC, and La MAPA, organizations who preach victimization rather than self-initiative.

In politics, there are many battles to fight. I learned that I could not fight them all. If I did, my colleagues would stop listening to me. This is a mistake many new conservative school board members often make. I had to take one issue on at a time and stay with it until it was won. When you are in a battle, you have to decide to win.

The district's global citizen mission statement, though it was the most disturbing, had to wait. It was actually the light that shined on what was really going on in our schools. Political correctness had replaced academics. My mission was to return the schools to their real job, not creating a new type of citizen but teaching children how to read, write, and do math. It was these skills that would enable young people to be whatever they wanted to be, to be free to think whatever they wanted to think. The fact that children were not learning English had to be the first thing to address.

The ending of bilingual education became my signature issue. Finally, I was able to get our bilingual teaching methods on the agenda so I could talk about it. The school board president caught me in the hall and said, "You only have five minutes to talk on bilingual education." I shot back, "When I was a community member, I had five minutes. Now I am a school board member, and I will say what I need to say."

I knew the board did not want to discuss it. After visiting many classes, I wrote an article exposing bilingual education that was published in the Editorial Page of the local newspaper, *The Orange County Register*. I immediately received 200 letters asking me to resign from the board. Later I learned they were generated by one person, my soon-to-be nemesis on the school board. I also heard the article was pinned up on school bulletin boards across the state. I found out others cared, too. Even today, almost twenty-five years later, I will get a call occasionally from college students who read my article and want to interview me for a class project.

Once the issue was out in the public, the district was forced to deal with it. I then asked for a study on bilingual education in our school district. A committee was selected. To make it look fair, people with different views were selected. First, the committee leaders were carefully selected and trained. Then the district selected topics, controlling the discussion, missing the real issues, of course! It was the "divide and conquer" method. No one could hear the whole conversation because everyone met in small subgroups. And when the subgroup leaders reported out to the larger group, opposing comments were carefully censored, downplayed, or misrepresented by the subcommittee leaders. It is called the Delphi technique, developed by Rand Corporation in the '50s. The technique is used to make it look like everyone in a diverse group came to the same consensus, when the reality is that the dissenting opinions were not shared or allowed to be discussed with the group.

It was all controlled by the Superintendent and his staff, and little or nothing came out of it. Like so many studies and committee work, our taxpayer money is squandered on maintaining the status quo or moving a group to a predetermined position.

The elementary teachers seemed to like bilingual education methods. It seemed compassionate; why put children through the tough transition into English when they are so young? I came to the United States when I was six and spoke only Spanish. I do not remember the transition being very hard. My first day in kindergarten, the children were in a circle singing, "Put your right foot in, put your right foot out, and shake it all about." I joined in, and it was fun. It seems that within six months I was functioning in English, though for my older brother and sister, it took a little longer. While claiming that this method would give children two languages, the real issue seemed to be the money. The district received $350 for each student who was classified an "English Learner." Teachers received more money for teaching the children in Spanish.

But the intermediate teachers were pulling out their hair! With teens entering with such low reading levels in English and with second-grade vocabulary levels, how could they get these vulnerable intermediate students ready for high school? I think the public discourse emboldened them. All of the teachers at one intermediate school signed a petition asking the Governor of California to end bilingual education.

School Board Member Audrey Yamagata Noji, a strong proponent of the failed methods, wrote a letter to each teacher, "Dear Mrs. Applebee, I understand that you signed a petition to the governor asking for an end to bilingual education, obviously you do not understand our program. We need you to come to a meeting with myself, the Superintendent of Schools and our

Director of Bilingual Education so that you can learn about our program and take your name off of the petition." How intimidating is that?! The wise principal protected his teachers. He told the district that none of his teachers would be going to a private meeting in the superintendent's office. If the district wanted to share about their program, they would have to give a presentation to all of the teachers at the school site.

A second-grade teacher in our school district, Gloria Matta Tuchman, who taught first grade at Taft Elementary School, worked tirelessly at the state level to try to end bilingual education. She got together with wealthy Silicon Valley entrepreneur Ron Unz and wrote Proposition 227, a ballot initiative called "English for the Children" that would end the failed bilingual teaching methods in California. Now the entire state was forced to discuss the issue.

Most people agree that children should know two or more languages, but these teaching methods produced poor Spanish speakers and poor English speakers and destroyed our children's future. I began debating for Proposition 227, the "English for the Children" Initiative at schools, civic clubs, and at town hall meetings.

I believed children should know other languages. I presented a "Four Language Plan" but realized I first had to discredit the current system. I recommended that Spanish speakers be given an extra year of developmental kindergarten to slowly acclimate to English and get a firm foundation of the most used English words, particularly those they needed for learning. Then from Kindergarten to sixth grade, the children should be immersed in English all day long, with the exception of forty-five minutes of Spanish instruction in the afternoon. After seven years of English instruction, and Spanish classes each day for seven years, students in seventh and eighth grade should have two years of Latin. This will help them with English vocabulary and science in high school. Then they can learn French easily, as it is another language with a Latin root. Many private schools teach children two modern languages and Latin. Upon graduation, students can take a test to show their abilities in four languages and receive a card to put in their wallets to let future employers know they have had instruction in four languages.

One day I was invited to debate bilingual education at Fountain Valley High School and was told it was going to be televised on cable TV. That was great; I was excited. Later the teacher called and said, "I just wanted to let you know that you will be debating Stephen Krashen." That was all she said. "OK," I said and hung up. Then someone explained who Mr. Krashen was. He was the architect of the bilingual education teaching methods and had written many books on the subject. "OK, so I have to do a little more homework!" I reassured myself. Actually, debating Steven Krashen was fun.

My neighbor Heidi attended and thought I won the debate, and I agreed.

The statewide initiative Proposition 227, "English for the Children," won! The voters of California had spoken; children would now be required to learn in English. That was the end of it. Well, so we thought, but not in Santa Ana. By now the district had elected two new Latino activists: Nativo Lopez and John Palacio, and they joined forces with Dr. Audry Yamagata Noji. They were determined not to implement the law. The new education law stated that if after thirty days the child could not function in English, parents could request waivers and the child would be placed in Spanish class, provided there were twenty other students who could not function in English. The idea behind the waivers was that if children truly struggled in class, had learning disabilities and could not process language well, exhibited great stress like wetting their beds at night, and so on, they could get a waiver.

But our board members and the district devised a scheme. It was an evil scheme. And yes, I call it evil because what they did to the children was indefensible. They created a special thirty-day curriculum to purposely confuse and inflict pain on the children. The children were given poems and rhymes to read. "I clean the house with a train. I go to sleep on a fork. I see the cups do their homework." The school district purposely tried to make the children confused and frustrated. Children were also asked what they would rather do than go to school. They fed the children lines to say, "I don't want to go to school, no, I want to stay home and ride my bike." "I want to stay with grandma." "I would rather stay home and watch television." It was unbelievable. I complained, but the board heartlessly did nothing about it.

Board President Nativo Lopez forced the district to have special meetings and set up tables so parents could sign up for waivers to pull their children out of English classes. Even at PTA meetings, parents were encouraged to sign up for waivers. He personally stood outside the schools encouraging the parents to go inside and sign up for the waivers.

As a local Latino activist and community organizer, Board Member Nativo Lopez, had his nonprofit organization Hermandad Mexicana National stripped of its nonprofit status when he encouraged his English and Citizenship classes to vote before they had been sworn in as citizens. Previously, the State of California was asking him to return one million dollars for not providing verification that his nonprofit organization used the money for English and Citizenship classes. Now he was again disregarding the law that children needed to be taught in the English language.

We had worked so hard, but the district was completely bypassing the law. What were we to do? We called the Grand Jury! That is what we did!

Grand Jury members asked to visit the schools. I personally escorted them to see that the children were still learning in Spanish. The district was livid; "Why didn't you warn us they were coming?" It is as if they missed the purpose of their visit. They wanted to see for themselves what was really happening. The

Grand Jury put out a scathing report reprimanding the district.

Thank goodness this put a little holy fear into them.

There were times when I was so furious at their lawlessness that I told the superintendent that I was going to sit on the roof of his district office and stay there until the district complied with the law. My husband firmly said, "No, you will not be doing that; you will probably be the target of a drive-by shooting." I felt like Moses: "Let the children go!" How many times did we have to say it? It was time to free the children to let them learn and succeed.

Now that English became the rule at the district, I could move on to the reading and math battles.

California brought in Whole Language Reading. And when the results were in, California schools came in dead last in the nation. California Superintendent of Schools Chief Bill Honig apologized for the fiasco. But did that stop the district from re-adopting these failed reading programs? No!!

It was time to get back to explicit phonics reading instructions rather than having children learn to guess words or try to read by osmosis with the Big Books.

Schools order or adopt new textbooks every seven years. It was time to select our reading textbooks. Whole Language books were recommended by the district. I called for a fair and balanced debate at the school board meeting. Each side could present their views and question each other, give statistics, and present their case with final arguments.

The board voted 3 to 2 to go with the Open Court reading series, a proven phonics-based program. Hooray! But the next day, the teachers demonstrated. They had given their input and wanted the Whole Language books. With all of the pressure, particularly from the teachers' union that supports school board candidates, one of the board members called to change his vote. We met and held his feet to the fire.

I objected to the new fuzzy math, but the board still adopted the books. Teachers would hide real math books in their classroom and sneak them out when the principal was not looking. It only took two years before the crazy politically correct math textbooks were thrown out.

One thing I learned from being a public school board member is that the facts did not matter. *What matters most is what is politically expedient.* Unlike private schools, where people personally pay for education, there was no incentive to do what actually works. In fact, the incentive was to fail because low test scores brought in more federal money.

I was naive when I first came on the board. I thought if we just looked at the facts, we would make good decisions. But the facts did not matter. Factual reports, carefully prepared by members of the community, received but a glance and were immediately tossed into the trash can, next to our seats. They did not even take them home to look at them. Years before being a school board member, I had been the parent and community member preparing those reports. I knew the tons of hours of hard work that went into gathering that information. Their disrespect broke my heart.

The facts just seemed to irritate the board members because it was not the easy way. They wanted to be nice community members—certainly they did not want to ruffle feathers and be marginalized by going against the establishment's agenda. They may have told themselves they were doing the right thing, but to me it seemed they were saying, "To hell with the children!"

Due to failed teaching methods, our children have struggled. How tragic! A generation of children has not learned to read well or master math facts and processes. Businessmen ask, "Where are the scientists and engineers?" We have to say we have none. They cannot read well enough to understand the science books or use high levels of math to become engineers. The results are that now we have to import scientists and engineers from China, India, Guatemala, and other nations. And our economy is floundering.

Meanwhile, many of our children are selling drugs, struggling to feed their families, and sitting in prison cells. Shame on us!

After years of fighting and winning the failed Bilingual Education Methods, we now won the reading and math wars, defeating Whole Language Reading and The New "New" (Modern) Math, or "fuzzy math" as it was called. We were on a roll, thanks to the other angry women who rose up to fight. There were special teachers that provided invaluable information, encouragement, and actually pushed me forward. Through published opinion columns, we garnered the community pressure that was needed to change votes.

Test scores rose. The kids were becoming proficient in English, improving their vocabularies, learning to read well, and mastering their math facts so they could go on to higher math levels. Prayer, wonderful support from friends and teachers, a love for the children, and a determination to win is what won the day!

Chapter 13
Defending the Constitution

It was the year to adopt the eighth grade history textbooks. I asked friends to help me read the textbooks. One textbook said that the Constitution was made so that it could be easily changed. It stated that the second amendment, the right to bear arms, was only a reaction to the revolutionary war, like quartering of soldiers, implying that these rights were not needed today. I obviously disagreed.

At the public board meeting, right before the vote, I shared with the board what was in that particular book and objected to its adoption. Board member Nativo Lopez, the community organizer, said, "Well, that is what I believe; I will vote for it." And the textbook passed. So that is what the children will learn for the next seven years.

I was disappointed and upset. All the work we had done reading the textbooks. Perhaps I should have said nothing and advocated for this terrible textbook that twisted our history. And then, seeing my support, they probably would have voted against it. Most of the board members would never have known the difference, as they did not read the textbooks or bother to find out how US history was portrayed. In fact it saddened me that no one in the community cared to read the textbooks. This was the time for people to speak out about what was being taught in the schools. Sadly, there were never any public comments on the textbooks.

Perhaps this was because parents who cared put their children in private Christian schools, Catholic schools, or in our more patriotic fundamental schools in the district. While Santa Ana has wealthy homes in the north, a large low-income central area, and middle class homes on the south, most of the students, 96 percent, were low-income Hispanic children. Parents worked hard, often six days a week, and some could not read. They were new to America, and did not understand its history. In fact, many parents who vote on election day rely on their older children to advise them. The young people have better English skills, and their parents assume they know more about America having gone through the schools.

Years before the Latino activists and community organizers took over the board I realized that students did not have to pass a United States Constitution test. When I grew up, the eighth grade Constitution test was a big deal. You could not go on to high school until you passed the test. Our fundamental schools required children to memorize certain parts of our founding documents. But it was not a district mandate to do so in all of our schools.

I was new to the school board, and to my amazement, the battle for a Constitution test was an incredible fight. Several times I put it on the agenda, and it was continually rejected. "How could they object?" I was surprised that the schools were not requiring the children to pass a Constitution test. I thought it was just expected. This was such critical knowledge for all children, but especially for our new immigrant children! They were living under a constitutional republic form of government. Certainly they needed to know the principles and the system that governed the nation.

When our family became naturalized citizens, five years after we arrived in America, I remember my parents studying American history and the Constitution. I heard them discussing it as they prepared for their citizenship test. I asked mom, "Why don't we have to pass a history and Constitution test to become a citizen?" "Oh, you will," she said. "They will teach you in school."

I tried five times to require a United States Constitution test, but failed. The district wanted to make it a US history and Constitution test and wanted to include very strange concepts. One bizarre concept was "civic virtue," which according to the new global civics education materials meant giving up your personal rights for the common good—the good of the world.

This definition of "civic virtue" is the exact opposite of what is taught in the US Constitution and Declaration of Independence, where it is clearly stated that men possess God-given individual rights, and it is the duty of governments to protect those rights. It is not civic virtue to ask people to give up their God-given rights.

I found that these strange civic concepts came from the Center for Civic Education out of Calabasas, California. The books and materials were beautiful and looked very patriotic with pictures of the founding fathers signing the constitution. Their main curriculum initiative is called "We the People." The Center for Civic Education and books were created and distributed with funds from the US Department of Education, under Goals 2000, Clinton's educational programs. The books with their beautiful patriotic pictures look wonderful. Most parents and educators would glance at them and believe that our children are learning about the greatness of America. And many, even if they read the books, may not have picked up on the subtle themes. But my father had taught me well.

I knew these supplemental books were not American textbooks; these were world textbooks. And indeed they are being used all over the world in many nations, including the United States.

To my knowledge, these supplemental books do not go through the regular state adoption process. Nevertheless, history teachers are invited to the County Department of Education to take workshops on how to include them in their classrooms. It is also interesting to note that the lesson plans are being funded by multiple funding sources in our government. One lesson plan under the topic of "authority" carried the notation that its development was funded by the National Endowment for Humanities, the US Department of Justice, Office of Juvenile Justice and Delinquency Prevention, and the Office of Justice programs.

Our federal government is using our tax dollars to develop these books, provide teacher training, and to help other nations use them as well. Imagine! We thought the federal Department of Education was overseeing education in America, but it is also exporting global education to other nations, reinterpreting American history and redefining American values.

The superintendent changed my agenda item to require a US Constitution test/US history test. It appeared the district was trying to trick me into including these new strange global concepts in the Constitution test. I had to insist that the teachers use only the language in the Constitution when they studied. It was also mandatory for all eighth graders to pass the test before going on to high school, making it a high stakes test. Thank God I saw through their masquerade.

Other nations probably welcomed the curriculum because they wanted the freedoms of the United States. In the books, young people are asked to embrace "democracy," participatory democracy. President Bill Clinton used that term often. Everyone thought he was talking about freedom and our form of government, but he was really talking about "shared governance," government by committee, a form of government promoted by the United Nations. I had learned from personal experience in several circumstances how committees are used to manipulate people, evade an opposing view, and give an appearance of consensus. It is called participatory democracy because everyone has to participate and go along with the pre-prescribed central plan. Dissenters are not tolerated and are always removed.

Because having a required Constitution test was such a battle,

I knew I was on to something—something important. And I knew restoring the knowledge of our nation's first principles was key. It made me all that more determined to make sure the children knew what was in our Constitution. I was on a mission.

Looking back, it is important to note that I do not think that everyone that fought against a required US Constitution test hated America and her founding principles. Tragically, most people are not aware of the battle. They do not realize we are losing the knowledge that made America great and prosperous. There are great forces out there that do not want our children to know who they are as a nation. Nowhere is there a greater stronghold than in our inner cities. And because our new immigrant children do not know differently, they are easily taught and manipulated. We need to care what happens in our inner cities because the students are the voters of tomorrow.

When I was running for Congress, I picked up a magazine that interviewed our very liberal Congresswoman Loretta Sanchez, my opponent. Even though the Catholic Church excommunicated her for her strong abortion views and votes, she wore a cross necklace on her sweater hoping to identify with the Hispanic religious beliefs of the voters. In the article, she urged young people to get their parents out to vote and help them cast their ballots.

Young people are key in elections. If the schools do not teach our nation's first principles, I do not know who will. And sadly, misled young people are dangerous to our nation's future.

Voting booths are now brought onto our high schools to make sure they capture the young Latino vote. MTV, watched by many young people, promotes voting with their campaign "Rock the Vote."

The Latino vote is very important to both Republicans and Democrats, as it can determine the direction of our nation. President George W. Bush understood that and with his compassionate conservativism was able to get 44 percent of the

Latino vote in 2004. And Latino young people influence much of that vote.

If our youth could just learn what made America great (its liberating values and sound founding principles) and become acquainted with the amazing US Constitution that has stood the test of time, it would be all over for those who want "to fundamentally transform" America. It would devastate the Left that wants us to become good socialist global citizens, surrendering our individual rights for the common good.

After several unsuccessful attempts to require the Constitution test, I let the issue rest for a while. But then I found the perfect opportunity to strike.

At our next board meeting, we would be swearing in two new school board members, Nativo Lopez and John Palacio, both liberal Latino activists. Surely they would not care about the Constitution test! Was all hope gone?

This was my last chance. We had a board of five members. I only needed three votes. I decided to place the item on the agenda. The two new board members stood up and were sworn in. In front of a large crowd, they stood to attention, proudly raised their right hands, and recited the oath of office. "I promise to protect and defend the Constitution of the United States against all enemies foreign and domestic." No sooner than they sat down, the agenda item came up. "Shall we require every eighth grader to pass a US Constitution test before they can go on to high school?" What could they do?

They just swore in front of the public to defend the Constitution. They voted yes!

Chapter 14

Recalling the Devil

The trucks with American flags waving in the wind drove up and down the city streets. Signs on cars and trucks read, "Recall School Board Member Nativo Lopez!" "Nativo Lopez Lied." "English for the Children" signs from the Prop. 227 state initiative campaign were placed on the sides of the truck. Cars lined up and formed parades driving through the neighborhoods, honking their horns. Drivers waved and shouted at people walking. "Recall Nativo Lopez!" The city was abuzz.

Grocery store managers called the police as the red shirts and the blue shirts battled it out in front of the stores and parking lots. "Sign the recall papers!" shouted the red shirts who were gathering recall signatures. "No, don't sign the recall papers!" shouted the blue shirts. "And if you did sign the recall papers, sign here, and your name will be taken off the list." It was hand-to-hand combat in the streets and at the supermarkets.

As signature gatherers marched door-to-door collecting recall signatures, they found that the community was with them. The people knew something was terribly wrong in our schools. Anglo residents, of course, had long been angry that they had lost their neighborhoods, that going shopping for groceries felt like going to a foreign country, as few spoke in English. But Latino parents too knew that English was important to their children's future. They personally understood that if they wanted to move up to become a supervisor or clerical person, they had to improve their English skills. Many mothers angrily said, "I will teach my children Spanish at home, but we want the schools to teach English!"

With the current failed bilingual methods, the children did not master Spanish, and they did not master English. Many spoke "Spanglish." Teachers and school board members falsely encouraged them, saying, "College is in your future," but it wasn't.

Two angry mothers, Vivian and Veronica, came to the school board meeting. They were fuming! The principal of their elementary school refused to translate the PTA meeting into English. The principal told the mothers, "Just come to my office after the meeting, and I will tell you what was said in the meetings." "No!" the Latino parents replied. "This is the United States. English is the language here. My kids need English and so do we. We want the meetings in English, and we want our kids to learn English!"

These angry women continued to complain week after week at the public board meetings. The principal stood her ground. The parents tried to remove the principal, collecting signatures at their school. But the principal was protected by the school board members and the district.

Other angry parents became concerned and joined the effort. They knew I was an advocate for English instruction. I had received English instruction when I first came to this country. It helped me graduate from high school and college with honors. They knew I was born in Guatemala and had spoken only Spanish when I arrived. These frustrated parents contacted me and pleaded for help.

It was time to channel their energy to constructively make changes in education. I advised, "Why don't we get some parents together and form a parents' group and work on educational issues." Several concerned mothers came to our first meeting. The parents complained and complained about different issues, special education, English instruction, and the lack of communication. The more they talked, the more the conversation centered on School board member Nativo Lopez, who refused to allow the district to implement Proposition 227, the "English for the Children" initiative. "We have to get rid of him!" they agreed. I only listened.

"We cannot wait for another election." "That's it! That is what we will do." "We will recall him!" "Yes, if he will not listen to us. We will take action. We will do it ourselves." Then the competition was on. Two mothers each wanted to be the first one to draw the recall petition from the Register of Voters. They ran out the door to file the paperwork.

"Do not mess with angry moms!" is what I say. Sarah Palin agreed. She calls them Mother Grizzlies. "Don't mess with our babies, our children!" Secondly, Latinos are passionate people. And angry Latina mothers are even more passionate.

Five angry mothers, led by Vivian Martinez and Beatriz Salas, led the recall fight. They came to the school district and complained that their children were placed in Spanish classes and they had to fight to get them out. They were outraged that the PTA meetings were in Spanish and not translated for them into English. They were fed up.

It was the perfect storm. Nativo had ticked off the parents. But he also ticked off the mayor by trying to sue him. The Latino activist school board, led by Nativo Lopez, also tried to build a school at the north end of town, where the more affluent residents of Santa Ana live. Some of the houses there look like the house in the movie, *Home Alone*. These residents are very protective of their tranquil, tree-lined neighborhoods. They meet regularly, have a neighborhood association and a neighborhood newsletter. You might call them a different type of "homie" who protects his turf. Many of the residents are retired, and the young professionals who lived there usually send their children to private schools.

Eyebrows raised, and soon the residents in the north were alarmed that a school that would serve the inner city would be placed in their neighborhood. The northern residents rented two buses and came down to the school board meeting to address the board. They were sophisticated folks, knew local government, and wanted to share their views on the proposed school with the school board. They were not really looking for a rumble.

Their message was "We do not want a school here." They did their homework. The closest child who was slated to enroll in the school had to walk over an hour to reach the school. The school would be next to the busy Santa Ana Freeway. They had scientific experts share stats on the quality of the air and the danger it posed to the children.

Their real concern was for the quality of their neighborhood. "There is only one way into the school, and we know parents have to drive in to pick up their children. Like they do at other schools, parents will wait in their cars for the children to come out, and they will leave trash and dirty diapers," they complained. They had done their research.

School board member Nativo Lopez knew they were coming to the board meeting, and he was ready for them. He had enlisted the help of young people from the MECHA high school clubs. According to their national website, MECHA stands for Movimiento Estudiantil Chicano de Aztlán (Student Movement for Chicanos of Aztlan). Aztlan is the name they give to a large part of California, or all of the land that used to belong to Mexico before the Mexican American War. They believe that "the land belongs to the indigenous people," the people of Mexican descent, and they "do not have to submit to any foreign invaders." Are they saying they do not need to obey the (immigration) laws of the United States? It is a Latino activist high school club found in most of our Hispanic high schools.

The district moved the board meeting to the junior high gymnasium next door. The chairs were filled with people. The MECHA young people sat on the floor in front of all of the chairs. When these older retired citizens, some with walking canes, came forward to the microphone, one by one, to address the school board in the large gymnasium, the teenagers stood up and disrespectfully turned their backs on the older residents who were speaking. The back of their T-shirts read, "You turn your back on us, we will turn our back on you."

Well, needless to say, this rude behavior did not go over well with these older citizens. Soon each speaker began their speech with, "We are not racists, but…." They had been taught that young people should be respectful of their elders, and they felt very disrespected. They had every right to address the board of education. They soon understood that board member Nativo Lopez had put the kids up to this disgraceful behavior. Not only was the city mayor mad at Nativo for a previous lawsuit but also now the more affluent residents of the north part of town were angered.

The recall brought out Lopez's Marxist tendencies. After all, his mentor was Bert Corona, once a board member of the Los Angeles Communist School who was also accused of inciting violence. Bert Corona was a fan of the Communist Sandinistas and their Nicaraguan leader Daniel Ortega, as shown in pictures of them smiling together. When Corona died, Nativo renamed his building "The Bert Corona Social Center." Community organizer Nativo Lopez showed his Marxist tendencies when he wrote his anti- recall campaign fliers in Spanish calling the residents in north Santa Ana "*cerdos ricos*": rich pigs.

Vivian Martinez, one of the angry mothers, had worked with Ron Unz, a former candidate for governor of California and a wealthy Silicon Valley executive, to pass Proposition 227, the "English for the Children" initiative. And now she in turn needed his help with the recall. Vivian called and received financial backing from Mr. Unz. Unz had spent millions of dollars to pass the initiative. He was not going to sit back and allow Nativo Lopez, as president of the school board, to refuse to enforce the law. He was not going to take Lopez's rebellion, distortion of the law, and his continued disregard for the will of the people.

Ron Unz also wanted to make sure the recall would be successful. Knowing I was on the school board and supportive of his cause, he called me and asked me if I knew someone who could lead the recall effort. I immediately thought of Tim Whitacre.

Tim had helped me on my campaigns, and I knew he was a hard worker. Tim Whitacre was a former Marine. And we all know, "once a Marine, always a Marine." Tim knew how to take the hill. Tim ran the recall effort out of his real estate office. He personally led the recall parades through town. And he even found an old army truck for the team. It was large and we called it the "Bomber." Each Saturday the large army truck was decorated with "Recall Nativo Lopez" signs and "English for the Children" signs. Recall team members rode around waving at residents and yelling with mega phones, "Recall Nativo Lopez!" They also honked their horns and threw out candy for the children.

Tim had red T-shirts printed with bright yellow letters, "Recall Nativo Lopez."

The red shirts took to the streets to gather signatures for the recall. Nativo and his gang did not sit still. They dispatched their team with the blue shirts and followed the red shirts around door-to-door and to the grocery stores. The red recall shirts asked a shopper to sign the petition. And if they signed the petition, a blue shirt would follow him to his car and intimidate him, often blocking the door of the car, urging them to sign the new petition to take their name off of the petition that they had just signed. Shoppers complained of this intimidation, and grocery store owners called the police. It was combat, and Tim was prepared.

Tim knew how to write press releases, and he kept the newspapers apprised of the effort. He also had a good relationship with the mayor. It was not difficult for the mayor to get behind the effort; he knew Lopez was a troublemaker.

The mayor raised the money. The older citizens in the north who had been insulted donated, and the angry mothers marched through the streets gathering the required signatures. Soon whole bands of people joined in gathering signatures. They knocked on doors. "Nativo Lopez, our school board member, will not enforce the law you voted on. He will not give our children English. He is denying our kids success in the workplace and in college." The Registrar of Voters required 8,000 signatures, but the angry mothers gathered 14,000!

It was an amazing effort; the north, the south, and the inner city all joined in. Everyone knew the children needed English. And it was obvious that once you pass a law, it should be obeyed. Ron Unz gave the startup funds, the north sustained the effort with their donations, and the passionate mothers worked tirelessly on the streets.

After all the votes were cast, the victory was complete. We had won in EVERY precinct by a margin of two to one!

The newspaper stands had large posters on the metal newsstand advertising the successful recall. The headlines in the newspapers read, "Nativo Lopez Recalled."

The victory was sweet. On election night, the hardworking recall team met at Tim's real estate office, our recall campaign office, to celebrate with sodas and pizza. Many wore their red shirts. We stood in a circle to pray and thank God for the victory. Ron Unz called: "Congratulations for a job well done." Then Mayor Pulido called: "Thank you for all of your hard work." "We are all celebrating here in the north. Why don't you hop in that army bomber truck and come have hors d'oeuvres and champagne with us?" After we finished the pizza, some of us headed north to celebrate.

Before we started the recall, a few of us met with the mayor. He said he would try to help. Before we left, Tim asked the mayor if we could all pray together. The mayor agreed, and we all held hands in a circle and committed the recall to God and asked for his favor. The recall victory started with prayer and ended with prayer.

While the city celebrated, the disgraced Lopez snuck quietly out of town. For him it was a resounding defeat.

It took a few angry mothers, mother grizzlies Vivian and Beatriz and others, to make a difference. They were hardworking, dedicated mothers who loved their children. They worked tirelessly. As I tell everyone, "You can never underestimate the power of five angry moms."

Before we left to celebrate with the others, some of the team wanted to take a picture. "Come here, Rosie, come here. We want to take a picture." I joined the group. They wore their red shirts that read "Recall Nativo Lopez." I wore my red suit jacket. The picture was taken. Then I turned around. Abie Garcia, one of the fathers, was still holding up a hand-painted sign. It read, "Rosie de Mama de Santa Ana." It was a wonderful tribute.

But what made the victory so complete was the unity of the city! It took all of us—the hardworking parents of the inner city, the rich residents of the north, the middle class in the south, and the city leadership—united and working together with a single focus. We the people….They call it people power. The American process worked. And it was powerful!

Chapter 15

Exposing Corruption

There was another traitor, a Benedict Arnold, in town. He was the Orange County Sheriff. He was greatly loved, a shining star. In fact, they called him the Nation's Sheriff. A young five-year-old girl was missing and found dead, having been sexually abused. The whole nation followed the story of Samantha Runion, a beautiful Orange County little girl who was abducted and murdered. Sheriff Mike Carona was very involved; certainly he was seen in all of the photo shoots consoling the distraught mother. In the end, the sheriff captured the bad guy. Everyone rejoiced!

The sheriff closely identified himself with after-school programs for children. He and the future California Governor Arnold Schwarzenegger campaigned for a state funding initiative for after-school programs. He became the poster child for after-school clubs. The sheriff was the Master of Ceremonies at the Boys and Girls Club, the Boy Scouts, and the YMCA fundraising events. He gave his Christian testimony at the Christian Businessmen's Committee breakfast. He was the county's "little darling."

He was a Republican, and I had walked precincts for his election and dropped his brochure on people's doorsteps. We even filmed political advertisements for the same Republican cause.

One day, we were surprised, maybe shocked is a better word, to see that he had endorsed Nativo Lopez, John Palacio, and Nadia Maria Davis, all Latino Activists, all Democrats, for the Santa Ana School Board race. I and another Republican Central Committee member Lupe Moreno were running for school board in the same election. How could this be?

I know school board races are supposed to be nonpartisan. It wasn't just that we were Republicans and they were Democrats, but Nativo Lopez was being sued by the state of California. They wanted him to give back a million dollars for not verifying that he had taught English and citizenship classes with the taxpayers' money. He did not return signatures and reports on the people he claimed took his classes. How could a sheriff who stood for law and order even want to be associated with someone who was already suspect of fraudulently spending the taxpayers' money? Previously Nativo had also been investigated for voter fraud. It just did not make sense.

We called the sheriff's office. Tim Whitacre and others who were helping our campaign complained directly to him, his assistants, and to the Republican Party. Nativo Lopez campaign flyers were now being circulated in the neighborhoods. Nativo had his picture taken in the sheriff's office, shaking hands with him. And the sheriff's endorsement quote was printed in large print alongside the picture.

Sheriff Mike Carona admitted that he gave the endorsement and was allowing the picture to go out. Later at a meeting, I asked him why he gave the endorsement. He answered, "Nativo is going to do after-school clubs for the children." I was shocked! Absolutely dumbfounded! "Didn't the sheriff remember that I had gone to his office earlier in the year to share with him about our after-school programs and our character clubs in the schools and teen sport centers? And why in the world would he support someone accused of fraud and considered a Marxist teaching our children? What's more, I knew Nativo Lopez did not have after-school programs for kids!

Lopez was also known for voter fraud in the infamous congressional Sanchez-Dornan race. He was already notorious for encouraging people to vote before they became citizens, and, as mentioned before, he was asked to give one million dollars back to the state for misuse of funds. Why would the sheriff, a law-and-order man, want to be connected to someone like him?

Now we had to run against not only Nativo Lopez but also "the nation's little darling sheriff."

But what made matters worse was that after the election in which both Mr. Lopez and I won, Sheriff Mike Carona publicly said that he was still allowing Lopez to use his picture and endorsement for his anti-recall campaign!

Even the liberal Congresswoman Loretta Sanchez, whom Nativo helped get elected, was smart enough to stay out of the recall. She wrote a letter to that effect.

We kept wondering why Mike Carona would give his endorsement. It was obvious that the county sheriff was planning to run for state office. He had promised when he first ran for sheriff that he would only stay on for two terms. He had his eye on the office of state attorney general. It now appeared that the sheriff thought Nativo Lopez could deliver the Latino vote on his behalf. It was obvious to us that they had cut a deal.

Ironically, Nativo Lopez was not the guy to go to for the Latino vote. I ran in several elections against him. As I walked from house to house for my campaign, I would see signs for Lopez but inevitably there were no registered voters at these houses. It appeared that they were renters who may have recently come to this country and could not vote. It occurred to us that they were probably using Nativo's services and were asked for a political favor. Once at a board meeting, Lopez told us he had traveled all over Mexico, putting up signs encouraging people to come to Santa Ana and that he would help them once they arrived. It is no wonder Santa Ana had become the gateway to the United States. And once again our tax dollars were funding his operations.

Two people who had attended his citizenship classes had shared with us that they had learned that the United States had forty-eight states. Obviously they were using old material, and the teachers themselves were unaware of it.

One mother came to the school board to complain. She complained that school board member Nativo Lopez refused to help her get her son's special education class changed until she first found him one hundred families to join his organization and pay the fees. Evidently he was running his organization like the PRI, a political party in Mexico. The PRI is known for providing services in exchange for political favors. And this was who the sheriff was cutting a deal with.

When the sheriff was up for re-election and wanted the Republican Party to endorse him, we were at the Republican Central Committee as voting members. Tim Whitacre, the marine, led the battle. "Come on," he said, "Let's speak out." "Speak out against the sheriff?" This was hard. We won the election. We won the recall. Was this necessary? Sometimes it is easier to speak in front of the public than to stand up in front of your own friends.

The sheriff's chief of staff spoke, asking for an endorsement. The mother of five-year-old Samantha Runion, who was killed by a sexual predator, spoke and cried and shared her story. She expressed her gratitude toward the sheriff and his support during the terrible ordeal. Sheriff Mike Carona shared what a great job he had done and he ended his speech with, "I love Ronald Reagan, and I love California Governor Deukmejian." (Both are greatly respected by this group of Orange County Republicans).

Tim spoke up against the sheriff's endorsement and laid out all of the facts. Lupe, who ran for school board against Nativo Lopez, and lost, gave a stirring emotional speech. And I took up the end. "I used to love Sheriff Mike Carona; I worked for his campaign. I trusted him, but I no longer have respect for him. For political gain, he betrayed the children of the inner city, betrayed his friends, and sold out his morals.... I know one thing for sure; Ronald Reagan would never endorse Nativo Lopez for school board, and he would never endorse Mike Carona for sheriff!"

President Ronald Reagan understood freedom, disdained class

warfare, and hated Marxism, and he could sniff a Marxist a mile away. No, indeed, he would never endorse a character like Nativo Lopez, and I do not think he would have endorsed Mike Carona!

The sheriff lost the Republican endorsement that night, and it was a front-page story.

But that was not the end of it. The sheriff lobbied the Republican leadership and the Central Committee Members and bent the rules. At the next committee meeting, they pushed the endorsement through. And Sheriff Mike Carona was endorsed by the Republicans for his re-election campaign.

But did that discourage the Marine? No! Tim fought even harder. Soon more and more dirt was coming out about the sheriff, and Tim Whitacre made sure the newspapers knew about it. He sent out weekly articles to the newspapers about the sheriff and his Mafia connections. Then there was the daily exposé about marital infidelity and his long-term mistress. Then accusations were made of his underhanded financial dealings, the bribes he took, and favors he gave.

The newspaper was relentless, carrying pictures daily of the sheriff being arrested, of his trial, of his corrupt business partners, of his mistress, and pictures of him at trial. Bribery charges, corruption charges, money laundering. You name it, and the sheriff had done it. He had become so corrupt that both he and his assistant were sent to prison. The downfall of the sheriff was so complete because it was so shocking compared to the image he tried to portray. It was a sensational story. Both Nativo Lopez and Sheriff Carona were disgraced!

Before his exposure, I ran into the sheriff at a dinner in a swanky hotel. I approached him and had the distinct pleasure of asking him, "How is the Jane Fonda of Orange County? Mike, why did you sell the children of Santa Ana down the river?" Obviously, he did not reply.

As I think back on it, it seemed God sent him down the river. God cares about the children in Santa Ana.

"Big Donuts in America"

Los Angeles Century Blvd landmark

"The American Dream"

Rosie, age 9

Coming to America

Rosie's parents   *Brothers served their country*

"High School Days"

Cheer squad - flag twirler

Honor Society - top 2% of her class

Homecoming princess

Homecoming court

"College and Marriage"

Biola student

Engagement photo

Wedding day

Avila received more votes than any other candidate in the last school board election by campaigning against school-based health clinics and higher taxes.

Santa Ana School Board's *Flawed Parenting* advocate "comprehensive" sex ed program, for kids in grades, school that led Rosemarie Avila for why to run as a seat on the board.

Santa Ana School Board

Rosie's school board campaign

"Politics"

Biola University Trustee at graduation

Congressional candidate

Rosie and her husband, Jim

Education presentation

"Mentoring Activities"

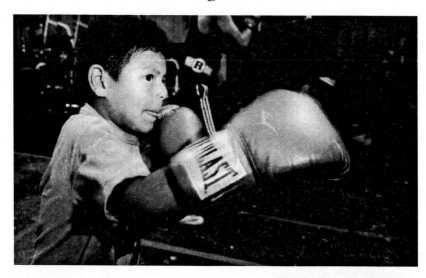

Clockwise: Neighborhood boxing club, School-based afterschool clubs, skateboard (and wrestling) sports clubs, character building activities

"Entrepreneurial Workplaces"

Entrepreneurial workplace boutique (thrift shop) in Garden Grove, CA

Clockwise: Community youth events at boutique: artwalk, live music night; Displays at second boutique "training older youth how to work and start businesses"

"The Future Vision"

Possible sites for Orange County Mentoring University (Ch. 26-27)

Architectural rendering of the old Santa Ana Civic Center YMCA

First American Title building

Part IV
Inside Education

Making Global Citizens

"The philosophy of the school room in one generation will be the philosophy of government in the next." —*Abraham Lincoln*

"Hopefully, some day, we can track children from preschool to high school and from high school to college and college to career."

—*US Secretary of Education Arne Duncan*

Chapter 16
Lifelong Learning

After so many victories on the school board: a successful recall, the teaching of English, a real phonics reading program, traditional math textbooks, a required Constitution test, and test scores rising not only in our fundamental schools but also throughout the district, it seemed I should have been triumphant. Instead I came to such great despair!

Something much more sinister than poor curriculum and faulty teaching methods was happening in our schools.

Education is key to "world changers," whether they call themselves Communists, Socialists, or Progressives. These "change agents" know they cannot always change the minds of the older generation, so they work hard to control the minds of the younger ones.

Conservatives have viewed education differently. We continue to think of education as the teaching of reading, writing, and arithmetic, along with science and history. And if teachers aren't doing a good job at giving children these important life skills, we should replace the teachers.

The priority of education in a Socialist country is no longer just to teach reading and writing and mathematics but to also make sure that everyone has politically correct views. It is important that the students walk lockstep with the statist agenda because their system is based on atheism and works only with tight control. Files, like the Ganglia files of Communist China, are kept on students and other individuals, and the contents in your file determine your career, your health care, and your place in society.

We scratch our heads and wonder, "What in the world has happened to education?" We know something is not right.

On October 17, 1979, President Jimmy Carter signed S.120 into law, establishing a federal Department of Education. The Department of Education Organization Act was Jimmy Carter's way of paying back the liberal teachers' unions and particularly the NEA, the National Education Association, for their help in his election.

After Carter, President Ronald Reagan commissioned a study on education called "A Nation at Risk." It came out in April 1983 and had strong Cold War rhetoric. The report stated that if another country had done to us what our educational system was doing to us, it would be considered an act of war! At the unveiling of this thirty-page report, President Reagan endorsed returning to school prayer, school vouchers and the elimination of the Department of Education.

"A Nation at Risk," with its strong language, was on the front page of every newspaper, giving impetus to a new education reform movement. The public was alarmed, and now everyone wanted us to improve education. As is usually the case, the findings may be true but what to do with them is where most differ. Conservatives, who champion limited government, tend to look for local solutions, while liberals look to government to establish their agenda though taxpayer dollars. Conservatives want to "Fire the teacher!" while liberals work to establish "Goals 2000," the eight *national* education goals, or whatever they name their new global agenda.

Now with a national Department of Education, the Progressives had the power to push their politically correct agenda on the schools. "A Nation at Risk," an educational crisis, was just what they needed to use as an impetus for their reform measures. "Don't let any crisis go to waste" is the Progressive or social revolutionist mantra.

The Department of Education created federal education

laboratories. At one point, there were around twenty-five education laboratories creating new curriculum and teaching methods.
These education labs were filled with social engineers and social
scientists such as William Spady and '60s radical revolutionary
Bill Ayers. Bill Ayers was the founder of the Weather Underground, a militant '60s antiwar group, involved in bombings of
the Pentagon and other criminal behavior. He is also an American elementary education theorist and is behind much of our
new elementary school curriculum. These socialist reformers,
using our tax dollars, brought in strange educational methods,
such as Outcome-Based Education, Whole Language, Collaborative Learning, and Thematic Units.

President Reagan had promised to close the federal Department of Education when he ran for president, but he did not.
I always wondered what happened. Recently I heard William
Bennett, Reagan's Secretary of Education, on the radio. He
explained that the Senate would not confirm him unless he
promised not to close the department. Reagan thought the
Department of Education with William Bennett at the helm
would make a good bully pulpit guiding the way to true educational reform. The Department of Education, under Mr. Bennett,
produced an excellent educational booklet titled What Works.
I ordered several copies and passed them around. It reaffirmed
my education philosophy and strengthened me in the education
battles that lay ahead.

Sadly, I do not know of anyone else that read it. In all of
our educational discussions, it never came up. What a shame!
President Reagan should have closed the department.

President George H. W. Bush (Senior) was elected, and after
"A Nation at Risk" he said, "I will be the education president."
In 1989, President H. W. Bush held an Educational Summit
for Governors and introduced America 2000, six national edu-
cation goals. Governor Bill Clinton of Arkansas and Governor
Richard Riley of South Carolina (President Clinton's education

secretary), and Marilyn McCune presented the goals. America 2000 came out of the World Conference of Education for All, sponsored by the World Bank. The goals sounded good and they were voluntary.

When co-Presidents Bill and Hillary Clinton were elected, they made the once-voluntary goals mandatory, added two more goals, and changed all of the federal education funding under the Elementary and Secondary Education Act to fund the implementation of the eight goals. They also changed the name of the goals from America 2000 to Goals 2000 because they knew they were not American but rather global goals.

President Reagan should have listened to Ed Meese III who told him not to support "A Nation at Risk," as it went against his stand to eliminate the national Department of Education. President George H. W. Bush should have known better too. Why did he invite the governors? Didn't he know that education was a local issue for school board members who were directly accountable to the parents and community? Children belong to parents, who have been given the responsibility to educate their children. Both the parents and the local community have to live with the consequences of our educational decisions.

National Education Goals, hmmm? As a school board member, I decided to become an expert on the new national education goals. The more I studied the goals, the more concerned I became!

I felt an urgency to tell people what I was seeing, but it was difficult. I felt like Matilda, a sweet six-year-old girl in a popular children's book of that name. Matilda was sent to a private school where the very wicked headmistress (or principal) Agatha Trunchbull would grab her by the hair and spin her around and throw her over the wall. She would also be placed in a closet for hours where spikes were pushed through so she could not move an inch. Her new friend, Miss Honey, a kind schoolteacher whom she confided in, asked her, "Why don't you tell your parents?" Matilda replied, "If I tell my parents, they will not believe me, and they will punish me for lying."

This was my dilemma. How could I tell people what I was seeing? No one will believe me. And everyone loves to punish the messenger.

Nevertheless, I tried to tell people. So I began my talks showing several popular new 3-D pictures. "The eight national goals, called Goals 2000 are like one of these 3-D pictures." We have all looked at these beautiful pictures with their colorful designs, but we were not sure what we were seeing. We were encouraged, "Look and stare, and after a while if you focus just right, you will see it. You will see a form inside...one much more real than all the colored designs." We focused and focused and there it was! We saw it. Sometimes it was a dolphin or the Statue of Liberty or a world globe.

As I stared at the eight national goals, the form I saw was frightening!

I set out to educate others, but soon realized that I could not simply tell people what I was seeing, I had to show them. It was important that they see the actual documents from the Federal Department of Education and from the school district education grant applications that funded the different programs.

There is not enough ink in this book to show you what was in my two-hour presentation. Rather, I will have to give you a quick summary of what is planned for you, our children, and grandchildren.

The national goals use the term *"lifelong learning."* To most people, this means that students will be well educated and will want to continue to learn independently all of their lives. Former Speaker of the House and presidential candidate Newt Gingrich mentions "lifelong learning" as he discusses education in his book *Renewing America.* He, like many others, believes that "lifelong learning" is a good thing. But when you understand the eight national goals, the term takes on a new meaning.

The national education goals cover everyone's life from the womb to the tomb. In other words, there is an educational program for every stage of your life. The social planners say they are bringing in "systemic change," changing our system. So it appears the government wants to make sure you are learning what they need you to know throughout your entire life. "Lifelong learning" is government prescribed and electronically monitored lifelong learning.

The goals set up a system of learning that starts with prenatal care and ends with continual re-education at the workplace. Local school districts are no longer K-12 institutions. They are now simply called education centers, and the goal is to have them open until late at night with education programs for parents. The ideal school, the "New American Schools," as they were called, according to former Secretary of Education Lamar Alexander, is open from 6 a.m. to 9 p.m. Schools were now asked to provide early day-care starting at three months, state-funded preschool, government funded after-school programs, and adult education programs at night.

State laws are now also encouraging corporations to provide additional education classes for their workers. Workers are asked to be constantly retrained and recertified, including parenting classes and mental-health classes, as well as workplace training.

Today our nation has signed several global educational treaties that obligate us to train everyone in a global education system. There are not only education treaties, but also treaties to govern almost every aspect of our life. To the elite global planners, it is important that everyone understands his responsibilities and are re-educated to accept new global concepts such as are found in the United Nations Rights of the Child and the United Nations Rights of Women and other global treaties. The United Nations Rights of the Child, though not yet ratified by the United States, protects children from parents who want to tell them what they can and cannot read or who they can associate with. It gives children more rights. Parents cannot force their children to go to church and children are given the right to divorce their parents. If you are bringing in a new global system, what better place than your local schools to educate the population and make sure everyone understands their new global responsibilities?

Vice President Al Gore came to Santa Ana to discuss over-crowded schools. It seems in preparation for his visit, Santa Ana schools were declared the most over-crowded schools in the nation. The event was billed as a town hall meeting. As a school board member of the "most over-crowded district in America," I requested to ask a question. "No," was the reply. I then asked if I could make a comment. The answer again was, "No." "We have created all of the questions and have already assigned who will ask them." "The vice president will make the comments." So much for an open town hall meeting!

Vice President Gore introduced a new concept. He wanted to have all the school facilities designed from Washington, D.C. The federal government would have all of the construction plans and designs, and local districts would just copy them. Our local Congresswoman Loretta Sanchez had authored a similar bill, wanting school construction to be a federal function rather than a state responsibility. Fortunately, it did not pass. But now I began to see an agenda here.

The average school building plans have to go to Sacramento, our state capital, an average of fifty-six times for approval. Can you imagine the waste of money and time if school districts had to make the Washington loop to get schools built?

Incidentally, our facility crisis was exacerbated by a previous state-funded program that instantly reduced class size from thirty-two students to twenty in the early grades. This forced the school district to scramble and quickly add portable classrooms to accommodate the new reduced class size. For every sixty children, we now needed three classrooms, whereas previously, only two classrooms were required.

Their global plans became clearer. If local schools are to be the new community centers that provide health care through school-based clinics, universal preschool, after-school programs, mental health programs, parent education, workplace certification, and every other government education program, certainly we would need a new design.

It was now no surprise when President Barack Obama allocated $17 billion in the Stimulus Bill to be earmarked for school construction. This was new school construction with federal dollars and of course that meant federal regulations. The federal funding for school construction was later removed.

It was at this time that I also began to notice that as new school district headquarters were built, they were no longer called just "unified school district" but given a broader name: "Education Center." It became evident that the local school sites were strategic in this new system as *re-education centers*.

When President Bill Clinton funded Goals 2000 through the "Elementary and Secondary Education Act," he established a cradle-to-grave educational system with personal files to track everyone's learning, certification, and workforce placement. Continuous "lifelong learning" was the goal. Academics were no longer the priority. The creation of a global citizen, the politically correct thinking and attitudes of each citizen, was what was important.

In the early '90s, California started requiring students to take a new state test based on state standards. Prior to this, districts could choose from several national testing companies. This kept testing competitive, and the local school districts were in control because they selected the test. The new California State C.L.A.S. Test surprised a lot of people because it asked psychological and politically correct questions measuring the student's attitudes. Only 15 percent of the test measured conventions or academics, actual math, reading, and grammar skills.

In my overhead presentation, I would show samples of the C.L.A.S. (California Learning Assessment System) test questions. "When would you throw rocks at the warehouse?" As I recall, the answer options were something like this: A) When you were mad at the owner. B) When your friends were throwing rocks at the warehouse. C) When you felt like throwing rocks. The question itself was illegitimate, but we were also upset that the students were not given an option to mark, "I would never throw rocks at a warehouse." Students must have questioned what the right answer was. After studying the goals, it appears the right answer might have been, "We throw rocks when our friends or group throws rocks." Maybe they were trying to get the answer that it is OK to throw rocks when others before you have broken windows. It was puzzling.

According to Joan Wonsley, in a Capital Resource report on the C.L.A.S. test (April 21, 1994), a test question called, *Just Lather, That's All*, "gruesomely describes a barber imagining cutting his customer's throat. The story describes his anger, describes the bloody act happening in his mind, and explains his eventual moral decision not to murder. The test prompts students to think about the emotions of the barber and how situations affect our own experiences. Students are told to list 'incidents from your life that have affected you in some way.' In light of this, aren't students asked to reveal emotionally-charged experiences which most likely deal with home life and morality?" Wonsley lists nine examples that clearly violate state education law that forbids asking students about family life, religion, and morality. Some reading prompts include, My Mother, Rachel West, which describes "children reacting to their mother's views on death and heaven." Additionally, the main character in Rosalily "questions God and the value of marriage."

According to the Capital Resource report, Dr. Richard Paul, director of the world renowned Center for Critical Thinking at California State University, Sonoma, (CSU, Sonoma), stated the C.L.A.S assessments "routinely ignore critical reading and writing skills essential for students entering the job market." He calls the C.L.A.S "a colossal example of educational malpractice" and "it systematically rewards the wrong set of values those which are subjective, idiosyncratic and irrational."

Another question, I recall, asked the students, "Have you ever been mad at your parents because you were hungry?" In my presentations after I shared the content of the C.L.A.S. test questions, I would show the back of the test booklet that showed who produced the tests. It stated in large letters "Psychological Corp."

The test questions were psychological and very guarded. Teachers were not allowed to share them. Parents were forbidden to see them. And when we, school board members, asked to see them, we were told we could look at them, but had to sign a form that we would never talk about them. So what was the use in seeing them? I never signed the paper and did not get to see the samples they gave school board members.

Fortunately, there were courageous teachers and other researchers who shared the information. Once again, it took five angry mothers who gave up a year of their lives to travel back and forth across the state, informing school superintendents, newspaper editorial boards, parents, and community leaders about the tests. It was these valiant mothers, led by Carolyn Steinke, a mother of seven, who exposed and defeated the C.L.A.S. test! They alerted parents to what their children were learning in school. Many parents across the state refused to have their children tested, and some districts refused to give the test, claiming the scoring and grading was unfair. Calls from twenty thousand concerned citizens jammed legislator's phone lines. Attorney Brad Dacus, now president of the Pacific Justice Institute, filed an injunction, and Governor Pete Wilson in 1995 pulled the test.

The exposure of psychological and attitudinal testing is perhaps what helped turn the tide toward academics. Now, at least for a while, the educational establishment knew parents were watching.

Unfortunately, we are again seeing this massive personal and attitudinal data collected through the new national Common Core tests, under Obama's "Race to the Top" educational funding. In fact, the massive data collection is not only disturbing, but also shocking, as educational manuals suggest that students are to be given wrist bands and other technical equipment to measure how long they take to answer questions, their breathing habits, and level of perspiration. The purpose, they say, is so they will know how hard the questions are so they can tailor-make new test questions for the students to bring them up to the next level. This new national educational system is individualized and has plans to use scientific methods to change our students' minds and attitudes. Constant, continual student testing and re-testing are required to make sure they are doing a good job at re-educating our children. Test questions, all given by computers, and out of sight of parents and the community, can be designed specifically for each individual child to make sure they are becoming the politically correct citizen of tomorrow.

After the educational establishment brought in state tests, President George W. Bush helped turn the tide toward academics by demanding every district, every teacher, bring students to a new federal education standard by the year 2014. And with the influx of "back to basics" school board members and other board members at the state level, our classrooms returned to more academics, but it was short lived.

This was because President George W. Bush, perhaps unknowingly, had his education plan, "No Child Left Behind," linked to a global education treaty. Under UNESCO, an agency of the United Nations, and Education for All (global education plan), students worldwide had to meet the same requirements by 2015, just one year later than the No Child Left Behind goal of 2014. Teachers hated the pressure, as along with the deadline came more prescriptive monitoring of each teacher and each child's progress. The love of teaching grew dim as teachers were forced to analyze data and develop an individual plan for each student. By pulling education toward more academics, many accepted the notion that the *federal* government could or should measure our children´s individual learning. Sadly, "No Child Left Behind" only moved the global agenda forward and took us further into politically correct, attitudinal education by giving our local control to the federal government.

Many of us knew something was wrong when Senator Ted Kennedy, a long-time liberal education advocate, was seen smiling and shaking hands with President George W. Bush as they celebrated the signing of the new federal "No Child Left Behind" education laws and funding.

The new Common Core state standards, a *federal* initiative, from President Obama's "Race to the Top" educational law and funding, continue to bring in "world class" education, which is linked to global treaties. It officially creates a *national* government education system through extensive computer-based testing which drives curriculum and instruction. Common Core violates three state and federal laws that prohibit the establishment of a national curriculum.

What is troubling is that it was forced on states, through funding promises during difficult financial times. Little information was given to the states, as the actual curriculum was not developed and therefore not available for review. Teachers are told they will be helping to create the curriculum, but teachers have secretly complained to me that most of the curriculum is set and their involvement is minimal or a sham. Without really being allowed to participate in the development of the curriculum, teachers are asked to sign the sign-in sheets to show they have.

Most of the program is computer driven, making it even more difficult for parents to see what their children are actually learning. It will undoubtedly be continually changed without parent and community review. Because it is global education, traditional American classical literature is omitted, and replaced by utilitarian technical materials such as workplace instructional manuals and Obama's Executive Orders. The new Common Core standards are linked to the "common good," or what the global planners want our children to know and accept. David Barton, a historian of America's founding, worries that cursive writing, or handwriting, is totally eliminated under Common Core education, making it impossible for future young people to actually read primary-source materials like the Declaration of Independence, the US Constitution, and the Federalist Papers (which explain the founders' intents) because they are handwritten in cursive.

Some states are starting to reject Common Core, as slowly we are learning more about what is taught, not taught, and how it is administered through prescriptive technology. It includes the same educational reforms of the '90s, such as thematic units, collaborative learning, and outcome-based measurements.

Through each of our past presidents, whether Democrat or Republican, the global education agenda has moved forward. Tragically, parents, through their local school boards, are no longer in charge of curriculum, teaching methods, or testing. They are but pawns, with very little power, in a larger global political scheme.

Chapter 17
OBE: Outcome-Based Education

The Eight National Goals are linked to outcomes, the end result. At first, some of the education reformers called the new education programs, "outcome-based education." So the question is, what are the outcomes?

I found the outcomes clearly stated in the Expected School-wide Learning Results (ESLRS) that each high school has to set and has to meet for accreditation. At Santa Ana High School, the ESLRS were: Multicultural Appreciator, Environmental Steward, Global/Community citizen, and Collaborative Learner. These were also some of the outcomes that were required for a Certificate of Initial Mastery, CIM, in an Oregon pilot program. According to these programs, once you pass the CIM at age sixteen, you are placed in a three-year career track, which includes one year of college. Once your career program is completed you receive a Certificate of Advanced Mastery (CAM), for your workforce training and can then be placed in a job identified by the Regional Workforce Investment Board.

The new certification was touted as replacements for the traditional high school diploma. When parents in Oregon saw that the high school outcomes for the Certificate of Initial Mastery (CIM) were not academic, they protested, and the district backed away. This is how educational reformers work: they take three steps forward, and with opposition, they take two steps back. But nevertheless they continue to move forward as long as the people do not notice. Once parents rise up, the social planners just reinvent themselves and rename their programs. But their plans move forward.

The desired outcomes create the ideal global citizen who has all of the politically correct attitudes. These are the ones who can move forward in the global economy and are rewarded with better jobs or a desired career.

A study of Goals 2000, the eight national education goals, shows us how this new system is brought in. We will not go into all of the goals here. But the first two goals give us a picture of what is being implemented in our local schools.

The first national education goal "Ready to Learn" brings children ages zero to five under the federal education system. It does that with three main programs:

1) Parents as Teachers (PAT) for children ages zero to three
2) Universal preschool for ages three to five
3) School-based health clinics for ages zero to five (through 18)

Parents as Teachers (PAT) covers children up to age three. It is a program that monitors parents to see if they are "at risk." It is modeled after the Hawaii PAT pilot program.

If the government finds you to be an "at-risk" parent during a prenatal exam or at the hospital when you give birth, you are placed in the PAT program, and government social workers or PAT home teachers may come to your home for a minimum of fifty home visits. Through home visits, the government will help you improve your parenting skills and monitor your progress.

The rationale for the PAT program is that "a parent is the child's first teacher." Due to new brain research, most of a child's brain development occurs during the early years. Thus it is important that the schools become involved. Particularly now that the federal government is in charge of education, we, in education, have to monitor the parents to make sure they are taking care of their children properly before they come to school. In California, the tobacco lawsuit settlement money is used to fund many "Ready to Learn" programs for ages zero to five.

I understand that there are a lot of ignorant parents out there. Today's young people come from fragmented families; many are self-absorbed and rebellious. Many are estranged from their relatives. It is also not fashionable to go to your parents or grandparents, who are looked at as old-fashioned, for advice or support. Tragically, many young children are being abused. With so much social chaos, this government intervention seems reasonable.

But is it right for the government to seek out potentially negligent parents and use the schools and hospitals to do so? Can people be suspect prior to any violation of law? Should parents be forced to have home visits? With a decaying moral society, is the answer surveillance of our homes?

The answer is that ideally it should not be this way, but the reality is that we need programs to help young parents. Again, I have seen many children in the inner city struggle and have wanted to remove them from their homes. But is that the answer?

The real question is, who should be helping young parents when there are no grandparents or stable support? Should it be the government or the churches? There are churches that host programs like MOPS (Mothers of Pre-Schoolers), but they are too few and are desperately needed in the inner city. Once older women, grandmas, and great-grandmas would advise the younger generation, but with fragmented families, churches divided into age groups, and the Internet, young people have turned to other sources.

When the child turns three and is ready for state preschool, the home is re-evaluated, and a determination is made on a PAT (Parent as Teacher) exit form. If the parents are still classified to be "at risk" by the Parent as Teacher program, they will now continue to be monitored in the state preschool program.

One other thing was disturbing. In Hawaii's pilot program, the list of at-risk factors are completely subjective: not enough toys, too many toys, not enough eye contact, too much eye contact, a death in the family, a divorce in the family, not having a phone or a car. Anything in your home that was not perfect or within normal could make you suspect. The "at-risk" factors were way too broad. Almost any family could be considered at risk if the authorities decided to monitor a child's home. While PAT may help prevent child abuse and help parents, it could also be used as a tool for intimidation. No one will want it to be recorded in his or her personal file that they were "an at-risk parent"; the file follows you the rest of your life and may later determine your employment.

There had also been talk at the California legislature about a parent report card. A *Better Homes and Gardens* article in the January 1995 issue explained how the new proposed report cards might work. A highlighted subtitle read, "Believe me, kids know if their parents are flunking." Report cards are given "on how well they are involved in their children's education. They set goals, approved by both their children and teachers, and are then graded on their performance in such areas as volunteer participation, providing a quiet time and place for children to study, how well-prepared a youngster arrives at school each day and how the child is groomed." It continues, "Parents graded below a 3.0 average must attend a parent-principal conference. And believe me, kids know if their parents are flunking," says Johnson. "And because the children also have to sign off on their parents' report cards, they are empowered as well."

While attempts to legislate a parent report card failed in the '90s, federal funding for low-income children, Chapter I funding, did require schools to develop a signed Parent Compact to tell parents what is required of them. Now we again see the notion resurface with new articles such as "Holding Parents

Accountable: Grades? Fines? Jail?" (Valerie Strauss, education writer for *The Washington Post,* washingtonpost.com, June 8, 2011, Blogs/answer-sheet).

Universal preschool is the second program under the first goal "Ready to Learn." Preschool is considered a right of every child, and many public schools now have a state preschool program at elementary school sites. Universal preschool has not been the tradition in America; in fact, even kindergarten, though generally offered, is not required in most states. But with so many mothers working, we have become accustomed to it being the norm.

But as my dad taught me, state preschool is the tradition in Socialist countries like the Soviet Union. The earlier the better when you are trying to create a compliant state citizen. And when parents have to work long hours to pay for big government programs, someone has to take care of the kids.

How very sad to miss out on your child's early years only to have to work longer hours so that you can pay for others to take care of your children at state preschool or day-care. Many of our children will miss out on opportunities throughout the day to learn our personal values. But saddest of all, the young children will miss out on lots of hugs and kisses that we generally give our young boys and girls throughout the day.

The third program under the first national goal is "school-based clinics." Here children ages zero to five can receive prenatal and medical care at school sites. According to the Academy of Pediatrics, our schools will be the new "medical home" for the children. The plan is to have school-based clinics serve students from prenatal care on through their high school years.

Growing up in public schools, I remember the school nurse. She was a great lady. She came to our classroom and showed us how to brush our teeth using those big model teeth. Those teeth were several times larger than our regular teeth! Sometimes she gave us samples of toothpaste or toothbrushes.

Other times she would come and show us the food chart,

reminding us to eat from the four food groups at every meal.
She was always there when we got hurt or had a headache. She
bandaged our cuts and encouraged our family. She even helped
my mother find a good low-cost dentist. My mother knew she
could go to the school nurse for advice.

Somewhere along the way, we lost the school nurses. Financial
shortages at the local level were said to be the reason. Now most
nurses are assigned to three schools. Long ago, elementary schools
had 500 children, but today some of our inner city schools have
1,000 students, and high schools have doubled in size. With so
many students, there is no time for classroom health instruction,
and nurses report they really only have time to do the special education testing and physicals. Part-time health clerks have popped
up to take care of daily first aid needs.

The community has always been concerned about the health
care of its children. Now, rather than returning to a model with
school nurses that has worked, schools are being asked to move
to a new system, a system that is much more expensive than
providing a local school nurse. Why? Why does it seem that there
is no funding for the personal care of a school nurse but somehow there are millions and billions of dollars for school-based
clinics? Has a crisis of school nurse shortages been manufactured
to bring in a new health care model?

One clue is the Support Center for School-Based Clinics at
the Center for Population Options. Rather than parents having
confidential visits with a school nurse, under this new model
parents are asked to attend meetings with a team of professional
experts, who will advise them on their child's health care needs
as well as their decision to have more children.

Children and parents are but one of the "stakeholders" at
the table; the clinic nurse, social worker, mental health worker,
district attorney's representative, and others from social services
might be there to encourage the parents to do what is in the best
interest of the common good. And according to today's elitists

or social planners, limiting your family is vital to the common good, particularly if the state is picking up the tab for health care, preschool, the evaluation of our homes, and every other program they find necessary. Often these recommendations to limit families run contrary to the parent's religious beliefs, cultural values, or family preference. Through intimidation by the so-called "experts," it is not difficult to see how parents would be coerced to limit their families.

And when health care is free and provided at the school, it may not be wise to buck the system. And what is the outcome? Evidently, according to the representative from California Tomorrow, who ran our parent meeting and brought in school-based clinics into low-income areas, the outcome is not only "land use" but also "ethnic balance." Did that mean fewer Hispanic babies...fewer black babies?

Again, the limiting of families is often part of socialistic Communist countries like China, who has a one child law.

In the late '80s, angry mothers, including myself, worked tirelessly to stop the implementation of school-based clinics in the Santa Ana School District. Today the "Building Healthy Communities" initiative is once again leading the march to train residents to advocate for health clinics at schools. Fourteen areas in California's low-income neighborhoods, including Santa Ana, have been selected and targeted for this initiative.

It is sad to see the Catholic Church involved. In Santa Ana, the meetings are held at their church, and many of the Catholic young people are being empowered to advocate for these programs. And it isn't a surprise because the programs are marketed as "accessible health care for the poor." We have been deceived by the rhetoric. Ironically, the real outcome planned is more abortions and parents who will be coerced to limit their families, contrary to Catholic religious beliefs.

The Catholic Church was abuzz. The cars filled the parking lot as I arrived. The group in charge had a public meeting to launch the California Endowment's "Building Healthy Communities Initiative." We were invited to come and learn about the plan.

The room was filled with community people. Immediately they put us in small groups, as the chairs were placed in round circles. For one full hour, the leaders mainly from Latino Health Access stressed that they had gone to all of the homes, done extensive interviews, and asked what the people needed. The written plan they claimed came from the residents' input. A pretty Latina walked back and forth stating the case for school-based clinics. "Why should we have to go to a city nearby to get health care when we can get it right here in our schools?!" she exclaimed.

A union man in our group was upset. "I walked in the neighborhood and conducted surveys for them and no one asked me for health care at the schools. They want jobs!" So much for community input.

The "Building Healthy Communities Initiative" was brought in with a big media effort. First Lady Michele Obama was the speaker at its launch in San Diego. Along with the initiative to create advocates for school based clinics, the California Endowment promised ten million dollars for community programs. Naturally, many people at the meeting wanted a piece of that pie!

The second goal of the national education plan is a 90 percent graduation rate. With dropout rates at 30 percent and some as high as 50 percent in our inner-city schools, this sounds like a great goal…very impressive.

Under Goals 2000, a 90 percent graduation rate will be easy to achieve because graduation is based on political correctness and correct attitudes, not academics. As stated before, students are tested at sixteen for their politically correct attitudes, the desired outcomes. Then once they are certified with a Certificate of Initial Mastery, they are allowed to enter their workforce training, which will enable them to work! Regional workforce boards will recommend career pathways and specific job needs in the local area, and ultimately most will be assigned to an employer for further training. No wonder we will have a 90 percent graduation rate. If you want to work or eat, you will need to comply.

Also required for accreditation at some of our high schools were senior exit interviews. These infuriated me! The letter inviting me to be on the exit interview panel explained the purpose of the exit interview. We, as members of the community, need to decide if the students were ready to graduate. How could the public make that decision? It should be up to the teacher, their grades, the classes they took, and the principal! It should be up to their academic achievement, not community opinion or approval.

The students came dressed up in white shirts and ties and neat dresses with their prepared portfolio, containing samples of their work. We all shook hands. It was a high-stakes interview, so I am sure they were very nervous and had help preparing the essays in their portfolios.

But what startled me was how political the writings were. They had to write about environmental issues, how they felt about the oppression of the poor, about women's rights. Their political views were highlighted, not how well they could summarize a story, or write down directions, or converse on a classic piece of literature. Most of the portfolios showed the liberal thinking of the students.

After participating in several exit interviews, I think only one portfolio stood out as being more conservative. Considering the tremendous emphasis on "peer review" for teachers and students, this new kind of community peer review was troubling. In the future, would the more conservative thinker be deemed not ready to graduate by a panel of carefully selected community members?

Chapter 18
School to Work

Dr. Ken Williams, a physician and surgeon, who was interested in the new "School to Work" initiative came to visit Santa Ana High School. Many of our inner-city schools now had workforce or career centers to help direct young people into their "career pathway." He decided to take an inventory test and see what work would be suggested for him. This doctor and surgeon answered the questions. He stated that graduation from college was his goal. Yes, he liked to work with his hands. Yes, he liked to work with people. The questions covered many areas. In the end, his results recommended that he could become a car muffler installer.

The doctor was curious. What if he took the test in a more affluent area; would the test results be the same? What would parents think if a student came home and said the schools suggested he become a muffler installer, mechanic, machinist, or model? Would career assessments in different areas provide a different outcome, perhaps encouraging him to be a doctor or a dentist? It seems the new system had lower expectations for inner-city youth. Whatever happened to the land of opportunity?

It was these concerns and others that caused Dr. Williams to run for the Orange County Board of Education where he has now served twenty years.

Another possibility is that these assessments might be linked to the work that is available in the specific area, as determined by the new Workforce Investment Boards. Since our city is a more manufacturing or industrial area, perhaps the Workforce Investment Boards were trying to fill jobs that might be available in the local area. In resort communities near a beach, young people probably would be encouraged to prepare for hotel management, entertainment, lifeguard, surfing instruction, or housekeeping work. But what about a boy dreaming to become a doctor in the inner city; would he become discouraged after taking these tests? And what if you wanted to become an astronaut? Would you be sidetracked because there were no opportunities for further training or employment in the region near your home? Why were we trying to manage the futures of our children? Why are we trying to meet the needs of a global workforce?

Millions, even billions, of dollars are being spent to bring in a School-to-Work system that changes our high school curriculum. Students are required to decide as early as eighth grade what career path they would like to enter. They are then placed in "career pathways," such as a business pathway, a medical pathway, or entertainment pathway, and their education becomes limited. A Regional Workforce Investment Board studies the workplace needs in the region. Career pathway choices and employment quotas, such as three doctors, seven lawyers, ten muffler installers, and eight machinists, might be determined for a particular region. Often the Chamber of Commerce is involved in the Workforce Investment Board that projects future needs.

If young people enter a medical career track, they will take more science and math classes. Those in the entertainment field will take more music and art or marketing. And those in business will take accounting, management, and other business classes. If you are in global business, you may be required to take more languages and learn geography.

At every School-to-Work Conference I attended, I would always hear, "Why should every student take Shakespeare?" This sounds reasonable and efficient. After all, not everyone likes Shakespeare. Why should every student take Shakespeare?" I would answer,

"Because the truck driver is going to marry a schoolteacher and may have to watch a Shakespeare play, and he may want to enjoy it." Everyone needs geography, whether they are going into global business or staying home to be the muffler repairman. Geography is important if you want to read the newspaper and understand the world. Learning is not always about a job; it is about being prepared for life. A well-educated person has more choices throughout his life. But under School-to-Work programs, now called *College and Career Readiness*, some of those choices will undoubtedly be limited.

American education traditionally has given all of our students a broad liberal arts classical education so students could be whatever they wanted to be. We never limited their choices. We never tried to manage their futures. A broad liberal arts or classical education prepares young people to be strong in many areas. It helps them be resilient and innovative in the workplace. It encourages young people to take advantage of present opportunities in a free market, because they have some familiarity with the line of work. A broad education also helps young people determine where their strengths and weaknesses are, helping them make better choices. I took art. I was good at drawing pictures, but bad at precision lettering.

Today most people change careers many times before they find what they really want to do. It is a self-discovery process. If they want to be a rock star in eighth grade and later when they break their leg decide to become a doctor, they will not have enough science and math to allow them to change careers. Having the government manage your career choices and corresponding education in this way limits your opportunities. And if you should later decide you want to be a doctor, it will cost the new system more money to allow you to later take different classes, such as science and math. Changing career paths will not be that easy.

Freedom is messy—but it is also challenging and rewarding. This new utilitarian education is just not American. American children will no longer be able to pursue their own happiness. They will be merely a cog or a resource for the new global economy. They will no longer be broadly educated, but instead be pushed along to meet a need in a government controlled pre-prescribed society. Sadly, we will have to say goodbye to the concept of upward mobility and the land of opportunity.

We found "The Human Resource Development Plan for the United States," published by the Carnegie Foundation in Rochester, New York. It is a letter explaining the School-to-Work plan, written by education guru Marc Tucker and addressed to Bill and Hillary Clinton when they entered the presidency. Hillary Clinton was on the Board of Trustees of the Carnegie Foundation with Marc Tucker. "The Human Resource Development Plan for the United States" says we are copying the German model.

Some of my friends had just visited Germany. They had told me about the large demonstrations they had seen. The people were angry about high unemployment. Doctors had to work part-time because they had trained too many doctors, and 60 percent of the people were not working in the career track they had been trained for. Haven't these social planners (at the Carnegie Foundation) heard that the German model does not work?

Once the plans are set, it is almost impossible to change them, as they have spent millions, in fact billions of dollars getting everyone to go along.

The free market and personal freedom is so much better than a carefully man-managed society. The freedom model is flexible and can adjust with the times, while the other is rigid. The arrogance! For who can really predict the future ten years out? Who would have predicted the Internet and how it would change our lives? People used to think we would die if we went over 15 mph. How foolish we have become!

Once again, we see the same attitude. Failed reading programs were re-adopted in our schools. Now we were running to copy the discredited German model. We are talking about our children's futures. "Doesn't anyone care?" To the elites it does not matter. "No, do not bother me with the facts; we are creating a new world, the '60s Age of Aquarius. Everything will be beautiful."

Chapter 19
Teaching Across the Curriculum

How do you change students' thinking? How do you make a global citizen? How do you create a politically correct student? Well, here is the recipe.

First, change your goal. The federal learning laboratories changed the purpose of education from academics, the learning of reading, writing, and arithmetic, and the attainment of knowledge of history and science to creating a new global citizen who has the correct political attitudes.

Secondly, once you decide on which new attitudes to instill, teach the new concepts or the politically correct attitudes across the curriculum all day long. Teach children to be multicultural appreciators in every subject. Teach children to be environmental stewards in all of the classes: science, history, math, and reading.

Prior to the 1950s, our public schools used the McGuffey Readers. The stories taught children how to read using phonics and a high vocabulary. The short stories uplifted children and produced good character. It could be called *education for greatness*. It taught America's Judeo-Christian values, stressing a belief in God and the need to obey the Ten Commandments.

These readers were well-written and introduced children to good literature. Using a phonetic approach to reading, the children learned individual letters and sounds and combined them into words. Children were asked to sound out words, form sentences, and then read paragraphs.

My daughter's third-grade reader had stories from all parts

of the world. It was evident that the purpose of the reading books was designed to create "multicultural appreciators." The individual stories were poorly written because the stories were translated into English from other languages and sometimes the grammar or story line seemed odd.

One story was different than our traditional fairy tales. It had the damsel looking for the prince rather than the other way around. The prince had run away from his parents because he was mad at them for not taking care of the poor. The King promised a damsel that she could marry the prince and receive one half of the kingdom if she found him. When she found him, she asked him to come home, but he would not. Finally she told him that she would get half the kingdom and that they could give it to the poor. So he decided to go with her and marry her.

Now I ask, "Where is the love?" I don't think they even kissed. At least the prince in our American fairy tales kissed the beautiful damsel. In *Snow White*, she had seen the prince and loved him in her heart and was dreaming about him. It was the same in *Cinderella*.

This story from Sweden seemed more like a marriage of political convenience, reminding me of some recent co-presidents. I did not like the role reversal, the feminist theme, where the damsel is searching for the prince rather than the prince seeking out his bride. I had to discuss with my eight-year-old daughter how to best help the poor. "Was it a good idea to just give all of the money away to poor people? What would happen when it was all spent? Would it be better if the prince and the damsel built a shoe factory so that the poor people could work for a living? How would that help the poor?" We discussed how the people would have money from working at the factory to buy many other things. As the shoes were sold, they could continue to work in the factory and make more money. "And more and more people would have shoes, too."

I had to teach my daughter that "capital," having money to

invest in factory equipment and leather and thread to make the shoes, was a good thing. I stressed that the money should be used in a way that would keep on helping, keep on producing, and continue to improve the lives of other people. I stressed that it was important to grow your money, create more money, and create more jobs for others.

The teacher, a wonderful Christian lady, liked the socialist story and had the whole class act it out in class. Unfortunately, she probably did not recognize the philosophical thinking behind the story. For her, it was an amusing story with a different twist. Perhaps she wanted the children to care about the poor and thought this had a good theme.

I think, out of the whole class only my daughter learned about the wisdom of wisely investing one's money so it could grow and do the most good. She probably was the only one who realized how important start-up money is for a business venture. Sadly, the rest of the class learned a more socialistic value, government redistribution of wealth, and a nontraditional view of marriage.

What could be more important than exposing children to well-written literature at an early age? What was more important than exposing children to important economic principles or their country's values or culture? It appeared that teaching feminism, socialism, and a multicultural mindset was the goal.

If we do not return to teaching children the basics and, most importantly, how to read well, none of our precious children will ever be able to read amazing classics from around the world like Hans Christian Andersen's *Grimm's Fairy Tales*, *Hansel and Gretel*, *Gulliver's Travels*, and *Aladdin's Magic Lamp*. These classics were well-written and do not replace reading textbooks and are not used as a means of indoctrination. Why are we sacrificing academics to create a "multicultural appreciator," an "environmental steward," a "collaborative learner" and a "global citizen?" Academics has to be at the center of education. The basic skills cannot be "embedded," as the educational establishment used to say.

At a reading in-service training for teachers, I was surprised to learn how the teachers were instructed to teach with the new reading textbooks. At the school district's fundamental school where my children attended, the school teachers prided themselves in finishing every page of the textbook, starting from the beginning to the end. These new reading textbooks were organized by politically correct themes and included a lot of group work. The teacher trainer said, "You can start in any chapter you want as long as you cover all of the themes. You can start at the back of the book or beginning or the in the middle; each lesson is on its own and is not connected to the others. In fact, if you have some children who are lower or higher in ability, you can use a different grade book." The themes were what was important, not the sequential mastering of reading skills.

No wonder a new teacher complained to me saying, "I am new, and I am teaching first grade, but no one will show me how to teach the children to read; every teacher around me is doing something different. So how do I know which is best?"

Math too was organized around political themes. Math problems asked, "How long would it take to reseed the forest if you could reseed five trees in half an hour? How much money would you need to repopulate the fish in the streams, if fish cost so much?" Fewer and fewer word problems applied math to everyday problems, like "how long will it take you to get to your destination if your car is going 40 mph, and you have to travel 20 miles?" These practical applications were replaced with environmental themes, in order to produce "environmental stewards," another outcome. New "New" Math, a repeat of the '70s failed Modern Math, lacked computation skills practice. The rationale was that children would be using calculators for math tests. Memorization of the math facts was passé, looked down upon as "mere rote learning," because it lacked critical thinking skills. Instead of having children learn arithmetic computation skills, we were told the schools were creating mathematicians.

No, they were creating politically correct thinkers, and it did not bother them that children could not easily go on to higher math. Without a solid foundation in computation, the basic memorization of the math facts and mastery of skills, it is difficult to do more complex problems that require adding, subtracting, multiplying and dividing. Common Core promoters admit that the goal of math is not to get the right answer but to have children explain how they tackled the problem. Their goal is to have children use creative ways to find the answer and to verbally express their mathematical thinking. Sadly, they do not realize that it puts boys at a disadvantage because most boys are not as verbal as most girls. And accountants who actually work with math on a daily basis will tell you that accuracy actually matters in the real world!

History textbooks revolved around tragic periods of American history. Again, a third-grade history textbook taught eight-year-olds that the explorers, rather than being brave men with keen insight and great visions, were greedy for gold and had callously killed off the indigenous Indians with disease. The California mission priests cruelly beat the Indians. Whites enslaved the blacks. The Japanese were interned in camps during World War II. And Hispanics are discriminated against and taken advantage of by the rich. This social justice negative view of America is what fuels diversity training and multiculturalism in our schools. They think that multiculturalism will make people who are different love, or appreciate each other more, but instead multiculturalism divides us. It is what we have in common as people, our values, that unite us.

The third grade textbook told a personal story of a Japanese child who lived in the internment camp. Every story was written to elicit sympathy. I felt sorry for the third graders. "Life is so sad; people are mean." History was all built around the victim mentality, the social justice view of "the oppressed and the oppressor." America was cruel.

And who do you suppose is helping to write these textbooks? '60s radical Bill Ayers, an associate of President Obama, at whose home Obama declared he would run for President, appears to be very involved. Ayers, a member of the college SDS (Students for a Democratic Society) founded the Weather Underground, an antiwar organization, who bombed the US Capitol, the Pentagon, and a judge's home, killing Americans, including three of his friends who were killed while making bombs. Bill Ayers is now a professor at the University of Illinois. According to Biography.com, Ayers graduated from college with a degree in American Studies, studied early childhood education at Bank Street School College of Education and earned a doctorate in curriculum and teaching. He is the author of several books, including *The Good Preschool Teacher* and *Teaching for Social Justice: A Democracy and Education Reader* (1998). Yet decades ago, in Bill Ayers' 1974 publication, *Prairie Fire*, he describes their group the Weather Underground: "We are a guerrilla organization. We are Communist men and women."

Evidently Bill Ayers has truly gone underground developing "social justice" curriculum for our elementary schools. America, of course, is the villain, as is taught in most university American Studies classes. Bill Ayers continues to have no sympathy for the innocent people he hurt or intended to kill in the bombings of the '60s. In 2001 he stated, "I do not regret setting off bombs; we should have done more." Why in the world would we now allow an unrepentant domestic terrorist to be teaching our young children? Have we gone insane?

There is a time and place for these historical facts when children are older and can look at events in the proper historical context, with the understanding of war, the nature of man and the role of government. This is certainly not appropriate for second, third, or fourth graders who are given little context. Why are we burdening young minds with the "evils of society"? It seems so cruel.

Certainly, statements from America's founding documents and a great religious awakening that gave impetus for ending slavery were not mentioned. For indeed the statement from the Declaration of Independence that "all men are created equal" provided inspiration to the abolitionists. The US Constitution, Article One, Section 9, included a provision to prohibit the slave trade within twenty years of the signing, to begin in 1808. It also provided for taxation of slave owners to slow down its trade. With wisdom, the authors of the Constitution sought out a way to phase out slavery, from the very beginning of our founding as a nation.

Our framers, in hopes of ending slavery, also incorporated the 3/5 count for slaves in the Constitution as a way to weaken the political power of pro-slavery representatives in Congress. Each Representative in Congress is chosen according to the population, the number of people that live in that state or area. The South, who always considered slaves to be but mere property, now wanted the slaves to have full representation in the new government and be counted. The slaves could not vote, but they wanted them to be counted so there would be more Representatives who wanted slavery to continue. Slave owners believed the South was growing, and soon there would be enough Representatives to ensure the continuation of slavery.

But those who hated slavery wanted to limit the South's representation to make sure slavery was abolished. It was a struggle, but creating a nation had to take priority. The compromise of partially counting slaves pleased the South. And the North believed that by limiting the count of slaves they could more easily end slavery. Limiting the count of slaves to 3/5 more accurately represented the sentiments of the slaves, enabling there to be more voices on their behalf to oppose slavery.

Why is it that instead of our real history, our students receive a twisted view of history? Instead we teach lies that our founders hated the slaves and devalued them counting them only as a partial person? How tragic!

President Abraham Lincoln led our nation during the terrible

Civil War and signed the Emancipation Proclamation, which ended slavery. America, like any nation or organization or group of people, can and does fall into sin and does evil deeds. But what is important is that we repent and turn from hateful ways, once we realize what we have done. The wise and loving leadership of Abraham Lincoln during such a difficult time propelled the Republican Party into great popularity for more than sixty years. President Ronald Reagan, also a Republican, publically apologized for the Japanese Internment. It was President Reagan who also signed the bill making Martin Luther King Day a national holiday.

Every year the Santa Ana Board of Education was invited to participate in the Black History Parade. It was great to meet many of the leaders in our own black community. We had our own convertible representing the school district. We sat on the back seat and waved to the crowds. The brave Tuskegee Airmen who fought in World War II drove in the car next to ours.

The marching dance bands were amazing! If you have never seen these young people's routines, you have missed something. The black community came out from miles around to participate in the parade in Santa Ana. It was great to see the many smiling faces that lined the parade route. During June, I was often invited to speak at the "Juneteenth" event, a celebration of the signing of the Emancipation Proclamation. Since I loved to talk about freedom, it was always good to reflect on what the Proclamation meant to so many people.

In 2013, we celebrated the fiftieth anniversary of the Civil Rights Movement. Before Democratic President Lyndon Johnson signed the Civil Rights Act, black people in the South led by Martin Luther King quietly protested the disrespectful way that black people were treated. Just because we had a great and terrible Civic War that ended slavery, it did not mean that hearts were changed. Blacks were still segregated and could not eat at most restaurants, drink from public drinking fountains, or ride in the front of the bus. As the blacks became adjusted to their new freedom, they soon rose up to express their disdain for these practices. Rosa Parks became a symbol as she refused to go sit in the back of the bus. As they rose up, angry whites became ugly and bombed homes and places of worship where black people were gathering to plan their protests.

On September 15, 1963, the 16th Street Baptist Church in Birmingham, Alabama, was bombed on Sunday morning during Sunday School and four innocent beautiful young girls died. This became a rallying cry. There had been more than eighty bombings in the city, but the loss of these four precious girls moved the people and ignited the movement. Ironically, the message given that Sunday morning was called, "A Love That Forgives."

Later Martin Luther King, a Baptist minister, led the people in peaceful and orderly demonstrations and a national march on Washington. Many joined the march from other states. The first amendment to the Constitution, in the Bill of Rights, states that we have the freedom of speech, religion, and the press, but it also says we have "the right to peaceably assemble, and to petition the government for a redress of grievances." And that is what the people did.

When some wanted to take up guns, Rev. Martin Luther King admonished them not to. The Civil Rights Bill was finally signed by President Lyndon Johnson in 1964 and officially ended segregation. The southern Democrats opposed the bill and tried to block it, while the Republicans urged its passage.

The laws have changed, yet it has taken years for hearts to change. Laws are needed, but change from the heart is what is most important.

Most of the United States did not realize the extent of the abuse and persecution that blacks in the South faced. We were not fully aware that they were not allowed to enter restaurants, ride at the front of buses, drink water from the same fountain, or use the same restrooms. I heard a black pastor from New York share that he too did not realize what it was like until he came to the South and saw it for himself. It took peaceful demonstrations and a publicized march to get our attention and show us the injustice and disrespect the black people endured in the South.

Most Americans favored the Civil Rights laws. It took those who lived in the South more time. Many had deep historical roots in slave ownership and class distinctions. They needed more time to adjust to new ways and throw off the evil of the past. In the last fifty years, blacks have made great gains, many have moved up, enjoying good jobs and personal wealth. We have had blacks rise to high offices, in the Supreme Court, two have become Secretary of State, many have joined the ranks of the United States Congress, and one has become the President of the United States. It is time to be thankful for all of these accomplishments. We should also give thanks for a nation who established the founding principles of free speech and assembly that allows peaceful demonstrations and public dissent. When people enter the public discourse and let their views be known, it is for the benefit of all. Awareness of injustice is necessary before real change can come. The message from the 16th Street Baptist Church reminds us that today, as always, we need a love that forgives. It is time to forgive, to heal, to love each other, and to help lift each other up.

Both black and white youth are ravaged by a culture that has turned from God and his values. It is now time, after fifty years, after a freedom movement, to have a new Jubilee, "a new birth of freedom," as Lincoln put it, that will set our young people free.

The Civil Rights Bill was signed in 1964. Shortly after the signing of the bill, in 1965 tensions flared up in Los Angeles in a South Central neighborhood called Watts, and a race riot ensued. It began when two boys were arrested, and a mother stepped in and angrily protested. Others joined in. People rioted in the streets, burned businesses, and looted stores. The riots lasted for days. This was not a peaceful, purposeful, planned demonstration, but began as an act of frustration and desperation. According to a PBS story by Huey P. Newton, the Watts Riots became "the scene of the greatest example of racial tension America has seen." In the end, the commission directed to study the riots stated that the "riots were not the act of thugs, but rather symptomatic of a much deeper problems; the high joblessness rate in the inner city, poor housing, and bad schools."

In 1966, when I was a freshman at Biola University, a group at the college recruited students to go into Watts and share our love with the people. For one year, I worked in the Nickerson Gardens government project in Watts, leading a girls club. I remember around February buying red and white material and lace for the girls to sew aprons for their mothers. After the riots, many ran to Watts to see what they could do to help, but as time goes by, these efforts are short lived. The report further pointed out, "no great effort was made to address them [the needs of the community], or to rebuild what was destroyed in the riots."

Perhaps there is a lesson in this, that, unlike the civil rights movement that was led by a great leader who urged restraint and calmness, the LA Watts Riots were just that, riots, the venting of frustration, not a planned means of communicating one's feelings and grievances. In the end, there were not many positive results but only a legacy of destruction. It is time to rebuild, time for fathers to come home and raise their children. It is time for women to speak kindly, pray, and be encouraging helpmates, supporting their men. It is time for good men of all races to go into the inner cities to mentor young angry boys and be a father to the fatherless. It is time to visit the prisons and bring liberty to those who are bruised. And it is time to set free those that are captive to drug and alcohol addictions.

One of my best friends and a mentor was a black man named Lewis Whitehead. He was the founder of the Orange County Rescue Mission. My husband and I worked with him on several projects and served on his board of United Christians, promoting unity in the city. We helped put on dinners, inviting the community to hear the heart of different leaders and pastors. We raised money and placed hundreds of encouraging billboards out on the streets. For the outreach to the 1984 Olympics, we placed 500 signs inside buses, 100 signs outside of the buses, and many others on bus stop benches, including a large billboard on the Santa Ana Freeway. One of our messages in three languages was "For peace…talk to Jesus."

Rev. Whitehead would come to breakfast at our house and we would talk, sharing our visions and dreams. He mentored me in how to be an effective board member. He set up the folding table and opened the folding chairs. I can see him leaning back in his chair and singing. We always sang before we started our board meetings. He asked my husband and I to give a testimony about him when he was selected as the Man of the Year for a local civic club. Rev. Whitehead was a man who believed in unity. We held hands at the United Christian's dinner meetings and sang, "We are one in the spirit; we are one in the Lord." And we meant it.

Yet every day, in every class, in our schools across America, we teach class warfare, the pitting of one group against the other. What is primary in these social justice elementary school textbooks is that the children receive the message that America is bad, that America is racist. What kind of a divisive message is that to give to young eight-year-old children? Certainly, after reading these oppressive stories, children were not encouraged to sing "America the Beautiful" or "God Bless America." Their little hearts were filled with hate, much like Obama's Pastor Wright, who preached, "God Damn America."

Chapter 20
Keeping the Peace

While on the school board, there was one elementary school that made me very uneasy. It was always receiving awards, yet scored academically very low. The awards were unusual. Even the principal received a celebrated $25,000 to be used for her own personal use. Award after award was given for producing such a great school.

While other schools had tigers, leopards, and eagles as mascots, this particular school had the dove of peace as their mascot. The school was considered a community center, open from early morning to late at night. The principal was very active in the community and successfully encouraged greater parent participation. Business professionals came to tutor children at lunch. Many classes were offered for parents. Community leaders, school personnel, and parents used the school to organize the community for other community projects. The goal was for the school to become the community hub.

As I recall, I first heard of this concept in the early '90s when Lamar Alexander, then United States secretary of education under President Bush Sr., was announcing the creation of the "New American Schools." He said that schools would be open from 6 a.m. to 9 p.m. for the community. Evidently, this was one of those "New American Schools."

At this particular elementary school, there were no safety monitors like I had in school in the '50s that wrote up students that were doing wrong things, like running in the halls, pushing, or hitting other students. Students would be punished, have to stay after school, or clean up the playground. Rather, at this school, selected children were called "peace officers." Their job was to bring in students before a panel of "peers" to discuss their behavior. In many schools, this is called conflict resolution, a new way of resolving problems.

The philosophy behind this new way of dealing with student misbehavior is: "No one did anything wrong; we just need to work it out." The attitude appears to be that if we correct people or punish them, we may hurt their feelings and destroy their self-esteem and damage their identity. And after all, there is really no right or wrong behavior. Who are we, the adults, to judge, and we certainly do not want to punish. In fact, "right and wrong" are no longer in the vocabulary. It felt a little like controversial police brutality victim Rodney King's plea, "Can't we all just get along?" The assumption is that all students are naturally good and just need some coaching. It appears that peer pressure, or what a select group of students think is the "common good" and the opinion of the group is what will change behavior, causing students to conform. The "consensus of the group" and "peer review" is now the force being used to compel acceptable behavior.

This is a completely new mindset. Formerly in America we assumed people were capable of doing wrong due to original sin, and needed to be punished for misdeeds. "Spare the rod and spoil the child" was the prevailing attitude. I used to get a kick out of reading the *Little School House Rules* used in the prairie schools with "three lickings" for pulling hair, and five lickings for putting someone's hair in the ink wells, and ten lickings for stealing." A "licking" was generally a sting on the behind with a thin tree limb. But now without right and wrong, without moral values, and without corporal punishment that was once used in schools, or in homes for that matter, we need to find new ways to keep people in line.

Designating school informants and modifying behavior, by intimidation through the use of peer panels is the new mode of behavior modification. Certainly it is not through outdated authority figures like teachers or parents.

A current trend in education is the use of journaling. Children are asked to journal each day, writing about their lives, activities, and thoughts.

A group of us from the school district visited a school in Houston, Texas, to learn about new teaching methods. We witnessed a teacher ask teens in her classroom to write in their journals about the last time they had a fight with their parents. "Was this legal?" I thought. According to the California Education Code 5151 it is forbidden to ask students personal or family questions. What was more troubling was that they were proud of the lesson. It was selected for our visit as a means of showing us the new teaching strategies.

As in the implementation of Common Core, the new federal curriculum, current laws forbidding the establishing of national education standards and the collection of personal data are arrogantly ignored and dismissed. Teachers are asking students all kinds of personal questions and requiring them to journal.

Government grants for teacher training in-service workshops sometimes require teachers to journal. Teachers are asked to journal their thought processes as they attend teacher training classes and are introduced to new concepts. I also have seen this practice used in a private Christian university when a teacher trainer, who held views contrary to the traditional views of the university, came to train carefully selected professors. Through journaling the trainers can see if the teachers are adapting to the new teaching methods or concepts. This is one means of monitoring the teachers to see if they are truly becoming the new teachers of the future. With so much data collected on children, it appears that journaling is a way to monitor "thought transformation."

In Harry Wu's book, *Bitter Winds: A Memoir of My Years in China's Gulag*, Wu recounts how he was called to go before a panel of his peers in the university and asked to change his thinking. He was required to journal his thought processes to demonstrate that he was successfully reeducated. Journaling is a way to control thoughts and re-educate people.

Now it is easy to see why even mathematics in the new federal Common Core curriculum is more concerned with students explaining their thought processes than actually getting math problems correct.

To save money, the Santa Ana School District was hiring a school police officer under a new federal program, President Clinton's 100,000 C.O.P.'s. The day Clinton left office, he proclaimed that the hiring of 100,000 peace officers was one of his greatest accomplishments.

Fortunately, as a school board member, I requested and was given a copy of the original US Department of Justice June 7, 1995, Universal Hiring program RFP, or "Request for Proposal," which explains the concept and requirement of the C.O.P. (Community Oriented Policing) funding. I also reviewed our district's written grant application. I say *fortunately* because I noticed that some of the original language was changed in later grant applications.

The schools were looking to save money to add a few new officers for our high schools. The grant paid up to 75 percent of the salary and benefits for an officer for the first three years, with the police department paying more of the salary each year, until the third year, when the schools or police departments would need to pay the complete salary and benefits. The Community Oriented Policing, or C.O.P. grant, was written for police departments across the United States. Every community in America, both rural and urban, was to have these new officers, not just high-crime areas. They were for everyone in the United States.

According to the grant, the new community policing would "address crime *and disorder*…enhance policing and *the quality of citizens' lives* across the country…improving the *quality of life* in the Nation's cities, towns and rural areas…*require police-citizen cooperation*...to maintain order and improve quality of life." It continues, "The community is an active partner with police in defining the problems...and *tactics used.*" Further, the Universal Hiring Grant says that the federal COP program calls for *"restructuring of the police agencies and refinement of their management techniques,"* and states, "The approach is dependent on an *effective flow of information* from sources inside and outside of law enforcement" and that "information coming from outside law enforcement" should be used to make the departments more effective (emphasis added).

Basically, the federal government, through this grant funding, would now be gathering information from local neighborhoods and restructuring local police departments to expand policing from addressing criminal behavior to addressing disorder and quality of life. While being marketed as a means to fight crime, it really is the addition of another layer of policing that is not directly related to criminal behavior. It rather puts a new kind of policing in place to monitor our quality of life and the kind of order the federal government wants for us. The words *quality of life* and *disorder* are vague and could mean lots of things. Also troubling was that all further training would be developed by the federal COPS Office in the Department of Justice, located in Washington D.C. "Future model community policing training guidelines will be developed by the COPS Office." New guidelines and federal training would be on-going, while local cities would eventually pay for the officers.

These new federal policemen are called "peace officers." According to early grants they were not allowed to do regular policing out on the beat. Everyone thought President Clinton's 100,000 C.O.P.s were regular policemen who would keep us safe from criminals. But this was not true. Rather we were given a new form of policing: "Community Oriented Policing" or "Community Watch" programs in our local neighborhoods.

The "peace officers" are federally trained. The Department of

Justice in Washington, D.C., creates the training for "Community Oriented Policing." C.O.P. cops are assigned to individual neighborhoods and are continually retrained by the Washington D.C. office. The peace officers assemble local neighborhood committees and empower self-appointed leaders or captains to patrol specific blocks and give information to these federally trained police officers. The non-elected neighborhood committees are encouraged to select local improvement projects. "This brings people together," they say.

In summary, the purpose of the program, known as Community Watch, is to provide information to the police, in this case, agents, for the federal government. The residents are kept in line through peer pressure, the fear that neighbors would report them to the police and the intimidation of being singled out by their neighbors.

These new peace officers reminded me of the "peace officers" in the elementary school. Student informants turning in their peers, and having to go before peer panels to have you change your behavior.

The "broken window theory" is used to justify this new type of community-oriented police work. As it goes, it has been proven that if a building has a broken window, others in the community will be encouraged to throw rocks and break more windows or graffiti the building. If a car is old, abandoned, and unkempt, community members will be encouraged to further damage the car. While on the surface this sounds good, but this new philosophy places the responsibility on the owner not the criminal. It is our responsibility to keep things up and be proactive. It is not necessarily the violator's responsibility to stop destroying property. The theory makes it seem like the owner's lack of proactive action actually prompted the criminal behavior. Those who throw rocks at buildings are only acting naturally due to our irresponsibility.

The key word again is "prevention"; the goal is keeping the neighborhood clean and in order to create a better quality of life.

Neighbors are encouraged to tell on neighbors when things are broken, furniture is left out, trash cans are not put away, or when house trim is unpainted, fences are broken, or grass is unkempt. Further, neighborhood informants are asked to look for unusual behavior, unknown cars on the streets, and open garage doors.

Block captains and neighborhood association leaders are told to report unusual activity to the police. They are told to watch out for their neighbors, learn their habits, and the times when they are home. A flyer that is passed out at every one of the meetings has the community watch program sign printed on the front, "Neighborhood Watch Program in Force: We report all suspicious persons and activity to the Police Dept." A Next-Door.com website was given on the back of the flyer. Residents are asked to join the Next Door website and provide a personal profile on the site. According to Next Door's website, even if you do not join, your neighbors will be asked to provide information about you and your family for your profile. With Next Door making contracts with city "community watch" programs, it appears the Federal Department of Justice and the COPS office will now have access to everyone's personal profile linked to their home address. This gives a whole new meaning to the words community watch!

Rather than enforce laws created by "local" elected officials, in open meetings, as has been our American tradition, these "federally trained" peace officers work with community committees or associations, empowering a select group of neighbors to enforce a new federal agenda. Of course, at first they are told they get to decide what projects to do in their neighborhoods, but in the end, it will probably be federal projects that they will be working on.

Peer pressure and neighborhood informants are used to enforce what the local group or federal government thinks is acceptable behavior. And perhaps in the future residents will be asked to exercise "civic virtue" and give up their personal rights (to privacy, to speak out, to freely use the Internet, to own a gun) for the sake of the "common good," as taught by the federally funded We the People civic education programs.

The city of Santa Ana has been at the forefront of Community Oriented Policing. In a city that is twenty-four square miles, we now have sixty-four neighborhood associations, some which have been in existence for twenty years.

When I was a candidate running in a Santa Ana school board election race, I was passing out campaign fliers on the sidewalk outside of an elementary school. One of these newly empowered (federal government) block leaders came out. "You can't do that!" he demanded. I explained, "Yes, I can; the law says I can pass out fliers on the sidewalk. It is my free speech rights."

"It doesn't matter," he said. "I am the block captain, and you have to do what I say!" Somehow people now believe they can make up new rules for their neighborhoods, even if they violate existing laws. In this case, it seemed that these newly established committees are setting themselves above the law, or at the least creating new neighborhood rules without the proper authority from the people. The Clinton C.O.P.s program expands policing authority and goes beyond the laws made by locally elected officials. Apparently, we will be receiving marching orders through regular ongoing training from the Federal Department of Justice in Washington, D.C.

This is a totally new concept for Americans. Policing has always been a local government function. If police abuse their power, citizens can quickly rise up, demand public officials or chiefs of police to step down. And if they do not listen, the people can recall their elected officials at the next election. It is important to keep policing local, accountable to the voters, accountable to the people they serve, so it will not be abused. When cities give this new authority to the federal government, they are violating the rights of the people. But then, "peace officers" sounds so peaceful, doesn't it?

One of the requirements of the grant for Clinton's C.O.P.s was that if the police wanted to use some of these federally funded peace officers on the beat, they had to train other beat police in Community Orienting Policing. In this way, more and more policemen were trained in Community Orienting Policing policies. Now most if not all police departments have accepted this new philosophy. A new mindset is settling in that unelected easily manipulated neighborhood committees are now becoming the new rule-makers for our neighborhoods. Breaking with American tradition, they are often self-appointed and not publicly accountable elected officials.

In a COPPS (Community Oriented Policing and Problem Solving) manual written in 1999, we can see that the federal government's goals are taking root. On page 88, the Torrance, California, police chief reports, "Implementing the COPPS philosophy has meant transforming the department from a traditional, rule-based organization to a values-based organization." (I ask, who's values?) On page 165, Fresno, California, reports in. Describing the outcome, it states, "A clear set of rules and regulations, established and agreed upon by residents, to maintain a clean, friendly, united neighborhood that shares a common vision." As you can see, our local police departments are being restructured by federal programs. Community Oriented Policing is a new philosophy, adding a new layer of policing, based on new rules and regulations made by unelected, self-appointed neighborhood leaders who will be under the guidance of the federal government.

In recent news, we have had George Zimmerman, a Community Watch coordinator, shoot and kill a young black male named Trayvon Martin. At the scene, Zimmerman instantly described himself as a Community Watch captain. Prior to the shooting, it was reported that Zimmerman called the police department almost fifty times to report unusual activity in his neighborhood. Some incidents included garage doors that were left open or suspicious people. He was the eyes and ears for the police and was looking for trouble in his neighborhood.

Community Watch tells its neighborhood leaders to not

confront suspicious people, but to report them to the police. Zimmerman was not trained to handle confrontational situations as the police are. He was empowered as a community watch captain, and took things into his own hands. In a sense, he was a vigilante when he did more than report and started following Trayvon in his car.

The death of Trayvon Martin divided the community. It was an opportunity for the Left to cry *"Racism!"* and for Conservatives to side with neighborhood safety. Both are right. We need to protect our neighborhoods and call the police when we see someone in danger. And black young people should not walk in fear. But from my perspective, the real story of George Zimmerman and Trayvon Martin was that community policing had run amok.

We have all heard good stories and the need for community policing. Back in the '90s, I attended Community Watch meetings, put a C.O.P. sticker on my front window, and invited others to the meetings. I did not know it was a federal program. But taken together with all of the other educational reforms, federal policing of our neighborhoods just fits in with the larger agenda. No one would be involved if it were not disguised in wonderful language and a great rationale. As our society crumbles and crime escalates, we are tragically opening the door to abusive, unconstitutional federal community policing.

Once neighbors were friendly folks who cared for each other. If the neighbor's grass needed mowing, we might just go find out what is happening and help out. Our first thought should not be *"I will report it to authorities."* If we saw a new car on the street, we could ask our neighbor if it belonged to them. Again our hands should not be on our phones providing information to authorities. But today we are told to report suspicious cars, peeled paint, trash cans left out, and open garages to the police. It is a sad day in America when neighbors have to fear their own neighbors. The federal government should not be policing our neighborhoods, and neighbors should not become informants.

Chapter 21

Collaborative Learning

The '90s brought in a wave of educational reform. There were reform manuals for high schools, middle schools, and elementary schools. I asked for the manuals and was greatly surprised by what was on the front cover of the elementary school manual called, "It's Elementary." Scrawled across the cover in handwriting were the words: "My Answer Is What Our Group Thinks."

"Collaborative learning" was now in. Everything had to be done in teams. *Group learning* they called it, but the official name was collaborative learning.

Collaborative learning is learning in teams, with group projects. Almost every class is now requiring group projects. Several students are assigned to a group, and they have to finish an assigned project. Often these projects take up a lot of time. Sometimes the children have to meet in groups outside the school hours.

Things have changed. Learning to master a subject and know specific information is no longer important; getting the facts correct is no longer the priority. It is the process of learning that counts. And this is true in every area of learning; history, science, and even math.

At the William Spady Education Conference in San Diego, we were shown just how these group projects worked. The speaker showed the teachers a large tag board that represented the front page of a newspaper. It was done in a group. The headlines read, "Civil War Breaks Out!" One student did the political cartoon, and another summarized the war. Another wrote about a hero of the war, and so it went. Each person in the group had a part.

One of the teachers stood up and asked some questions. "How long did it take the group to complete that project?" The speaker replied, "It took the group six months to do it." That is two-thirds of a school year! Then the brave teacher commented, "When we do this kind of learning, our test scores go down." The presenter did not bat an eyelash. "That's OK," he said. "It isn't important what they know. It is important how they learn. This is superior learning."

When my daughter was in eighth grade, I remember having to run to the drugstore at 11 p.m. at night to buy some plastic farm animals. My daughter had a history project to complete. She had to show how the rich aristocrats lived in beautiful homes or castles and how the poor people in England lived in hovels. It was a social studies lesson contrasting different standards of living. She took a cardboard box and divided it into two parts and illustrated the castle and the hovel, building a three-dimensional diorama. I thought why couldn't the children just make a line in the middle of a piece of paper and draw pictures illustrating both lifestyles? Why did it have to take so much time, involve the whole family, and cost money? It seemed like a waste of time and money. There was so much to learn. These kinds of projects are good once in a while but not *all* the time.

We carpooled to school. One of the boys in my carpool loved math. He spent all of his spare time doing tricky math problems and bought big math puzzle books. He had scored 98 percent on his math standardized test in fifth grade. He just knew he was a math genius. His mother was dreaming of having an engineer or scientist in the family. He even said to us as we drove to school, "At this new intermediate school, I am going to be the valedictorian." That was never a goal for my son. But hey, it does not hurt to reach high.

His mom called me. She was livid. "My son is getting a D in math! Something is wrong. I am going to sue the district! I am going to get a lawyer! You, as a school board member, have to do something about this!"

"How could this be?" There is no way that her son could have deserved a D in math. I asked to sit in on the math class. The children sat in groups, and there were five groups. The teacher put two fraction problems with numerators and denominators on the overhead projector.

"OK," she said. "Here are the problems. I want you to figure them out in your groups. You have twenty minutes." The kids scratched their heads.

"We have never seen problems like this."

"Let's try this."

"No, maybe we can do this."

In one of the groups, a boy already knew the answer. "I will show you," he said.

"No, don't show us. We are supposed to figure this out as a group."

"OK, I will keep quiet." This was indeed painful for the boy who understood his math. "You always know the answer!" his peers smirked.

Some groups came up with the great "Ah-ha, I get it!" Others, well, some never quite got it. Now the teacher said, "We will let each group share how they solved the problem." Each group took another five minutes each to discuss their thoughts on the problem. With five different groups participating, it took an additional twenty-five minutes. The teacher tried not to be judgmental about the students' approach to the problem. She discussed some of their thought processes, then said, "That is it; our forty-five minutes of class time is up. See you tomorrow." The teacher never taught. The class did one or two problems in forty-five minutes. And the smart kid was ridiculed.

So I stayed after and asked the teacher how she graded the students on their math. She said, "Oh, the group gives the grades for each team member." Now I had the great "Ah-ha."

"I get it!" "The smart boy got the D from his friends, who did not like a math show-off."

How sad is that! He will never be a valedictorian. No up-and-coming engineer or scientist here. Soon he hated math class. And his parents? They removed their son from the school and were paying high tuition payments to a private Catholic high school. Other children were not that lucky.

In a traditional math class, like those that use Saxon math textbooks, teachers introduce a new math concept each day. She then "teaches" the students how to solve the problem. Once the teacher explains a few problems, she shows them how to do them and lets a few children work the problems in front of the class. Then students are given twelve practice problems to solve on their own. While they work on the problems individually, the teacher goes around the room checking to see if the students are getting the new concept and helping those that need more direction. Then the students work on twenty-five problems. Some of the twenty-five problems include the new concept, and others are review of concepts taught in the weeks before. Children are constantly asked to review past learning while adding a new skill each day. The work is checked for right and wrong answers, and the results are recorded. At home, they can finish their math assignment and do some additional practice problems to reinforce the concept that was taught during the day. With the traditional approach, in one forty-five minute period, a student may work on thirty to forty problems, building their math skills with plenty of practice.

Unfortunately, this math teacher was not the exception. "Collaborative Learning" was in. Evidently, the right answer was what the group thought. Children were trained in the groupthink mentality. This was different. This was very different. Traditionally, we taught children to think for themselves, practice for mastery and success on their own merits.

With the new group learning, there were no right or wrong

answers. It was what the group thought that mattered. Children were graded on how well they worked together. They were graded and rewarded for going along with the group. Was I the only one that thought this was crazy?

I was troubled by the cover of the reform manual: "My Answer Is What Our Group Thinks." How could the manual be so blatant? Didn't it bother other educators? Wouldn't a title like that cause people to throw the reforms out? Why was the establishment so silent?

School administrators are just there to implement the latest trend in education. They have no say. School superintendents are also taught at their educational conferences how to bring in the new reforms and why they were so good for the children. Board members were unaware and look to administrators, the professionals, for direction. Most board members generally are not interested in how children learn. They leave the selection of teaching materials and teaching methods to the so-called "experts," the administrators and staff. And the poor overworked teacher has to constantly change her teaching methods to keep up with the latest reform. She is told working in teams is great. "Some children just never learn to work well with others. We need to teach them how. Business demands it."

I have a master's degree in organizational leadership, and I understand that in real life, in the workplace, people work in teams all the time, and this is an important skill to learn. There are a ton of new books out with titles such as Working with a Team, Inspiring Your Team, Selecting a Team, and Celebrating Your Team. And I have read many of them. It just seemed right to teach children to work in teams. There is always an element of truth in these initiatives; otherwise they would not be accepted at all.

The better educated you are, the more you have to bring to your team. A high level of education and competency, individual character, communication strategies, and good relationship skills are what make a good team member.

Elementary age students are just not ready to work in teams.

Remember the manual that said, "My answer is what my group thinks." That was directed to elementary age students! During this time in their lives, they need to be learning to read, to spell, to write, to add, multiply, and divide. They need to learn about plants and transportation and firemen and the history of California. They are building a foundation of knowledge. We cannot, and should not, let our children be cheated out of a comprehensive education due to social engineering in the classroom!

At recess the children are learning to share and take turns, to wait in line, to be kind and patient with each other, to build a sand castle together. In sports they learn the importance of rules and how to work together as a team. These are all skills they will need later on for work. There is a time and place for everything.

Business people say, "Give us workers who can read, write well, and do arithmetic. Give us well-educated young people with strong basic skills; who know their history, science, and geography; and we will train them." Again, we were putting the cart before the horse.

Character too makes a difference as to how you work within a team. Can you be trusted? Do you deliver on your word? Are you a hard worker or lazy? Are you polite and appreciative of others' efforts?

If our schools intentionally taught character, as we did when we used the McGuffey readers, perhaps our children would be more successful in the workplace and work better in a team setting. As I tell the young men in our workplace training program, "Your gifts and talents will get you a job, but it is your character that will keep you there." More than ever, our children need to develop character, a sense of what is right and wrong. Having stable homes and larger or extended families teach children how to get along with different personalities.

But teaching kids to be compliant team players rather than individual thinkers is a big mistake. Workplace teams are needed, but we have to remember that the teams are only as good as the individual thinkers of that group. Two heads are better than one, but there needs to be something in their heads. We cannot allow the groupthink mentality to replace our independent thinking. My answer is not what our group thinks! My answer is what I think.

I met a youth leader who goes back-and-forth to Hungary and Bulgaria in eastern Europe. It was a time when it seemed that the Soviet Union was weakening its hold on the people. I asked him, "How can Communist satellite countries like Bulgaria and Hungary transition to a more free society after having been suppressed for so long? He said, "It will be hard, because they are not used to initiating things or creating their own plans; everything has been done for them. They are used to just going along with the group."

I always felt uneasy when I heard the word collaboration. I couldn't understand why I hated it. At home, on my coffee table was a booklet, "Collaboration for Kids" from the California School Board Association. I had just gotten the laundry out of the dryer and was getting ready to fold it. A black and white historical documentary on China was on the television set. I was a history major in college and enjoy seeing these types of shows. As I folded the clothes, I looked up, I could not believe it.

In black and white letters on a white screen were the words, "CHINA BECAME COMMUNIST THROUGH COLLAB-ORATION." It now became clear.

Through these collaborative learning schemes, the elitist social planners have snuck into our school system, cheated our students of a real education, destroyed their future, and have decimated our workforce!

People in America are free to speak their minds. In *Downton Abbey*, the hit television drama, Americans such as Cora's sister, played by Shirley MacLaine, are characterized as those who have strong individual opinions and are not afraid to share them. We have been free to share our ideas, free to speak our minds, and free to disagree with the group.

How could this be happening to a nation like America? We are so full of independent thinkers. We are known for our innovation, thinking out of the box. People around the world watch us in admiration as we openly debate and challenge our government. We could never become docile, compliant people, who follow the company line. Or could we?

Chapter 22
Their Master Plan

In 2008, we had a financial crisis, an economic meltdown. Many lost 30 percent or more of their retirement income. The federal government acted. They passed TARP and the Stimulus Bill to put more money into the economy. It seemed these bills were quickly brought forward to address a huge economic crisis.

But it appears that the stimulus bill was *not* hastily thrown together. It was just another way to fund the master plan and move the Progressive socialist agenda forward by leaps and bounds. The government needed funds for school construction to federalize school facilities designing the new education centers, or the new American Schools that would be the hub of the community. The funds were needed to transform schools into school based clinics, mental health centers, day care centers, and parent education centers. Fortunately, the federal school construction funds were later removed.

Stimulus money is now being used to transfer paper healthcare files into electronic files. This facilitates a national healthcare program, like Obamacare. A plan that really begins with free healthcare in the schools, starting with prenatal care. According to the American Academy of Pediatrics, schools were now to become "the new medical home for children."

The TARP bailout funds placed more businesses under government control through excessive regulations that were codified into law. As Rahm Emanuel, President Obama's former chief of staff, stated, "We cannot let a good crisis go to waste."

The Left, the Progressives, are effective because they know what they are doing and where they want to take us. They have a plan to get us there and they know how to spend our tax money.

As always, remember to "follow the money." If you follow the money, it will take you to their master plan, as illustrated below. Being in education, I saw how education funding under President Bill Clinton was channeled to bring in the eight federal education goals, Goals 2000. The goals were introduced by then Governor Bill Clinton of Arkansas at President George H. W. Bush's Governor's Education Conference. Goals 2000 brings in a new system. The "change agents" call it "systemic change" because it changes our American system.

To some of us who were trying to figure it out, "lifelong learning" took on a different meaning. We called it "government prescribed and electronically monitored lifelong education" or simply "womb to tomb" or "cradle to grave" education. It was all about control, getting everyone to march lockstep with the new philosophy, enshrined in global treaties.

Lifelong learning starts with Goal One, "Ready to Learn" beginning with medical care at school based clinic, starting with prenatal care. The Parents As Teacher, PAT program monitors "at-risk" parents at their home. Thirdly, to get children ready, they are placed in universal preschool programs. Once children are "ready to learn," they then go on to regular school, where they will be continually monitored through their personal electronic portfolio assessments, or personal files. At school they will receive Outcome-Based Education monitored through the new Common Core federalized testing system. This will ensure the children are politically correct in their thinking and qualify for workplace training.

The outcomes, sometimes called SLERS (High School Student Learning Results), are to produce multicultural appreciators, environmental stewards, collaborative learners, good communicators, and global/local community citizens, not US citizens.

All of these themes are infused into every discipline, into reading, math, writing, science, and history through "thematic units." Students are exposed to selected political correct stories from around the world in early grades, and later given instructional technical materials to read, replacing much of our traditional American classical literature. Children will be taught that America is a bad, cruel, and hateful country with a terrible history. Children now will see history as a narrative between "the oppressed and the oppressor," a social justice worldview. Since the new outcome is the creation of a global (and community) citizen, the allegiance to America, or any nation, must be destroyed or weakened.

All of this transformation of thought is carefully measured by the state, actually national Common Core Standards Testing that is done through computer programs. It will become more difficult for parents to see what their children are learning. Each question and the students' answers are carefully monitored, and new learning is individually prescribed to get the individual young person to the desired political correct outcome.

Children keep a regular journal that includes personal information and records their thinking processes as they go through school. Children are taught to explain math processes, rather than compute and seek the right answer. It is the "thinking processes" that are now important, not the ability to solve math problems. Children are not given real history, stories of people and events of the past, but asked to view history through political correct themes and critical thinking schemes. Teachers are asked to do guided reading, and guided writing, with everyone working together. Individual learning and individual thinking is not encouraged. What an individual thinks is no longer important; what counts is what the group thinks.

And if you are a community member, an individual thinker, or have a dissenting position, you will be asked to join a school committee as a token stakeholder, to show diversity. But through the "Delphi Process," the group or whole committee will never hear, much less discuss your opinion. And you will be told that you are the only one with a different view.

Old report cards are changed and so are graduating diplomas and replaced with Certificates of Initial Master, CIM's, usually given at age sixteen. The CIM means that you have met the outcomes. It means that you are a "multicultural appreciator," an "environmental steward," a "collaborative learner" and a "global/community citizen." Having a CIM will mean that you have a "world-class" education.

Once you receive your CIM and have shown that you are politically correct, that you have become the new global citizen, then you can go on to receive your CAM. A CAM, or Certificate of Advanced Mastery will mean that you have completed your three-year workforce preparation. This internship program includes a year of college. Schools are no longer to be K-12, but K-14 institutions, including community college. Recently President Obama has proposed making community college free. This will facilitate the new system.

Eventually every young person will be assigned a job according to the needs of the regional Workforce Investment Board. Regional boards study the local economy and plan out into the future how many workers in each field are needed.

School Career Centers will take this information and assist students as young as eighth grade to select a career pathway. Once a career pathway is selected, a customized education is provided, which may limit science and math classes or Shakespeare classes if they do not parallel your career track. Education is now more utilitarian to help the student fill a need for the planned global economy.

The Chamber of Commerce is being used to bring in this system. School-to-Work looks good and is sold as a way to help students find their place in the workforce. Businesses are told they will have access to the student's records from high school in order to help them make better hiring decisions. It also puts pressure on youth to conform, as their files will follow them all of their lives.

This is a very different kind of education. Formerly, we provided students a broad classical, liberal education. They were encouraged to be individual thinkers and read all kinds of materials. Now they are being trained to be a compliant worker who will fill the needs of a carefully planned global workforce.

People have been reduced to a human resource. Previously the door to the HR office was called Personnel. Once we were considered individual persons. But now we are merely a human resource for the new global economy.

One of the superintendent's cabinet members, an assistant superintendent, knew I hated the term "human resource." One day he changed the name on the door of the HR department back to Personnel, just to tease me. He wanted to make sure I saw it. My hat goes off to the many administrators in public schools. They work hard and are talented. They, too, are helpless in stopping the changes in education. The names for the reforms sound good, the rationale for each new initiative is deceiving and compelling. They are very busy in the day-to-day operations and often do not see the bigger picture. They were patient in answering my questions, tried to make sense of my objections, and provided me with information I requested. And for that I am grateful. They are true professionals.

Dossier files are kept on all the students throughout their school life, including any prenatal care, parents as teachers programs you may have been involved in, healthcare, and state preschool. Even samples of your schoolwork from each year and test results are recorded. Once you are in the workforce, your personal file continues to follow you. Businesses can see your disciplinary record and files are used by the school, workforce boards, and others to determine your status and work in life.

Businesses are encouraged through government grants to continue to retrain their workers. Employees will receive continual recertification, and workplace classes may include parenting skills and mental health assessments. This is important because we will soon have to parent the new way, according to the United Nations Rights of the Children and other global treaties that take away our God-given rights to direct our children. Parent re-education classes may take place at your worksite or at the local education center, at your local "New American School" that will be open from 6 a.m. to 9 p.m. at night.

In the '90s, First Lady Hillary Clinton, as you will recall, moved into the Oval Office with her husband President Bill Clinton and immediately started to work on healthcare. It was the first time we heard words like managed care, HMOs, and health care rationing. She advocated for universal health care, coverage for all people enforced by the federal government, but we pushed back. In 1994, the Republicans won control of both the US Senate and House of Representatives for the first time since the early '50s. We were proud that we had stopped her. But in reality she was happy to move the agenda forward. "Three steps forward and two steps back," they call it. First schools, through school-based clinics, were to bring in a government funded health care system for children zero to eighteen years of age. Then Hillarycare, which pushed for an enforced mandate for employers to provide healthcare for all of their employees made it the expectation that employers take up the responsibility of providing health care. Both schools and employers would, of course, eventually be governed by federal regulations.

When I was young, I remember an insurance agent came to our house to sell medical insurance to my parents. We could pick any doctor we wanted and then send in doctor-signed forms to our insurance company so the doctor could get paid. Life was so simple.

Health care has become so complicated, adding layer upon layer of administrative management costs, making the price of health care go through the roof. Managed care has not simplified things; it has made the whole system extremely burdensome.

And with employers and corporations expected to pay for health insurance, costs further skyrocketed.

Many small insurance companies disappeared or merged to compete for large company contracts. When our school district, with 4,000 employees, looked for health care, we only had a few large carriers to choose from. Having fewer providers makes it easier for companies to set prices. And with prices rising, sadly, we had to cut the hours of our teacher's aides just to avoid providing healthcare.

With millions of dollars at stake, I am sure there are secret commission deals that line the pockets of negotiators, administrators, and school board members. This behind-the-scene corruption, of course, continues to drive up healthcare costs. And in the end we are asked to pay billions more through higher premiums and more taxes.

Obamacare now adds thousands of healthcare panels, exchanges, regulations, and management costs to a health care system that is already out of control. Rather than fixing the problems, it adds gasoline to the fire. It is totally unworkable. But to the social planners that is okay. Another healthcare crisis is just what they need to give us completely government-run healthcare, as in a single-payer system. Managed care, excessive regulations and state exchanges are just the beginning.

Tragically, as we have seen, the purpose for the government getting involved in health care is population control. That includes advocating for abortion, encouraging families to limit children, and in some cases limiting care for the elderly.

President Obama at one time named former Senator Tom Daschle as his healthcare Czar. At Reason.com Senator Daschle's approach to health care is analyzed in an article called, "How the Healthcare Czar Would Save Money by Limiting Care." His views are portrayed as advocating rationing, having more and more government panels decide who should get health care, what procedures are effective, and when people should get the services.

Others wonder if a new government healthcare system is not on a collision course with the national debt. Some are concerned that way down the line, government may have to choose between curtailing health care or eliminating people such as the disabled, elderly, and political enemies. I understand this is extreme. It is unthinkable. Yet, historically, we have seen that controlling regimes like Hitler's, who gave out expensive benefits to the German people and confiscated guns, also ended up eliminating the disabled, the vulnerable, and other "undesirables," such as the Jews. We must stand alert.

I mention guns, because when I was watching *Shindler's List*, a movie about the Holocaust, I wondered how could a few German officers round up thousands of Jews out of the ghetto, where they had been placed, and pack them into trains headed towards the gas chambers. I was saying to myself, "Come on guys, rise up, resist, don't let them do that to you!" Then it occurred to me, they could not resist, the German soldiers had the guns, they had none. Our founding fathers were so wise to add the second amendment to the Constitution.

Back to the education goals, Goal two calls for a 90 percent graduation rate. This sounds great! Especially when you consider some inner city school districts have a 50% graduation rate. This will, of course, be easily achieved because you cannot go on to get a job without first being certified that your attitudes have been changed. Similarly, you will not be able to get certain healthcare procedures unless you meet the right criteria. Through coercion, peer intimidation, and neighborhood informants, most will comply with the system.

It is now understandable why Common Core, the new education reform initiative under President Obama, requires massive data collection of individual students and their parents. According to the Department of Education, in their manual, *Promoting Grit, Tenacity, and Perseverance: Critical Factors for Success in the 21st Century,* students' "attributes, dispositions, social skills, attitudes and intrapersonal resources–independent of intellectual ability" will be collected.

As Orlean Koehle, author of *Common Core, A Trojan Horse* pointed out on a recent television show, "data collection techniques may also include hidden cameras to record children's facial expressions, electronic seats that judge posture, a pressure-sensitive computer mouse, and a biometric wristband on a child's wrist." While these may not be at your school yet, they are all described in exhibit 11 in the the the same manual.

In a March 13, 2013 commentary article in *The Orange County Register* newspaper, called "Data Mining Kids Crosses the Line," Joy Pullman, a research fellow on education policy at the Heartland Institute, referenced the above department report, and also stated that "the government will be collecting a dossier on every child, containing highly personal information, without asking permission or even notifying parents."

Big names like Microsoft founder Bill Gates and David Coleman are pushing Common Core, the new national standards and education testing system. David Coleman is the president of the College Board, a private New-York based organization that administers the advanced placement exam and produces the SAT, college entrance tests. Sadly, they are pushing a controversial testing system that excludes a large portion of American classical literature, reduces math to thought processes and minimizes or revises U.S. history. It makes sense because inevitably in the end these collaborators will probably receive large lucrative contracts from the federal Department of Education. It is this "crony capitalism" that certainly gives true capitalism and free enterprise a bad name.

History professor, author and National Council on Humanities member Wilfred M. McCay shares his concern that the College Board 2014 framework for AP history classes has greatly changed from the 2010 framework. "If the framework is permitted to take hold, the new version of the test will effectively marginalize traditional ways of teaching about the American past, and force American high schools to teach U.S. history from a perspective that self-consciously seeks to decenter American history." He asks, "Is this the right way to prepare young people for American citizenship?"

In the grand scheme of things, the United States is but one of the many "Nation States" of this new world where students are to become global citizens, not American citizens. According to the Center for Civics Education, that creates new curriculum and lesson plans for teachers, everyone is expected to exhibit "civic virtue" by giving up his or her God-given rights, for the common good.

In a man-managed society, it is the elitists and social planners who decide what is the common good, what is good for the environment, what is good for the people of the world, and what is good for the local group. The central committee does the central planning and ensures local committees participate in their plans as they implement their schemes. It is kind of a two tier system, the *(smart)* planners and "the little people" who need to cooperate. And it is all done in the name of equality!

In the early 1700's, our founders did not want to be under the whim of a mere man, a king. They did not want to be under a man-made society but under a loving, all-knowing, wise God. They wanted their elected leaders who looked to God for wisdom to make decisions for them. In America, "We have no King but King Jesus!" the founders shouted. They wanted the *people* who had to live by the laws to make the laws, not some king or chairman and his central committee.

For many in the educational establishment, the educational reforms are still like the 3-D pictures; each color or part looks good. They have not learned how to focus, how to see the real form within.

As I looked at the different educational elements, I was not sure what I was seeing. But one day it all came into focus—I saw the form. It was a totalitarian system, a seamless lifelong, government-controlled society. Yet it is not a new system. It is as old as the Tower of Babel. Nevertheless it is a frightening form, and many wars have been fought resisting these oppressive regimes.

Their plans for us are nothing but the controlled society my father described to us as we talked around the dinner table. Now as a school board member, whenever I gave a presentation on the education goals, sharing the government documents on an overhead projector, someone would inevitably stand up. At the hospital community room, an old simple couple exclaimed in broken English, "Why, that is what happened in Czechoslovakia!" At a meeting at the beautiful Newport Beach Balboa Bay Club, a sophisticated lady raised her hand to say, "We fought that under Mussolini!"

When I shared about Goals 2000, the eight national education goals, I would end my presentations with one question. "What is wrong with this utopian, wonderful, just society?"

I reviewed, pointing at the Lifelong Learning chart. Everyone comes to school "ready to learn," starting with prenatal care. There is no child abuse because parents are monitored; there is no unemployment because students are guided through school into their place in the workforce. We have a 90 percent graduation rate because students understand the importance of school, their personal dossier or file, and how it relates to their ability to find work. There is no bullying at school, as hate speech is monitored, through "safe schools", another goal. Everyone has government- or employee-provided and regulated healthcare. Teachers and police are constantly retrained. Everyone works together for the common good. Neighbors are involved in monitoring our communities. Employees are continually reeducated and recertified in the workplace. What could be more wonderful?

"Isn't this an amazing society?" I asked the audience. "What is wrong with this utopian, man-managed, carefully planned society?"

And again, giving them time to think, I asked, "What is missing?"

I gave a hint. "Just three things are missing."

"Life, liberty, and the pursuit of happiness" are missing. America is missing!

Part V
How We Respond

With Malice Toward None

"Of all tyrannies, a tyranny sincerely exercised for the good of its victims may be the most oppressive. It would be better to live under robber barons than under omnipotent moral busybodies. The robber baron's cruelty may sometimes sleep, his cupidity may at some point be satiated; but those who torment us for our own good will torment us without end for they do so with the approval of their own conscience." —*C. S. Lewis*

"With Malice toward none, with charity for all, with firmness in the right, as God gives us to see the right, let us strive on to finish the work we are in, to bind up the nation's wounds." —*Abraham Lincoln*

Chapter 23
With Malice Toward None

C. S. Lewis got it right. "Of all tyrannies, a tyranny sincerely exercised for the good of its victims may be the most oppressive. It would be better to live under robber barons than under omnipotent moral busybodies. The robber baron's cruelty may sometimes sleep, his cupidity may at some point be satiated; but those who torment us for our own good will torment us without end for they do so with the approval of their own conscience."

What I saw was disturbing. It was a heavy burden. I had to share it with someone.

It was time to give a Goals 2000 presentation to another group. "Why should I go?" I asked myself. People think either I am crazy or they are afraid. They ask, "What can we do with this information?" I replied, "Expose the evil. Share this information with others!" "Write letters to the editor at your local newspaper." "Talk on the radio." "Talk to your elected officials." "We need to sound the alarm!"

But something bothered me. I knew that would not change things. Was it too late for America? Every program that would enslave us had a wonderful rationale, a funding mechanism to bring it in, and committees to make sure it was implemented. How could we fight that?

I fell into great despair as I realized, America left God and now we were going into captivity! Our churches seemed ineffective. It did not seem to matter what party was in office. Our culture was spiraling out of control, our mothers' hearts had grown cold, fathers were absent, and men were doing evil deeds. Judge Robert H. Bork, one of America's most distinguished conservative scholars, wrote a book called *Slouching Towards Gomorrah*, meaning that we were sliding towards judgment. Are we doomed to lose our greatness? Or worse, lose our freedom?

I greatly despaired! There was nothing we could do.

Why was I going out to speak? Why was I leaving my five children, going out to yet another meeting room in a hotel or community center to share with others what I was seeing? We are powerless to stop the decay of our nation, and we are powerless to stop the elitists' plans.

My despair turned to anger! I yelled out, "God, I am so mad at you! Why did you show this to me? It is too great a burden. Why would you spend all this time showing me these things! I will never read another grant proposal again! I do not want to know anything else."

"I see it, and it is cruel for you to show this to me. I love America, what she has stood for! I love freedom! I love righteousness! Why have you wasted my time?" I raged at God. "I will never go out and speak again." I cried out in great despair, "There is nothing we can do!"

There was a pause, then God spoke: "What are you fighting?" He asked. "I am fighting Communism, world Socialism, the New World Order, a totalitarian, god-less society!"

"What are you fighting?" he asked again. I tried to appeal to God's better self: "If we have an oppressive form of government that hates Christians, we will not be able to share the good news of your love and forgiveness with the people. I am fighting the loss of our freedoms, and that includes our religious freedoms!"

"No, what are you fighting?" He asked, a third time. "Well" …I paused…"It is all just a pack of lies. Their utopian, man-managed society has never worked. It has killed millions, caused many to starve to death, increased poverty and created so much suffering." But it all sounds so good; every program seems so compassionate. It is based on false compassion.

"I am fighting a bunch of lies and false compassion!"

God said, "Yes. And how do you fight that?" he continued.

I thought for a moment. Lies and false compassion...

"You fight lies with truth and false compassion with true compassion."

He said, "Raise up an army to tell the truth with real compassion!"

It all made sense. The truth would drive out the lies.

Instead of false compassion, we need true compassion.

Then it hit me...Truth and Compassion..."That is Jesus!" He is "full of grace and truth." He is the truth. And he was filled with compassion and healed the sick and fed the hungry. He preached and he healed. He spoke the truth with love.

Why is it that Jesus is always the answer?

I thought, "Raise up an army." After a while, I asked God, "What kind of army? Big? Small?"

In my mind, I began to see thousands and thousands coming. My mission now was to raise up an army, to call out a group of people to march out together with the truth and with hearts full of compassion for the people. We will fight with truth and genuine compassion!

We have a generation of hurting people, not just in the inner city but in every segment of society, who have been devastated by the destruction of the family, and by drug, sex and alcohol addictions. In the '60s, the hippies were rebelling against the materialism of their parents, which resulted in a disintegration of our families. This increase in divorce led to poverty which produced welfare policies that encourage fatherlessness and abortion. Today, particularly in the inner city, we have a generation that is devastated by the drug culture, street gangs, violent crime and incarceration.

But in contrast, we also have a generation of young people who want to make a difference in their community. They are cause-driven. They too have felt the pain and want a new society. And with the aging of the baby boomers there are more and more retired people who want their life to count. They want to leave a legacy. The church is also talking more about going outside the four walls to reach out to people. The timing for a great movement of truth and compassion could not be better! God had prepared the way.

But here is a question. Will the social justice advocates mobilize our youth and our churches to work for a just, utopian society, or will the church call young people out to share the true gospel, the good news that God can forgive, save, heal, and transform individual lives? It was time to make America good again!

Our founders believed that freedom, or our form of government, was only good for a religious and moral people. Patrick Henry said, "The great pillars of all government and social life are virtue, morality and religion." Samuel Adams believed that, "Religion and morals are the only solid foundation of public liberty and happiness." John Adams said that "Liberty will not long survive the extinction of morals." And Benjamin Franklin noted that "only a virtuous people are capable of freedom. As nations become corrupt and vicious they have more need of masters."

John Adams summed it up, "Our Constitution was made only for a moral religious people. It is wholly inadequate to the government of any other."

A revival of righteousness and moral values will restore America's goodness and, in the process, restore our greatness. And it will allow us to remain free. This was a daunting task, to turn a generation around.

The time is right. The cause is urgent. We have to move quickly. It was time to raise up an army!

The first thing in war is to listen to the commander-in-chief and follow his instructions. He said, "Raise up an army to tell the truth with true compassion." These were his marching orders.

And if God thought this was the answer, who was I to argue with him. And if it was time to move the people out into the battle, we first had to unite them behind the cause. A winning plan, an offensive strategy, and an understanding of the enemy was absolutely necessary.

I switched gears. I already knew all I wanted to know about our school's education agenda to transform America. We now had to get ready to mobilize an army. But what if thousands of volunteers came to fight what would we do with them?

First, we had to get ready to receive them. Along with some concerned community members, we started a nonprofit organization and I earned a master's degree in organizational leadership and we set out to change the world! Rather, we wanted to change our city, our county and the nation. We knew God had a plan, and that was enough.

Still the question lingered: how do we respond to this devastating information? It was a question that I had been asked many times. How do we respond to the hijacking of our schools, the destruction of our families and the loss of our freedom? Do we sit back, complain, fret, and wring our hands? Or do we rise up and do something?

But before moving out, first, God had to break my heart. We had a club membership store near our house called Fedco. It was a forerunner to Costco or Sam's Club. They published a great little store magazine with ads. It also had interesting articles on little-known historical places in California. I read that there was a Lincoln Memorial Shrine in Riverside. I had a brother who lived up in Arrowhead, up in the mountains. At times we would meet in the middle in Riverside at a mall. The Lincoln Memorial was near that area. Our family also had recently gone to Forest Home Family Camp up in the mountains, and I was familiar with the area. I knew just where that memorial site was. I decided to go visit. The memorial had a few marble walls with inscriptions surrounded by lovely rose bushes. I sat there on a bench and read what Lincoln said concerning the Civil War. I started to cry, and I cried and I cried. I began to see the devastation of the Civil War, where brother fought against brother. How tragic, to fight your own countrymen. Both Robert E. Lee and Ulysses S. Grant, the top generals on each side, were greatly respected. Even family members fought on different sides!

The southern states needed slaves to help with the cotton and tobacco plantations. When the federal government wanted to end slavery, the south objected. They claimed that the federal government did not have the right to tell the states what to do. They stood up for state rights. The northern states, although they enjoyed the cheap cotton and tobacco, wanted to end slavery. As you recall, even at the founding of our nation when the Constitution was written, it was the framers intent to end slavery. They believed that "all men were created equal" and that all people had been given inalienable rights by their Creator "the right to life, liberty and the pursuit of happiness."

The 1852 publication of *Uncle Tom's Cabin*, a two-volume novel by Harriet Beecher Stowe, a young wife and mother, changed forever how people viewed slavery. According to the Harriet Beecher Stowe Center website, the book sold 10,000 copies in the first week and 300,000 in the first year and "galvanized the abolition movement and contributed to the outbreak of the Civil War."

When the government started talking about ending slavery, eleven southern states left the union and elected their own president, Jefferson Davis, who served as president of the Confederacy for four years. This was of great concern to President Lincoln. He had to preserve the union. He needed to keep us together. Some were fighting to keep the union while others were fighting for state rights. To each of the sides both reasoning appeared to be noble causes.

While many southerners stood up for states' rights, the real issue was slavery. If the South prevailed slavery would continue. Once the war began, the north decided that we had to end slavery once and for all. And this was the time.

What a tragic war! Americans fought against Americans. What about "E Pluribus Unum," our motto—*out of many, one?* What about the Declaration of Independence statement that "all men are created equal?" America was divided.

The inscriptions at the Lincoln Memorial were about the widows and fatherless children that were left behind in the aftermath of the war. I had never thought about that before. War affects not only the soldiers who died but also their families. Of course, with 620,000 men dying in battle during the Civil War, there were children and women who were left behind, fatherless and widowed. Perhaps there were 500,000, or maybe a million or more. The pains of the war continued in so many hearts.

My heart began to break. I saw the similarities. In a sense, today, we are once again divided, engaged in a new type of civil war. We too have been ravaged with a cultural war since the '60s, when many young hippies hitchhiked, left home, and essentially became motherless and fatherless. They rejected their parents' lifestyle and their parents' values. Alone, lost and without values, they tried to fill the emptiness with drugs, alcohol and sex.

They wanted *peace* and *love.* And the cost of "free love" was high. Babies were unwanted. The women's liberation movement and the ravages of divorce had left so many women in poverty and left young boys and girls without their dads. As I sat on the bench at the memorial, I thought of the sweet boys and girls who had to grow up without the guiding hand of a father. Our prisons, too, are full of hopeless young men and women who also are casualties of our cultural war. They are in anguish and crying. And I cried and cried some more. My tears were more for this generation, the fatherless children and widows or single mothers who have struggled alone.

Then there are the innocent babies who have died from abortion, never knowing their parents, never fulfilling their purpose. Fifty-seven million are gone. What a tragedy! Almost ten times that of the horrific Holocaust! This has been a generation of death.

Also tragic is the neglect of so many children due to absent or abusive mothers or fathers. This will have repercussions that will haunt America for generations to come.

A generation of children will continue to struggle in life because they were not taught to read or write well. They think they are dumb, but they are not. They were just caught in a different kind of war, the Reading and Math Wars.

And what about the children who have to grow up with the daily trauma, brokenness, and scars of sexual abuse? Yet they are expected to perform and keep up.

What was Lincoln's response to the death and destruction of his day? Lincoln came to Gettysburg on November 19, 1863, to dedicate a final resting place, a burial ground, for those who died on the battlefields of the Civil War. What did he say? First he reminded them of our history, that we "were conceived in liberty and dedicated to the proposition that all men are created equal." He said the battle was about whether a nation "conceived in liberty and dedicated to equality could long endure." We, too, worry if America can long survive. We are again divided and a nation divided cannot stand. The stakes were the same in Lincoln's day. "Can a nation so divided, continue?" Lincoln asked. We need to choose. Do we give up, or do we bring our people together and resolve to advance the cause of liberty?

President Lincoln said the people were gathered to dedicate this resting place, to consecrate it and hallow it. He reminded them that the brave men, living and dead, who struggled, have already consecrated it. They suffered and struggled that the nation might live. Then he called the people, the living, to renew their dedication for the unfinished work. The war was winding down but it was not over. He called for a rededication to the great task remaining before them.

Abraham Lincoln ended his speech at Gettysburg with these words: "...that we here highly resolve that these dead shall not have died in vain—**that this nation, under God, shall have a new birth of freedom—and that government of the people,**

by the people, for the people, shall not perish from the earth."

Lincoln called for a rededication of the people to the cause of freedom. He said we needed *a new birth of freedom*, so that government of the people, by the people, for the people, shall not perish from the earth. Let us resolve, today in the 21st century, to pick up the torch and once again fight for freedom and personal liberty.

Over the years, many brave people; our military men, President George Washington, President Abraham Lincoln, President Ronald Reagan and Rev. Martin Luther King and many others have fought to keep us free.

President Ronald Reagan stated that, "Freedom is never more than one generation away from extinction. We didn't pass it to our children in the bloodstream. It must be fought for, protected, and handed on for them to do the same, or one day we will spend our sunset years telling our children and our children's children what it was once like in the United States where men were free."

It looks like it is our turn to join in this battle. Let us also resolve today to dedicate ourselves to the unfinished work and task ahead.

In our fight, we are not called to take up arms, we are asked to join in a revolution of love, a movement of real heartfelt compassion for the poor, the disenfranchised, and the hurting. Love never fails; it wins out every time.

As we fight to stay free, we must also realize that there are many good men and women on both sides of the aisle. Many are just unaware of the battle for freedom, and others are deceived by the rhetoric, the double speak. While some of our leaders truly understand the consequences of tyranny, the plan and agenda of our enemies, there are many others who do not understand the battle. They have believed the language of the enemy. And to some extent, we all have been deceived at one time or another. We need to share what we are seeing with patience and love. Lincoln, who knew the destructive forces of *disunity*, said we need to move forward "with malice toward none."

Seeing the master plan of the enemy brings despair. We have

been lied to, our children have been stolen, and our families are devastated. We feel violated! We should be mad, angry, and resentful. We have to come to a point of despair before we can experience real change.

Our personal liberties are at stake and our entire existence as a free nation is on the line. Yet it seems that no matter who is president or who has the Congress, the Progressive global agenda just moves forward. That is because we have been deceived by the rhetoric. And without the truth, we are powerless to stop it.

We called our nonprofit after school clubs "Sports Plus." We offered structured sports instruction, academic tutoring and character lessons. But an elementary school principal kept saying we do not want you to emphasis sports we want you to make a real difference. We want the children's test scores to go up with your homework help. We want them to learn respect and responsibility with your character lessons. In response, we changed the name to "Making a Difference Clubs." Soon everyone was calling them M.A.D. Clubs. At first I did not like it; it seemed so negative. Interestingly, the pre-teens in our intermediate school clubs loved the name. It must be their age.

I have discovered that it is true—we first have to get M.A.D. before we can really Make A Difference. We have to be mad enough to do something! We have to hate the evil in the world and the destruction it causes to so many lives.

In I Samuel, a book in the Bible, David, the future king of Israel, and his men came back home to Ziklag. They found that their wives and children were captured by their enemies and that their possessions were missing. David's men were angry with David, their leader, and wanted to stone him. He prayed, sought God's counsel and God encouraged his heart and told him what to do. David told his men, "God has a plan. He is with us. Let's go!" They pursued the enemy, recovered their wives, their children, their goods, and they even took a spoil. God restored everything and gave them more!

Like David who looked to God, in my despair, God encouraged my heart. He said there is a winning plan. "Raise up an army to tell the truth with real compassion."

So let's go! Let's take back what has been stolen from us. Let's take back our families, our children—our cities and our nation!

This is a big battle. It is more than an educational battle. It is more than a cultural war. This is the battle of the ages, the battle between good and evil. It is a battle between truth and deception, a battle over freedom or slavery...a battle against tyranny.

Lincoln knew the Civil War was a war over the slavery of men, but it was also a battle for the union, a battle to preserve the nation. It was a fight over whether we would stay together as a united people. America is divided today also. And a nation divided cannot stand. Let's get mad at the great destruction, allow God to break our hearts for the people, for those who are enslaved, and as Lincoln said commit ourselves to the task at hand.

Let us respond in *love* "with malice toward none" and work to bring people together.

Once people understand the deception and learn the truth, their eyes will be opened. We also must realize that evil plans do not work and in the end will not succeed. They fail every time. And as in the Tower of Babel, when the people tried to create their own utopia, God knows just how to confuse their plans.

We also must respond in *faith*, knowing God has called us to the battle and he has the winning plan and the winning strategy.

For ages, men have wanted to rule the world—Alexander the Great, Napoleon, and Hitler, to name a few.

I remember as a child growing up in the '50s watching a cartoon show called *Felix the Cat*. It was about a black cat with big eyes that laughed a lot and his friends Poindexter and the Professor. The theme of the cartoons was generally that someone evil wanted to rule the world, and Felix and his friends had to stop them.

And as I recall, in every cartoon, Felix and his pals did stop them.

Chapter 24

Freedom and Tyranny Chart

I have a friend, and I think he is a genius. He graduated from Yale and probably did other important things. His name is Eric. He likes to write and at times will send me a packet of his writing. Sometimes he is hard to listen to because he seems to go over my head. But if I try to stay with it, I am not disappointed. One day he showed me a little simple chart. I do not know if he thought it up or if he got it from somewhere else. But it changed everything. It is the key to understanding freedom and tyranny.

Before we talk about the winning plan, we first need to understand the philosophical difference between freedom and tyranny. Knowing the difference will show us how we can win. Once you see the chart, you will see what is happening to America. America is flipping out!

Here is the *Freedom and Tyranny Chart*:

Freedom	Tyranny
Individual	World
Family	Nation
City	State
State	City
Nation	Family
World	Individual

While the Constitution gives us a limited role for the federal government, we acknowledge that we need government at every level; that is why we have some world agreements, a federal government, a state government, and a city government. We also have rules for our homes, and through self-government we have standards that we each live by.

Abraham Lincoln gave his view on the role of government. "The legitimate object of government is to do for a community of people whatever they need to have done, but cannot do at all, or cannot so well do, for themselves—in their separate and individual capacities." This is a good rule of thumb. The more people can do for themselves, the better. National defense is definitely a function for the federal government, given by the Constitution, as it is something we cannot do for ourselves.

While it sounds like a foolish question, it must be asked. "Do we want to live in freedom or do we want to live with tyranny?" There is much confusion out there. I have sat in a restaurant, across the table from a nonprofit counselor, and she stated as a matter of fact, "I like Socialism. Government should provide for the people. It should provide health care for everyone."

On a recent trip to Washington, D.C., I asked my black taxi driver, "Are you concerned about President Obama's plan to redistribute the wealth?" He answered, "No, no one is saying that!" "Don't you think that that is where Obamacare is headed, for example with the rationing of health care?" Again he said, "That is not what is going on."

Then he went on to share how he admired Cuba, how they provided education, health care, and jobs for its people. I then asked, "Don't you know that Cuba is a Socialist country?" "If you like Cuba, I think you do want to redistribute the wealth—you like Socialism." People give lip service to freedom, yet they now believe in tyranny, the confiscation of a man's labor, and the forced redistribution of goods. They say they are against slavery, but they willingly accept a new kind of slavery, a new kind of tyranny to the "common good." We have shifted from a belief in individual rights to a belief in the world's needs.

We need to settle it once and for all: freedom is better than tyranny. Free countries have trouble because people from other parts to the world want to get in. People want to live free. Countries with an oppressive government, Socialist societies or Communist countries, like Cuba and Russia have to keep people from leaving. They often erect fences, like the Berlin Wall, to make sure the people do not leave. People all over the world want to be free. They want the freedom to enjoy the fruits of their labor. They want the higher standard of living that a free society produces.

This *Freedom and Tyranny Chart* can help us to see the difference clearly. It will help us see behind the smoke and mirrors to what is really happening. It can help us understand that we need to make individuals important once again.

As you can see above in our chart, freedom puts the individual first, then the family, then the city, the state, the federal government, and the world last. Individual rights are the most important. They always have to be at the top of the list. Our United States Constitution states that it is the responsibility of government to protect our God-given individual rights.

Tyranny puts the world first, the nation second, then the state, the city, the family, and finally what is least important is the individual. That is why books that teach global citizenship are teaching young people that "civic virtue" is giving up your individual rights for the "common good," for the good of the planet, the world. The priority under tyranny is the good of the whole, the world, not what is good for the individual. We cannot or should not give up our individual rights for the common good, or to another government. Our form of government was created to protect individual rights. They were given to us by God.

The framers of the Constitution had a big debate over whether they should list the individual rights that God had given man. Some wanted to be very explicit and list the rights so there would be no questions. Others felt a list might limit rights if some were left out. In the end, they decided to add the Bill of Rights to the Constitution. Americans have not only the right to life (to live), the right to live free (without excessive government control), and the right to pursue their own happiness (pursue their individual dreams) but also other rights. The Bill of rights was specific and stated that Americans have the right to freedom of speech and that they could speak their minds. Individuals also had freedom to express their religious sentiments. They could express their viewpoint in print, in newspapers, for distribution without worry of retaliation or censorship. They also had the right to own a gun, and that no one could infringe on that right. There were other rights like the right to privacy, the right to live without someone snooping on them, without Internet email monitoring, or without neighborhood informants. It was the role of government to protect the rights that were listed and other rights that were not listed.

We cannot have a free country if individual people are not free. Freedom always starts with the individual. America has been known for its individualism and self-reliance. If there were a problem, we would not look to government; we would try to solve it ourselves. Sometimes we would create a business or a nonprofit organization to solve the problem. That is why we are known for our ingenuity and innovation. Individuals were rewarded for their efforts, hard work, or great inventions. Their labors and property did not belong to the national government.

Next to the individual, the family is the most important. Parents are given children as gifts from God, and parents need to look to God for help. They need to be free from government interference as they make decisions for their children, whether they are health care decisions or educational decisions.

Cities keep our roads in good condition, collect our trash, make sure we have streetlights, bring us safe drinking water, and provide for security and emergency services like police, fire, and paramedics. As we have seen, policing should always be a function of the local government and never a federal program.

Recently, we have heard stories about police brutality or abuse. It is up to the people to hold their local police department accountable for how they treat the people. It cannot be addressed at the national level. City by city, there needs to be a discussion. We all want to be protected from criminals who would steal from us or kill us. But we also want to know that the police respect our individual rights to walk around freely. What kind of force do we want, and what kind of restraint do we need?

According to the tenth amendment in the Constitution, states have the authority to do whatever the national government has not been given the power to do. The federal or national government has a limited role and should only be involved in what the Constitution allows.

The writers of the United States Constitution limited the role of the federal government. Its main goal is to provide national defense and to keep us safe from other governments that may want to harm us. They were given the responsibility to control commerce across state lines, provide for a national transportation system, and other limited services. Due to the limited nature of the federal government, US Representatives and Senators used to only work part time.

President George Washington warned us in his Farewell Address to not be entangled in the affairs of other nations. We are not to be the world's policeman. We are not to fix everyone else's problems. We are not to sign treaties that limit our own right to govern ourselves. We are a sovereign nation. Our elected officials, who are our representatives, make the laws for the American people. And they, too, are required to live by the same laws.

Needless to say, we have strayed from many of our first principles.

Tyrannical regimes want to scare you to give up your rights so they can control you. Hitler would not have been able to kill so many Jews had he not first confiscated their guns. He had to first take away their God-given right to protect themselves.

As you can see by the chart, freedom is the opposite of tyranny.

So when you hear people talk about giving up your individual rights for "the common good," our "collective" selves, "social justice" (the redistribution of wealth), and the "need to save the planet," your antennas need to go up.

I am not saying that everyone who uses these words hates freedom. In fact, they would all say they love freedom. It is often that they just do not understand freedom or our American system. It has not been taught correctly in many of our educational institutions. These collective words are creeping into our vocabulary, and many of us just go along and use these words without understanding their implication.

When I first was elected to the Santa Ana School Board in the early '90s, all the children, I particularly remember elementary children, had yearbooks with a picture of the planet on the cover and the words SAVE THE PLANET. This seemed strange. These were yearbooks. It was about each child, the teacher they had, the friends they made, pictures of things they did, field trips, and clubs they belonged to. It was "their" memory book. So why SAVE THE PLANET? It just bugged me.

Later I began to see that so much of the curriculum was about saving the planet, saving the eagles, the owls, the water, the rain forest, and it just went on and on! These poor children, first and second graders, who were helpless to save the beautiful Scarlet Macaws in Brazil or the cute, furry polar bears, were being asked to worry about them. What a burden these little kids had to carry. Soon there would be no more clean water to drink, the polar icebergs were melting, the sun was burning our skin due to the depletion of the ozone, and so many of these magnificent animals would be gone.

Frankly, I thought, "This is child abuse!" These precious children should be learning about our wonderful world and how it has survived thousands of years. They should be learning about Thomas Edison and how he wanted to create a light bulb and tried and tried, failed and failed, and then finally did it! They should be reading about Dr. Salk who invented the polio vaccine that eradicated the dreaded polio, and George Washington Carver who came up with so many uses for peanuts. If they spend their youth learning about how we had solved problems in the past, they would be full of hope rather than despair. They would have a "we can solve it" attitude.

Topics such as world hunger, water shortages, and endangered species should be taught in high school or junior high after the children have learned about the many great men who were problem solvers. They can tackle these problems after they have learned to do research for themselves, are able to read scientific documents, and know how to integrate their learning, using their excellent math, reading, writing skills, and historical knowledge. Then they are prepared to approach these problems with confidence and hope. Apparently, the purpose of this horrific education is to scare these children into becoming global citizens. And if the globalists have to indoctrinate children before they have learned to think for themselves, they probably are wrong about a lot of things.

Captain Planet, a children's television environmental cartoon show created by Ted Turner, uses the scare of environmental disaster to promote population control. On June 7, 2012, it was announced that the world had seven billion people. Ted Turner, who also is the founder of CNN, in a 2012 television interview, advocated that we stabilize the planet by reducing the population by five billion people, leaving two billion. He also advocated that everyone limit families to one child (a policy Communist China is now rethinking). His interview appeared to be serious. While Ted Turner is extreme, he is not alone, and he is influential. It now seems that many of us have a bull's-eye on our heads and will need to give up our right to life for the common good of the planet. It is indicative of the hysteria that surrounds these issues and explains the huge push in our schools and on television.

The answer to solving our environmental problems is not killing off two-thirds of the planet or forcing everyone to comply with onerous regulations. But it is the teaching of character. If you learn to be principled and responsible when you are young, chances are you will not pollute the rivers with your company's toxic waste when you are older. The solution is creating good people.

I have always taught my children that when we go to the beach, we need to leave it better than when we came. We need to not only pick up after ourselves but also after others. If you want people to do the right thing, we need to develop good people with excellent character who innately will do the right thing.

The children need textbooks that teach character, not political correctness! In the early 1900s, America's children learned to read with the McGuffey Readers. As a teacher and school board member, I checked them out. They were amazing! I read them all to my children at home. They taught children to fear God and to be people of character.

In one story, an older man found a baby on his doorstep in a basket with a note. He wondered, "How could I ever take care of this baby?" His neighbors heard about it, and everyone helped out. They brought him baby items and helped him with the care of the child. In his old age, the baby girl now grown would wait by the gate for him and was a great joy to him. Selflessness, community, and the value of life were passed down to the next generation.

Another story was of three boys who wanted to go out and play. One of the boys said, "I have to do my chores first, then I will go out and play." So the other boys waited for him to do his chores and helped him, then they all went out and had fun. I had just read that in the McGuffey Readers. As I walked through the schoolrooms as a board member, I flipped through a reading book. To my surprise, the new reading textbook had a similar story. A child was swinging on a swing trying to decide if he should do his homework first or stay out and play. After thinking it over, as I recall, he said, "I live only once; I will play first. I can do my homework later." I read and reread the story, was I missing something? Didn't this have a lesson at the end? No, this appears to be the message we are giving kids today. There are no real principles, no truths, no right and wrong, just do what you feel like doing." No wonder our environment is hurting, not to mention the culture.

Character education would solve a lot of these "world" problems. If you are used to practicing responsible, honest behavior as a young person, you probably will grow up to be a responsible, honest businessman. And if you were taught compassion as a child, thinking of others first, you might not want to send out poisons into the air near school buildings. And if you were taught to love principles and people more than a fast buck, you might be generous using your wealth to help others, instead of being greedy when you grow up. I know we do not live in a perfect world, and people do not naturally have character, and that is exactly the point. We must teach character if we want to live in a better world. Passing laws to fine businessmen may be needed today due to our lack of character, but the real goal should be to have businessmen who put others first above profit. Our goal should be self-government, not oppressive government regulation.

We need to raise good children. We need to teach them that great men can solve difficult problems. And responsible people care about others. We have to start with the individual.

Let us not forget that "the one who rocks the cradle rules the world." If fathers and mothers spent time with their children teaching them character, we would not have to worry about saving the planet. The planet would not need saving. Save the children! Save the individual! That is the answer.

It is the chaos in our society that opens the door to tyranny. America is upside down. We are losing freedom and accepting tyranny when we dedicate ourselves to the collective whole, to the common good, to forced redistribution, or to a beautiful, man-managed utopian society. We need to dedicate ourselves to loving, caring and making the individual the most important thing.

When you look at the chart, it seems that America has already flipped out. We need to exert energy and pressure to flip America back in the right direction. Do we have the will to flip our country back? Are we willing to get up and join others in rolling back the tyranny that we see creeping in? How can we once again enjoy the blessings of liberty? You will see that, although it takes effort, it is not that hard, and it will not take long to flip America back because there is a plan.

Chapter 25
Whole vs. Individual

I was asked to speak at an education conference on teaching methods for reading. Reading was but one of the many battle grounds in education. But the surprise was on me because it was then, just as I was about to speak, as I reviewed my remarks, it hit me. It was one of those moments where you can remember where you were when it happened. It dawned on me, "We are talking about the same thing! It is the same battle. How could this be? Why did the teaching of reading mirror the battle of freedom and tyranny?"

Yes, I knew reading was important to freedom. It takes an informed educated citizenry to vote correctly on an issue. And yes, our forefathers believed that everyone needed to read so they could read the Bible and make wise decisions. But what I was seeing in these reading battles was a bit spooky. Why were we talking about learning individual sounds versus the whole piece of literature?

Basically I wanted to promote the teaching of "intensive systematic phonics"—the mastery of the individual letters and the sounds they represent. The entire State of California had gone hog-wild over "Whole Language Reading," an opposite approach. So it was a battle.

Once I understood the *Freedom and Tyranny Chart*, it truly amazed me how educational teaching methods mirrored these priorities. Remarkably, it was this understanding about the importance of the individual that helped me quickly decide what teaching methods would be successful and which ones would destroy the future of the children.

The new teaching methods centered on the "whole" rather than on the "individual" part. After a while, I could tell a bad teaching method instantly whether it was whole language or whole math, or whole writing? And there was even whole history and whole science!

In the '70s, we removed prayer from our schools and soon after took down the Ten Commandments. It was as if God was saying, "OK, you educate them." They tried. As God was removed from schools, the schools fell into great confusion and accepted failing educational methods.

It seemed elementary: to be a successful reader you have to know the "individual" parts, the letters and sounds. That is why a systematic, explicit phonics approach works. It has worked for two hundred years. In the same manner, to move to higher levels of math, you have to master the basic individual math facts of addition, subtraction, multiplication, and division. The memorization of these facts enables you to move quickly through more and more difficult problems, through algebra and geometry and calculus. Without this basic understanding and quick recall, higher math is almost impossible, if not brutal. Paying attention to the individual parts gives you a better end result. Teaching methods that emphasize and start with the whole always fail!

Amazing flower arrangements require fresh beautiful flowers. If half of the flowers are dying, the end result is not good. Each individual flower adds to the beauty of the whole.

Leave it to California to lead the nation! Whole Language Reading was introduced to California by Superintendent of Schools Bill Honig. It was characterized by BIG BOOKS—very big books made out of thick poster board, expensive, of course, and beautifully printed in color. The teachers held them up and read them over and over to the children until the children kind of memorized them or learned to read them through osmosis.

This was called teacher-guided reading. Children did not get intensive systematic phonics. Instead they read whole stories along with their teachers from the Big Books. Phonics was said to be "embedded" in the instruction, as teachers talked about some of the letters and sounds as they came across them in the stories, as in *The Flim Flam Man*.

The question I always asked was, "If it is embedded, why don't the children know the letters and sounds?" Children were asked to guess at words by looking at the pictures or studying the context. "But why guess if instead you can quickly know what the word is by reading or decoding the sounds?" It seemed the teaching of Reading had become a guessing game.

After years of Whole Language Reading, California State Superintendent of Education Bill Honig publicly apologized for the Whole Language Reading failure. The results were in. California came in last in the nation in reading test scores!

But did that stop school districts? No, many districts, like our own, again adopted Whole Language Reading. How could the Santa Ana School District adopt another set of Whole Language Reading textbooks after these failed results? Why were teachers and school board members married to these failed teaching methods? It seemed it was not about the facts; it was not about the children; it was not even about the methods. It was a philosophy that centered on the whole.

Could this be the politically correct way of teaching reading?

The one thing that surprised me most about being a school board member is that board members did not care about the facts or the results. I naively thought if I could show them facts, charts, test results, and other proof, it would make a difference. I worked so hard to present reasonable information, to verify my sources, to patiently and respectfully show them my perspective. But the facts never changed anyone's mind. Board members voted on what was politically expedient. They did not want to look radical, opposing the prevailing views and bucking the educational establishment.

One board member asked me in the back room, "How can you be right and all of these educational experts be wrong?" My reply was, "The kids are not reading! They are failing! The parents know it, and I represent the parents and the community." Nothing seemed to change their mind, not even an apology by the California superintendent of schools.

Like the Bilingual Education teaching methods, these teaching methods appeared to be a part of a liberal philosophy, a mindset, a foundational belief, perhaps multiculturalism and diversity. Their native language had to come first. And it did not matter if the way we were doing it was ineffective. It did not seem to matter that the children were neither proficient in English or Spanish.

I hated when the newspapers called me an "English Only" school board member. It was the failed bilingual teaching methods that I objected to. I advocated that the children learn several languages, proposing a four-language plan with English every day, Spanish for an hour in the afternoons, two years of Latin in junior high, and a fourth language in high school. I was never "English Only." I was "English First." We had to make English a priority. It was the language of success, the language needed for college and for the workplace.

Whole Language Math fared no better. Rather than teaching children in an sequential order the value of numbers, then adding, subtracting, multiplying, division, and then decimals, fractions, and on to higher math like algebra and geometry, children were given the seven strands of math at the same time. As they say, they got the whole enchilada! In kindergarten, children were expected to begin basic concepts of algebra, geometry, decimals, adding, subtracting, and multiplying. The curriculum was said to be "a mile wide and an inch deep" (http://www. catalyst-chicago.org/2005/07/math-teaching-in-us-inch-deep-mile-wide/). There was too much material to cover and no time for practice and mastery.

They threw out "incremental" math, a step-by-step, "precept upon precept" approach, which required mastery of each skill before moving on to the next. Instead they used "integrated" math that integrated all of the math strands at the same time. Poor babies! Memorization was characterized as mindless rote learning, while "higher order thinking skills" with tricky mathematical questions and the recognition of patterns were considered superior. "We are making mathematicians," they said. "Proclaiming themselves to be wise, they became fools" is how the Bible puts it.

My son was in the All-American Boys Chorus, a group like the Vienna Boys Choir, and we went to practice two times a week. We met in a large historic house at the fairgrounds. While the parents waited, I saw parents sitting around in groups working on math problems. I asked, "What are you doing?" They said, "We have formed a math co-op so we can figure out the math problems our children are bringing home. These tricky pattern ones take the kids over an hour to figure out, and they have no time for the other problems."

Imagine that. We keep our children ignorant in math, while parents and teachers were doing all the work of guiding kids through the disaster of "whole math."

Is it any wonder why businessmen are scratching their heads, "Where are all of the scientists and engineers?" If children cannot read well or master math, they cannot become scientists and engineers. The National GNP (Gross National Product) is directly proportional to our children's science and math scores.

While incompetent teachers certainly affect teaching, they are not the cause of our educational demise. Excellent teachers who are forced to teach with these new teaching methods often give up because it is impossible to produce good results. Teachers who knew better often had to sneak in good phonics and math practice sheets so their children could learn. During the fuzzy math debacle, I was secretly told, when the principals came by, they took out the crazy math books, and when they left, the teachers taught real traditional math. Thank God those fuzzy math books were thrown out after two years rather than kept for the seven years they were adopted for.

Once a group of teachers begged me to go to their principal and ask for math worksheets for adding and subtraction practice. They were tired of spending so much of their money acquiring and copying these practice sheets for the children. The textbooks did not include any math practice. I talked to the principal, and she agreed to make separate math practice books for the children.

Boy, was I surprised when I saw the books! They were only for the parents to use at home, not for the teachers to use at school. According to the principal, these hard-working, low-income parents were supposed to teach the children the math facts while the teachers did politically correct "whole" group activities at school.

We need to have great sympathy and respect for teachers. It is not their fault. The schools have fallen into confusion, and the system has forced on them politically correct failed teaching methods, created by the social scientists. These are the social engineers who worked at the twenty-six education laboratories developing new teaching methods and creating textbooks. The teachers' hands are tied.

After wasting seven more years of our children's lives and destroying more futures, the district finally adopted the Open Court reading textbooks that stressed systematic phonics instruction. This was a huge battle and an important victory.

I was greatly encouraged and assisted by a wonderful teacher, Jennifer Charles, whose students consistently scored high. In fact her principal referred to her class by saying, "She has the advanced students." She knew differently: "The children were just regular kids when they came into my class, but certainly left advanced." Later she taught a different grade, and still her students were the "advanced students." She was passionate that all of the children in the district could succeed like her students. It always puzzled me why we do not copy success.

With the help of other teachers, we decided to demand a formal hearing on the reading textbook adoptions at the school board meeting. We allowed textbook publishers to present; one teacher for each textbook also spoke, with questions for each side, and concluding statements and questions from the school board members. The vote was 3 to 2 for the phonics Open Court books!

To make sure the teachers gave input, I had requested that both sets of textbooks be placed at each school, and teachers were asked to fill out questionnaires on their level's textbooks.

We wanted to read what they had to say. "The vocabulary is too high; my kids will never get this," were some of the comments on the phonics books. "The teacher's edition has bullet points, making it easier to read," was a comment on the Whole Language Books. It was easy to see which books would advance our children in reading.

We asked that each teacher be given an opportunity to give the board input. The textbooks were sent to the schools, and forms were given out. Unfortunately, the district added a sentence at the bottom of the evaluation forms, "Vote on the textbook you want." I was furious. The teachers were not to "vote" but just give input for the board considerations. It is the responsibility of board members to vote and approve curriculum, particularly textbook adoptions, not the teachers.

Once the teachers and the teachers union heard that the phonics books won the vote at the school board meeting, a protest march was organized. "We voted. You did not respect our vote!" the signs read. "At our school, we chose the other book. We voted." A squishy school board member tried to change his vote. But we held his feet to the fire and won the day!

With the end of bilingual education teaching methods

and whole language reading, our district reading test scores soared! Some of our lowest-performing inner-city schools amazed the district. One school in particular, Madison Elementary, raised their test scores from the low 400s to the 700s. The goal was 800. We proved that inner-city schools could raise their test scores significantly when they used phonics and taught in English.

No sooner had we gotten rid of whole language and whole math, we had to fight whole writing. The district brought in "Write from the Beginning." Like the reading of the Big Books, a guided "reading" approach, the teacher's used a "guided" writing approach. The teachers would write essays together with the whole class. The children would copy the group essays. The children would print them in their best printing. "Wow!" Parents came in, "The kids are really writing well!" The reality was that the teachers were doing most of the work. Children became dependent on teachers and had trouble writing on their own. Before we had these whole writing methods, we taught writing by starting with letters, then words, then paragraphs, then whole essays, building sequentially on their skills. .

Yes, and we even had "whole" history. I can remember when the teaching of history changed. In the late 1960s, I went into college as a history major and came out a social science major in the '70s. I was surprised the school had changed the name, but it was fine with me; "social science" sounded very intellectual and sophisticated. When I studied to become an elementary school teacher, I noticed the new children's textbooks were called "social studies."

Just like in math, where the curriculum wanted to create mathematicians, now we wanted to make young children into social scientists. Boys and girls were no longer allowed to just learn about the world around them, their community, California, US history, and different nations. They had to do "higher order thinking skills" that asked them to compare and contrast, to predict, to project. These were the tools of the social scientist.

How can young children be asked to compare Brasilia with New York? Yes, some of the buildings are different, the products are different, but the children have not had the lessons of history to understand what makes them different or alike. This kind of critical thinking needs to be done, but not until eleventh or twelfth grade, after they have learned the history and background of each of the cities and acquired research skills.

I felt sorry for young children who were asked difficult questions without the tools to truly answer the questions. Children need a knowledge base, a context of time and place, and research skills to truly answer these "critical thinking" questions or social science concepts. This abuse of young minds saddened me. Because the textbooks did not provide the knowledge they needed, the children were fed the correct answers, again guided by their teachers. I began to see critical thinking as, "I will tell you what is critical that you should think!" Critical thinking at young ages is a form of indoctrination.

We need to teach history sequentially, not with an integrated approach. It is like building a house. You have to build it one step at a time. First, you have to lay the foundation of knowledge. This is taught in kindergarten through third grade. Children need to know about travel in cars, boats, airplanes, and trains. They need to know the parts of the flower, and how plants grow. They need to know how people live in different places, in the mountains, in the desert, by the ocean, in the cities, and in the country. They need to know about the fireman, the doctor, the banker. They need to learn about great presidents, holidays, their city, and community. They are building "a foundation" of knowledge. These should be happy, carefree days full of wonder.

Secondly, they need a framework of time and place to hang their knowledge on. In fourth through eighth grade, they learn to place that knowledge in its proper context of time and place. Generally that is when students learn about US history, the history of the fifty states, and different countries of the world. "Now I understand why President George Washington wears a wig and has a ponytail and a lacy shirt!" "Everyone dressed like that then!" "President Abraham Lincoln wore a hat, and other men wore hats, too." It was a different time than today and a different place. The context of time and place is where they place their knowledge. It is "the frame" on which they support their building.

In ninth through tenth grade, students are ready to build their "roof of protection." While they have learned to do simple reports, now is the time to learn real research skills, reading primary sources, looking up facts on the Internet and in their local library, reading scientific journals, checking things out with other commentaries. Research skills will protect them from being misled or misinformed. They can have the assurance that what they are learning or thinking is true.

With the foundation of knowledge, the framework of time and place, and the protective roof of research, they are ready to develop true social science skills in eleventh and twelfth grade. They should now debate, compare and contrast, analyze, and project out into the future. These are the critical-thinking skills they will need in life. Now they can develop their own personal beliefs, their own worldview. And depending on what they read, each house or building can be uniquely different. Everyone does not need to think the same. Their individual structures can be continually repainted, new windows added or remodeled as they read more, view media, or discuss their opinions with others. This is true lifelong learning: individuals who have all the skills they need to learn and grow in their opinions and thought processes.

Social studies, in contrast, feed the children the politically correct response. The social planners need everyone to view the world through their lens. They want all the students to think the same. In the past, we gave children the tools to learn and the freedom to think. Instead we are asking children to come to their own conclusions before they have the knowledge, context, and research skills to do so. This is nothing but indoctrination!

No wonder everyone is surprised that this generation knows very little history. Rather than learning about great men and women and reading exciting stories of the past, today they are given boring social studies textbooks starting in elementary grades. And somewhere along the line, as they are bombarded with "critical thinking," the children never learn what really happened. Rather than becoming "higher order" thinkers, they have become New World Order unthinking robots.

Recently, I saw the movie, *A Wrinkle in Time*, a classic children's story. In the movie, social planners tried to make an equal society. The loud speakers would sound through the neighborhood of look-a-like houses. "It is now time to play, for one hour." Children like robots opened the doors to their houses, came out with a basketball, and bounced the ball in the prescribed manner. It was spooky.

The girl in the movie, while observing this uniformity states, "Equal does not mean the same."

Equality means everyone is special and has unique gifts and talents, and they should be free to express their uniqueness and pursue their own happiness, their passions and dreams. *Equality* means we all have the same individual rights and opportunities to use our unique gifting.

The children who were trying to understand what had happened to this strange society were told darkness covered this part of the earth. But in the end, it was unconditional love, the love for an individual, (their brother, who was deceived by the system) that broke off the darkness. Another movie with a similar theme is *The Giver*. The state controls everything even the birth of babies by state approved carefully selected or certified parents. A boy, who had been assigned the task of taking care of the new babies in the state nursery, notices that a baby is marked to be discarded. His heart is moved by compassion, he rescues the precious baby, Gabriel, and flees. It is this act of love for the individual that once again dispels the darkness.

During the Cold War years, a science fiction movie scared the heck out of me. It was called, *The Invasion of the Body Snatchers.* In this movie, someone mysteriously placed big seed pods next to people when they were sleeping. Bubbly slime came out of the seed pod and soon enveloped the person. In the end, the people who once had unique personalities and opinions would get up and walk like mindless robots, displaying no feelings or personal opinions. They left where they were, with blank looks on their faces and joined the others who no longer were individual thinking adults. It was a very popular movie in the '50s during the Cold War because it reflected the view that Communist societies, in trying to make everyone the same, took away a person's soul and made each one a robot-like creature.

Compliant workers now seemed to be the goal in education, not well-educated thinkers. Our youth are soon becoming the politically correct global citizens of tomorrow who are but a human resource, a cog in the new global economy. Jobs will not be assigned according to the desires of the individual, but according to what is in your file, and the needs of the local economy. "It is the economy, stupid." I believe that is what President Clinton used to say? Or was that Karl Marx? We have had enough of the "whole," "the statist common good." We will not give up our God-given rights for the common good, to save the planet, or to usher in an unworkable utopian world.

But we will make a better world. And we will do that by focusing on the individual. God loves the individual. He works through individuals. He wants to pour out his love upon each person. He cares about their pain, their struggles, their needs, and their individual dreams. And so should we.

If we are to make America great again, we need to make America good again, and that starts with the individual. John Adams, one of our nation's framers, said that "our Constitution is only good for a moral and religious people. It is totally inadequate for the governing of any other." Since our nation has lost its religious and moral compass, it can no longer be a free nation.

On the school board we have passed wonderful programs like "Sex Respect", only to see that they were not implemented correctly, and eventually were phased out. We have passed a required Constitution Test. Yet we know there are people in the system who want to replace the concepts of the Constitution with false notions of "civic virtue" that calls for us to give up our individual rights for a global society. We are asked to give up free speech, stop expressing our religious views, and accept a press that is censored and tows the company line. We are asked to give up our guns that protect us and our right to privacy. It is these individual rights which are all protected by the Constitution under the Bill of Rights.

When the foundations are destroyed, what can good people do? The answer is we must rebuild the foundations. And America's foundation is our trust in God. It is time to strengthen our two pillars of religion and morality. The only people who can impart these values are people who share these values, a religious and moral people. We cannot wait for the schools to do this. We cannot point a finger at the system when we ourselves have been entrusted with that responsibility.

We cannot live free if we do not love individuals. We cannot live free if we do not impart our Judeo-Christian values to the next generation. We have been told to love our neighbors like we love ourselves. We need to go out and visit our neighbors, spend time with them, love them, and share the truth we know with a deep compassion for their well-being.

In the '60s, a small church called Calvary Chapel, in Orange County, California reached out to the disenfranchised hippies, dirty, straggly, long-haired, bearded youth. And a world movement was born. Today we need to go to the "gang-banger," tattooed, pierced, and lonely young person. And that is how we will save America. We must love the vulnerable, those, like in the movie *The Giver*, who have been tagged to be disposed of by the system. It is love for the individual that will shake off the darkness.

Do not think that we can just teach our very own children, grandchildren, or great grandchildren. In fact, sometimes our own families are the hardest to reach. That is not enough. We have millions of new immigrants who have no concept of America's founding or who do not understand how our religious and moral values laid the foundation for our amazing way of life. If the schools do not teach these values, who will?

Immigrants and the next generation have a right to know why America became the greatest country in the world. They have a right to understand our Judeo-Christian Protestant roots. They have a right to know how much God loves them, how his son suffered on the cross for them, taking their sins on himself. They need to understand that Jesus took their punishment, so that they can be pardoned and not be punished. They have a right to know that God offers them not only forgiveness and a clean slate but also a new power to do what is right. They need to know that God wants to help them, provide their every need, and transform their lives. This is what will fundamentally transform America—helping individuals to start again and once again do what is right and good.

An atheistic system can only control society with political power, forcing people to do what a few deem best. It isn't based on a system of right and wrong, but on a system of control through peer pressure from the local group. The elitist world changers hope those of us who understand these values will just die off, and with a new population-control-based health care system, they may just facilitate our departure. We, and those who share our values, are the only ones who can restore America. America is, as England's former Prime Minister Margaret

Thatcher stated, "a nation of ideas." It is our ideas and values, hopes, and dreams that bind us together.

As Ronald Reagan stated, "Freedom is never more than one generation away from extinction. We didn't pass it to our children in the bloodstream. It must be fought for, protected, and handed on for them to do the same, or one day we will spend our sunset years telling our children and our children's children what it was once like in the United States when men were free."

We must share these American ideals. We must make America good again. We must repair our foundation and restore the two pillars of religion and morality…that is, if we want to live free.

Part VI
The Winning Plan

America Needs a Superhero

"Apathy can be overcome by enthusiasm, and enthusiasm can only be aroused by two things: first, an ideal, which takes the imagination by storm, and second, a definite intelligible plan for carrying that ideal into practice."
—*Arnold Toynbee, Historian*

"A large and exacting undertaking is easier than small ones."
— *John R. Mott, YMCA Movement Leader, Nobel Peace Prize laureate*

Chapter 26

Big Vision

We had our orders—"Raise up an army to teach the truth with genuine compassion." It was a big vision. Where would we start?

In 1997, I was asked by the California Speaker of the House Curt Pringle to help with a small citizenship training effort. My task was to find an office in downtown Santa Ana. They were looking for around 400 to 600 square feet, nothing big. One Saturday morning, I set out for downtown with my handicapped daughter. She is generally my sidekick, and comes along with me to keep me company.

When I saw For Rent signs, I wrote a few addresses and phone numbers down. As we started to leave the downtown area, I remembered that a young adoption attorney in Santa Ana told me that he drives daily by the old abandoned YMCA building and prays for it to be reused to mentor young people. I first met Ted Youmans at a public hearing on adoption and foster care hosted by State Senator Teresa Hughes.

"Where could that building be?" I wondered. I asked a few people and drove a few blocks back into town, and there it was. "Wow! This is huge! This is magnificent!" This was an extraordinary building with arches and stonework and beautiful architectural features. The building was boarded up, abandoned. I wondered what it was like inside.

My daughter and I sat on the front steps and soon heard noises. We discovered that men from the city were working in the building. They came out and were standing next to the door.

"May I see inside?" I asked, pulling my "I am an elected official, a school board member, here in Santa Ana" line. It worked.

"OK, come on in. We will take you through the building with flashlights, but be careful; it is wet. The rain left water on the floors, and there is a lot of pigeon poop." It was like going into a dark cave, crossing streams, ducking for low-hanging places. But as I looked at each room, vision filled my mind. Yes, this would work. This was not only a beautiful place but also a strategic location to mobilize and train thousands of volunteers to go out into the community.

This amazing four-story, 44,000-square-feet building was in the exact center of Orange County, in the County Seat, across from the County Board of Supervisors' office, the Hall of Records, and the Orange County Treasurer's and Assessor's buildings. As they say in real estate, "Location, Location, Location." It even had three massive fireplaces, a pool, and spa. What more could you want?

And just think, back in 1924, community leaders thought young people needed adult mentors and built this magnificent building! Surely now in 1997, at the height of an era of gang violence, there was an even greater compelling need to call people to mentor young people!

The instructions were to raise up an army. I pondered what that would look like. In ancient Israel, a judge named Deborah was concerned about her nation and gave out a call and 10,000 enlisted. Orange County is about the same size as Israel. What if 10,000 arose?

If God needs an army, then evidently it is time to go to war—a war to recapture our children and our families and all of the greatness America has lost. But what if thousands showed up and asked, "What do you want us to do?"

"What would the volunteers do? Where would they go?" I wondered. I began to read articles on recruiting and sending out volunteers. I read about the need to screen, train, and monitor and celebrate the work. An effort of this magnitude will take a larger office, training rooms, connecting and planning spaces. We might just need a whole building! Perhaps it was this magnificent building.

I heard that the mayor was flying to Philadelphia for a volunteer summit with Secretary of State Colin Powell and former presidents Jimmy Carter and George H. W. Bush and then-President Bill Clinton. They were calling the nation to volunteer. This was a perfect time to share with the mayor the vision of mobilizing thousands of volunteer mentors. I quickly typed out a proposal for the building.

I received an email from the mayor's office that he would be reading my presentation on the plane as he headed to Philadelphia. I was excited. Little did I know that the mayor was not only going to Philadelphia for the volunteer summit but also going to Washington, D.C., to request funding for a digital art school that UCI (University of California at Irvine) and Santa Ana College were planning for an empty YMCA building.

In one of our classes for my master's degree in organizational leadership, we were assigned to read the book *Built to Last* by Jim Collins and Jerry Porras. The book is a blueprint on how to build organizations. One chapter emphasized the importance of buildings, as they often represent the work. This greatly encouraged me. The YMCA building had such a rich heritage of mentoring youth, it was in a perfect central location, and had magnificent architecture. It would be a perfect symbol of our work. And by giving the work visibility it would be a catalyst, encouraging others to join in the effort.

The plans for a digital art school by the University of Irvine and Santa Ana College fell through, and so did the plans for Chapman University to use the building for its film school. The Mind Institute, Claremont Health Spa, and the High School of the Arts have all sought to use the old magnificent YMCA building, only to see that it did not go forward. The building now had been vacant for more than twenty years.

Years later, the city held a special committee meeting to discuss the future of the building. A few of us attended and sat on the side. The mayor called for me to sit at the table with the committee. He stated that I had a long-time interest in the building and asked me to speak. Then he suggested I consider another large building, the Delhi Center, with lots of classrooms and fields for kids. All I could say is, "Oh, no, Mr. Mayor, the important work of changing lives needs a magnificent building like this civic center YMCA!"

Somehow it was difficult for people to understand that this building was not for the actual youth programs. Why would I put the 800 young people that were enrolled in our after-school programs under one roof when the programs could be out in the community where the children lived? There really was not enough room for them. And it would cost to have them bussed in. The building was needed only for administrative offices, training classes for mentors, and connecting people with a vision for the community. It was a mentoring university. The work would be done out in the community, at local schools, neighborhood sport centers, and workplace training sites. This would just be the hub, a training center, and a hangout for the O.C.(Orange County) "yuppie" volunteers.

I soon found out that the mere mention of the name of the YMCA building generated great emotions and wonderful memories. One Sunday morning, I showed Pastor Chuck Smith, the leader of the Calvary Chapel movement, a photograph of the building. He exclaimed, "I love that building! I know every inch of the building. I used to work there when I was in college and set up for events. We had such great events there!"

At Polly's Pies, I met with Manuel Esqueda for breakfast. Mr. Esqueda was a special friend of the community. He had raised thousands of dollars for scholarships for young people. When I mentioned the YMCA building, he exclaimed, "That building made me the man I am today! I used to polish shoes there and the men brought me more and more shoes from home. I made a lot of money. I watched the men who came there. They wore shirts and ties. 'When I get older, I am going to wear shirts and ties every day,' I purposed in my heart." And so he did. He became a banker and wore a shirt and tie every day!

While on the school board, we named an elementary school after Manuel Esqueda. At our Boxing Club Street Fiesta, Manuel Esqueda spoke to the teens and their families from the stage. Mr. Esqueda began, "When I was young, like many of you, I loved to box. In fact, I made enough money boxing to buy my mother a house." Manuel Esqueda not only inspired the young people but also supported our work and gave a donation to the boxing club. He toured the historical street boxing gym and watched the boys demonstrate their boxing skills. He was also seen in the gym giving money to the teen boxers so they could go buy a hot dog or some carne asada from our Street Fiesta food booths. He was mentored at the YMCA building and became an outstanding citizen and was now giving back to his community.

A former Santa Ana Mayor, Lorin Griset, also had a great interest in the YMCA building. His father was on the Board of Directors in 1924 when they built this magnificent building on Civic Center Drive. As mayor, Lorin Griset founded the Human Relations Commission. Lorin was still very active in the community. He founded and dedicated himself to the Christian Business Men's Committee, a group of businessmen who held a breakfast once a month. He called everyone in town once a month to urge us to go to the breakfasts. We could always count on his call. At the breakfasts, well-known men in the community shared their life stories, particularly how Jesus Christ changed their life.

My high school son enjoyed going with me at 6 a.m. to hear the men tell their life stories. He also learned about all the crazy things they did as young people. I think it inspired him to do many of the wild fun things he did in college, like bringing in a Jacuzzi into his dorm and trying to break the Guinness Book of World Records by making the largest hopscotch in history throughout the Biola campus! Not to mention his public art project where he had his art colleagues paint designs on his white car with spray paint. Everyone could see him coming in that crazy car!

As a Trustee for Biola University and a member on the facility committee, I panicked when I heard about the Jacuzzi. Although he said he had a sheet hanging on the ceiling to catch the drops of water that evaporated from the steam, I immediately ordered him to take it out. And what about the Biola hopscotch on the side-walks? I knew Parents' Weekend was coming up. I encouraged him strongly to wash off the chalk hopscotch before the parents came. I sometimes wondered if taking him to those breakfasts was a good idea. That is, until he had his first date. Her name was Destiny. So he had a date with destiny. Mom could relax.

Lorin Griset, the founder of the Christian Business Men's Committee was also on the Board of Trustees at Biola University with me. One thing that drew us together was that my mother was born in his uncle's house in Guatemala in Central America. His uncle, Cameron Townsend, was the founder of Wycliffe Bible Translators, and my grandparents lived in his home near Lake Atitlan taking care of the house while he was on furlough in the United States. I always imagined that Cameron Townsend came back and held my mother, a newborn baby, in his arms and prayed over her. Perhaps it is because of this blessing that she was the first in her family to come to faith. And now at age eighty-eight she is leaving an amazing legacy.

Lorin Griset loved to tell stories of his father, who was on the YMCA Board of Directors when the building was built. "Poppi would drive through Santa Ana, see teenagers on the street, and ask them if they wanted to go swimming. He would load his car with kids, take them to swim at the YMCA, and in the process he had a chance to mentor them. At the school district, we wanted to honor Lorin Griset. His health was failing, and we were unsure he would be with us for the Lorin Griset High School's grand opening. He sat demurely, expressionless, in his seat at the school board meeting. But when asked to speak, he became alive and animated. He shared the story of his father who had helped build the Santa Ana YMCA. His talk that night was his last public message; he died shortly after that.

All of these men have had a great impact in our community, and the YMCA had a big part in that.

Toastmasters, a worldwide organization that teaches people how to be effective public speakers, was started in the Santa Ana YMCA building.

When I had lunch with Sheila Schuller Colman, the daughter of Pastor Robert Schuller, Sr., I shared my vision for the YMCA building with her. She said, "My brother, Robert Jr., learned to swim at the YMCA." Later Sheila brought Dr. Schuller, Sr., to visit the boxing club gym. I can still hear him say in his old gravelly voice as we walked around the street boxing gym, "In—all—my—days, I have never been to a boxing club!"

Dr. Schuller gave a wonderful talk to the kids. "What is wrong with failure?" he asked. He shared about his daughter Carol who lost her leg in a motorcycle accident at age thirteen. She was on a baseball team at the time. He went to see her at the hospital where she spent eight months, and she told him she was going to still play baseball. "That poor girl," thought Dr. Schuller, "she does not realize she just lost her leg." He sadly replied, "I am not sure about that." "No, Dad, I studied it, and they have to let me stay on the team because I am handicapped. I may not be able to run to the bases, but I have strong arms. And I know how to hit the ball. I can hit home runs, and then I will not have to run to the bases." Sometimes what seems like failures are just ways of learning what we are not good at and pointing us to other strengths in our lives.

One day I was reading a small devotional book called, *My Utmost for His Highest*, and I noticed in the preface that the short individual lessons in the book written by Oswald Chambers were prepared for and shared with young people at the YMCA.

That month Rodney Page, the Secretary of Education for President George W. Bush was coming to town! He came to speak at the YMCA Youth Service Day at Willard Intermediate School, one of our district schools, and as a school board member I was going to be speaking right before him. I had just learned that President Bush and his wife Laura were reading the devotional *My Utmost for His Highest*.

From the stage, I talked about the wonderful history of the YMCA, how they recruited caring mentors, and sought to instill character in the children. I brought a copy of *My Utmost for His Highest*, and held it up: "The messages in this book were once taught at the YMCA. Today I would like to give Mr. Page, United States Secretary of Education, a copy of the book. Secretary Page" I continued, "since I hear that President Bush and First Lady Laura are reading this book, I wanted you, to be on, well, on the same 'page' with the president." Later he thanked me for the book in a wonderful letter, which I hung on my office wall.

Just think! Material that was once given to young disadvantaged youth was also encouraging the president of the United States and hopefully his Secretary of Education! As I write this, the old magnificent YMCA building still stands unused, abandoned, and in great disrepair. It seems to symbolize the state of our communities, and our young people that are in great need of rebuilding. The police have used the building for urban warfare practice, a sign of our times. It seems that our national roof is leaking. The windows are cloudy and broken, and vandals, graffiti taggers, or the homeless are writing on our walls. Who will repair this building? Who will repair the broken lives?

I began to share the vision with a select few. A local pastor said, "Rosie, don't talk to the mayor. He will pat you on the back and say that you have a great idea. Talk to the city manager—he will tell you if it is workable. He will let you know if the building is available."

The pastor was right. The city manager was direct, affirmed that the building was not available due to UCI's plans for a digital art school, and suggested that we look at the vacant Church of Scientology building on Main Street or the old Masonic Temple on Sycamore. My heart sank. "No, I want the building that was built for the 'Glory of God' to mentor children."

Nevertheless, we looked at the old Masonic building and Church of Scientology anyway. A crew of eight accompanied us. Two were architects who had worked on the Crystal Court at the beautiful South Coast Plaza Mall. We looked through boxes of beautiful, very old certificates that were used for fundraising purposes for the building campaign of the Masonic Temple. We saw the places where Masonic rituals occurred. It was like we were able to go into the inner sanctum. The stage had a low, five-foot-long metal trench with gas pipes; it seemed to be used for fire in their rituals and theatrical performances. We walked up the narrow stairway that led up to the gazebo structure on top of the five-story building. It reminded me of an ancient ziggurat with tiny narrow steps leading to the top. There was only a sink at the top, a low flat sink. And the long, thin windows around the top of the gazebo seemed to stretch out into the sky. Needless to say, I felt uncomfortable, and this was not the place for us! The architects advised us that a building like the Masonic Temple would nickel-and-dime us to death. It would cost over $10 million dollars. They were right. In the end, Mike Harrah, a local developer, spent $18 million to retrofit and remodel the old Masonic Temple. Today the Church of Scientology owns it and is using it as one of its world headquarters.

Chapter 27
The First Step

Just when the door closed on the YMCA building, a peculiar thing happened. The Chamber of Commerce CityLine News had an article about the First American Title Company building that was located downtown on Main Street and Fourth Street in the Fiesta Marketplace area. "Now this was a beautiful building!" I thought. It looks like the White House, with elegant white pillars and a triangular pediment. While simpler, it also had many characteristics of the Capitol building. An elegant gold eagle logo set it off perfectly.

Parker Kennedy, the fourth-generation owner and current CEO of the largest title company in the world, was interviewed in the CityLine newspaper article. First American Title had plans to move their offices from the downtown Main Street area to a new location on the 55 Freeway. These elegant buildings might become available. The two buildings took up one whole block!

In the Chamber of Commerce article, Parker Kennedy was asked, "Who will be taking over this historic location?" We were going through a short recession, and he answered, "We have not made a decision about that yet. We have actually considered different options…selling, leasing, or even donating the building to a charitable or civic organization."

Now this was interesting. Very interesting. The more I thought about it the more excited I became. Wow, this was just what I was looking for, and it did not need retrofitting! This would be a turn-key building and an amazingly beautiful one; and the décor was just right for someone who was going to save America. I called immediately. The secretary answered. "I have not heard of anyone giving this building away. But you might as well be the first one in line." I couldn't ask for more!

"Thank you," I said, "Keep me posted."

A few days later, I realized I had never been inside. Yes, I know I just asked for a building I had never seen! I called again and asked for a tour of the building. The secretary hemmed and hawed.

"I do not know," she said, "Let me have you talk with the president directly; I will put you through."

"Mr. Kennedy, I am a school board member here in Santa Ana, and I have a great vision for the children," I started. "I read that you might be interested in giving this building away to a nonprofit....That is, if you cannot sell it or lease it." I could sense he was a little hesitant. But I continued, "I am interested in your building to be used to train mentors to help our young people. I have never been in your building; do you think I could have a tour?" He paused and said, "I can do that. I will have Mario give you a tour."

We again assembled a team and we walked through the building. It was beautiful, with wooden floors, mutton windows separating offices, exquisite lighting fixtures. Especially interesting were the black and white photographs of Orange County's history that decorated the walls. What a perfect building for an Orange County mentoring movement. Incredible!

As we walked and walked, I began to laugh, "How can this thing be? Am I crazy?" More and more offices and still more offices. What would we do with all of this space? To my surprise, there was another floor underground in each of the buildings. These two three-story buildings filled a block and were a 100,000 square feet! That was twice the size of the YMCA building. After we toured the building, I soon was dreaming and drawing. Vision filled all of the floors. "God must be up to something big!" was all I could say.

I am sure you think I was gutsy, perhaps crazy, with these two buildings. You are right. I was. And no one was as surprised as I was! I am generally a shy person, especially one on one, but become animated when talking to large groups. I tease and say that I am at my best in front of two hundred angry union men.

Some of you may doubt that God talked to me and asked me to raise up mentors. Well, if you do not believe that, you can see that something happened to me. I had a new assignment, and it changed the course of my life. It was time to raise up an army of volunteers. I immediately started a nonprofit organization and earned a master's degree in organizational leadership so I would be ready.

With a vision for the First American Title buildings in hand, our new Board of Directors prepared a presentation requesting these buildings. Eight of us began to meet every week at the adoption lawyer's beautiful wood-paneled boardroom. We used their important board table to begin an important work.

We began in earnest. We took several weeks to create our mission statement. We all wrote out words on pieces of paper that we wanted in the mission statement. We mixed them up and thought about them in different ways. Then we added more words, and soon concepts started to come forth. In the end, it seemed to all come together without any great debate.

MISSION STATEMENT
"…to bring hope and purpose to inner-city children and youth by developing a partnership with the business/private sector and the Christian community to create wholesome activities that educate, train, inspire, and transform lives."

That was it. It says it all. The words were broad enough to give us latitude on programs.

And our final goal was to transform lives. We knew if we could change individual lives, we could transform the whole community.

Then we set our goals and objectives: first we would create a beautiful volunteer center in the heart of Orange County. Then we would establish character clubs in the schools, develop neighborhood teen sports centers, provide workplace internship programs for older youth and present inspirational high energy entertainment events for youth.

Later we created our five Organizational Values:
We value God's Glory: *"Is God glorified by what we do?"*
We value a Changed Life: *"Are our activities changing lives?"*
We value Volunteers: *"Do we serve our volunteers, and do they feel appreciated?"*
We value God's Provision: *"Are we good stewards with the resources*
we are given?"
We value Professionalism: *"Do we handle our business in a professional manner?"*

Later we evaluated our staff using these values. As we prepared to make a presentation to Mr. Kennedy for the building, we created large presentation boards for each of our programs. Each board member took a program that we wanted to do and showed how the building would help us accomplish our goals. We practiced, timed each other. It was a forty-minute presentation with twenty minutes for questions. We had to be disciplined and prepared.

Finally, we were ready. We were all on the same page. We knew what we wanted to accomplish and how we were going to do it. I called Mr. Kennedy, "We are ready and would like to give you a presentation on how we might use your buildings." He said, "We have not decided what to do with the buildings, and we are not ready for a presentation."

"Well," I paused. "OK, I understand. Thank you." After catching my breath, an overwhelming feeling of relief filled my heart.

Praise God! What if he had given us the building? What would we do with it? How would we keep the buildings up? Our nonprofit had not even been federally approved to collect money. We had no funding and no programs. Thank God we did not get the buildings!

A few years later, I prepared a large state grant requesting three million dollars to fund the YMCA building, but it required the city to approve the project and three million dollars of matching funds. And wouldn't you know it, just as I finished the grant proposal and turned it in, a wealthy donor showed up. He went to the city with me and committed to give six million dollars to the project. With the three million in state funds and his six million, the total needed for the project was just about there. That was a good day, a very good day!

But as things worked out, it was hard for the donor to liquidate his funds. He said, "All hell broke loose." And without city approval, the time ran out on the grant. It really showed me that if I take a step, God will come and take the next step. But I was also learning it was time to start small. When and if we would need a large building, it would be up to a different type of board of directors, who had experience with larger projects and who were fully committed for the long haul, to decide. As always it would be up to God to bring in the funding. And it would all need to happen in his perfect timing.

I often wondered what caused community members in 1924 to build such a beautiful, expensive building dedicated to mentoring youth. It seems that the need is even greater today.

In Guatemala when there was a concern about Communist advancement, the businessmen noticed that it was the evangelical Christian community that resisted the notion of socialism. I think it is because Christians tend to trust in God to take care of their needs not an all-powerful, often oppressive government. The businessmen knew that when Communism took over a country, the new regime often confiscated the businesses and sometimes personal property. Rather than free enterprise and the free market creating wealth, the state manages the economy. And in many cases the state owns large sections of the economy. The businessmen, though not religious, got together and funded large Christian rallies in stadiums, hoping to strengthen the church, so that Guatemala would not fall to Communism.

While we had these two magnificent buildings in view for a large work, we understood that we were not ready for such a large endeavor. After meeting weekly for months, we regrouped. I encouraged the troops, "You know we have a big vision, a big task ahead. We are all united in our vision. We have our mission and goals. But we have to start small. We need one child and one mentor. Let's rest; we have worked hard meeting weekly. Let's meet in a month and see where we will start. Jim and I are going to Israel with Calvary Chapel for our twenty-fifth wedding anniversary, with Pastor Chuck Smith, who married us. After we get back, we will figure out where and how we will start." Little did I know what was ahead for us in Israel!

Chapter 28

Starting Small

At a hotel in Jerusalem all 450 people from the tour were seated in the beautiful elegant banquet room. Israeli Prime Minister Benjamin Netanyahu was the speaker. But first the waiter brought us a piece of cake with lit candles, the crowd sang "Happy Anniversary," and Pastor Chuck Smith said from the podium, "I married them!"

We felt honored that the Prime Minister was able to attend our anniversary party!

As I shared earlier before, Jim and I met a Santa Ana police sergeant and his lovely wife at that banquet. I shared the vision for reaching young people in our city. The next day he and his wife came up to us and said he would ask a friend if we could use an old street-boxing gym. The old gym had opened in the '70's but had not been used in five years. When we got back home, we got the call that we could use the gym. Now we had a place to start. It is amazing that when you decide to start, and take a few steps forward, things just fall into place. And God gives you the next step.

The cop's wife shared her story growing up in the Bronx, living in fear, never knowing if she would get beat up or have dinner each night. She shared how two teachers made a difference in her life. They noticed her and asked her questions, showing a genuine interest in her. She also shared how she was given some used clothes and found a beautiful jumper to wear. Because it was too small on the sides she used safety pins to hold it together.

At school the students laughed at her. She ran home crying and jumped into her bed where she purposed to become rich and make something of her life.

This was our mission statement: we wanted to bring the children hope and purpose—a hope that they were someone, someone valuable. We wanted them to purpose in their heart to accomplish something, finish school, raise and support a good family, and live an ethical lifestyle.

Now we knew where we would start! I couldn't wait to tell the Board. We had our first program, a boxing club. But what did I know about boxing? I was an elementary school teacher, had tutored for a private business, and taught character at after school clubs. Maybe we could do a children's club there and invite the children from the elementary school across the street. "No, this building is too closed in, smells sweaty, and parents would not want their children to cross the street to go to an after-school program. We decided to start an elementary after-school character club at the elementary school across the street from the boxing gym. Later we launched an intermediate after-school club at Carr Intermediate, where one of our Board members taught. We found a boxing coach and decided to do a boxing program for teens at the historical boxing club. We were well on our way. With three model programs serving children, pre-teens and teenagers we now had something to show potential donors.

Each of our programs provided homework help and academic tutoring, structured sports instruction, and character education using stories of biblical and historical heroes. Additionally we tried to provide character development service projects, such as visiting the elderly, planting flowers at the school, painting out graffiti, or collecting shoes for relief efforts.

In 1998, we had our first teen entertainment event, a drama called "Cry of the Young," put on by Victory Outreach. It was a drama presentation featuring domestic violence, gang involvement, drug addiction, and many of the problems our inner-city kids face. We rented the auditorium at Santa Ana High School, five hundred attended, and fifty asked for further counseling. Many had tears running down their faces.

After working out of our cars, at home, and Ted's law office for meetings, we decided to rent our own 400-square-foot office. These were exciting days. While this was not 44,000 or 100,000 square feet, we were thrilled to have our own space. Now we were really a nonprofit.

We were not sure how we would be able to pay our monthly $400 rent. As a Santa Ana School Board member and Trustee at Biola University, I attended a lot of fundraising banquets. At one banquet, a man at my table said he knew of a donor who might be interested in funding after-school programs. I later called for the potential donor's address and wrote a letter requesting funding.

I first typed, "Could you give us $3,000." "No, that was too much to ask for!" I rewrote the letter and changed the request to $1,000. A representative from the foundation came to visit our office, and I shared the vision. He said, "You have a big vision: you have programs; you have to ask for more money." "More money? How much more money?" I asked. "Figure out a budget of what everything costs, include some salaries, and send it to me." "OK." I wrote a budget for $66,000. And he sent me a check for $66,000!

And each year after that, for nine years, they sent us $30,000 to pay the salary for our elementary and intermediate after-school character club director. We had an angel!

From that wonderful beginning, we were able to grow steadily each year, adding more and more clubs. By 2008, we had eighteen programs in different schools and neighborhood locations and three clubs in progress. Each week we served an average attendance of 650 boys and girls and had more than 800 enrolled.

Through the years, we had developed four skateboard clubs, at two intermediate schools, a high school, and at City Lights

Dream Center. City Lights skateboard center was located at an old Victorian house and was just across the street from Willard, another intermediate school. Our skateboard club at Godinez High School was located next to a park where there was a new city skateboard facility. Professional skaters such as Christian Hosoi and Richard Mulder taught the young skaters. Other professional skaters judged the young people's routines and gave out trophies at our larger competition events.

With city funding, and under the direction of Wrestling Coach Scott Glabb from Santa Ana High School, we funded two intermediate wrestling clubs and a few elementary school wrestling clinics. We also had our flagship program, the boxing club, which served about sixty teens each afternoon, five days a week. Qualified teen boxers also entered competition meets on Saturdays.

For a short time, we taught karate at our elementary school clubs and also used the Wells Fargo Computer Education Bus at our intermediate after-school technology club. The sport centers were funded through private donors, city grants, and later a federal grant.

Wrestling Coach Glabb has written a great book called, *Saint in the City.* "Saints" is the mascot name for Santa Ana High School, so it was a great name for the book. When you read it, you will see how Coach Glabb has used wrestling to build character into the lives of these vulnerable youth.

As Scott tells his story, he came to Santa Ana High School to coach wrestling with the desire to develop a winning team. But at each wrestling meet, the boys lost their matches. No matter how hard he tried, they kept losing. He was discouraged. "OK," he thought, "if I can't make them wrestling champions, I will just work on developing their character." He talked with them, brought in great motivational speakers, and took them to wrestling summer camps sponsored by Fellowship of Christian Athletes. Soon they were winning their matches! Now everyone in town was talking about the great wrestling team at Santa Ana

High School. These wrestlers took CIF, (California Interscholastic Federation) were State Champions, and won National Meets!

ABC Eyewitness News covered our boxing club program on prime-time television. It was a very professional and inspirational telling of our story, and a wonderful promotion. Several donors called to help fund our program. One businessman called me on my cell phone and asked, "What does it take to run the program for a year?" Back then, we were only running the program part time. I told him it cost $26,000 a year. He said, "Twelve into $26,000...." I heard the adding machine in the background. "That comes to $2,166 a month. I will send you that much each month." Wow! That made our day.

Another time, we had completely run out of money. It looked like we were not going to make our next payroll. Then a call came out of the blue from two women. "We are down at the boxing club. Can you come and let us into the gym to see it?" I quickly got in the car and drove down to open the gym. They said they felt like they were called to link donors with nonprofits, and they heard about us. A day later they called back. "We have a donor who wants to give you $50,000." We sent them a plan of how the money would be spent, and they sent the check. We had a wonderful celebration at the gym, with the boxers, the parents, and the new donor. The donors, a local family-run market, provided all of the food and sent family members and several of their business managers to the celebration.

Santa Ana Police Sergeant Richard Murg took to the microphone: "I am a boxer and I have been in most of the gyms in California, and no other gym does for the kids what this club does. They not only provide great boxing instruction, help kids compete, but they also mentor them through life and provide academic tutoring."

One of the boxers who was sixteen years old, stood up: "I have been here for three years, and these are the happiest years of my life."

We learned how to start clubs at school sites for younger children and how to develop teen sport programs, and we had put on eight different teen entertainment events at high schools. Now if thousands of volunteers answer the call, we know where to send them. We know exactly what they should do. If 100 volunteers show up, within a month, we can have them trained and out in the community mentoring thirty or more young people each and every week. And if 1,000 volunteers come at once, we will hire more staff or use volunteer staff to open up more school-based character clubs or neighborhood sport centers.

In 2007, we celebrated "Ten Years of Making a Difference" with a beautiful banquet at the Hyatt Hotel. Two hundred guests attended. The jazz band played, the coffee bar was open. White table cloths and white flowers gave it a classy feel. We were ready to share our vision and showcase our model programs!

We showed videos of the after-school programs. Then one of the teen boxers came up to the microphone to share. He just stood there. We waited. He stood there. Then tears rolled down his face. He looked at the crowd of well-dressed donors and friends and slowly said, "I did not know that all of you cared about us at the boxing gym!" Needless to say, he brought the house down.

Chapter 29

Running for Congress

I was in the midst of my election campaign, running for my fourth term on the Santa Ana School Board when the phone rang. The election was just a few days away. "Can you come down to meet with me in my office?" the caller asked. "Look, we need to get out the vote! I have to make phone calls. Can I meet with you next week?" "No, this is important," I was told.

"OK," I said. "I will come." It was November, and it was pouring down rain. "Why did I have to come now?" I questioned, "Can't this wait? It is pouring rain, I can hardly see through the windshield!" I complained. But when the Republican Party calls, you need to answer.

I walked into the office and we talked. "We want you to think about running for higher office, perhaps United States Congress." I was flattered, but protested, "But first I have to win my school board race!" Didn't they know you have to give it all you got, down to the wire? I had won three elections before serving three four-year terms, plus an added year when they realigned the election. This would be my fourth term and before I considered a bigger political move, I needed to win again. "I will talk to my husband and let you know later. This is a big decision."

A few months after I won the school board election and a fourth term, my husband and I took a cruise to the Caribbean for our thirty-second anniversary. This was our first and so far our only cruise. It was wonderful! We prayed and discussed the possibility of a Congressional race. Soon I was off getting ready to run for Congress.

I ran for several reasons. First, I enjoyed politics and thought I was successful at it. I had won four elections and was generally the top vote getter. Winning was fun! When I first ran, I beat out the three incumbents, surprised everyone and was on the front page of *The Orange County Register* newspaper. Another time I received more than double the votes given the second contender. Winning big was great! At one of the elections, Nativo Lopez, my political nemesis, spent more than $200,000 on our school board race, the most that was spent on a school board race in California, perhaps the nation. Despite the three hit pieces sent out against me I still won, having been out-spent by nearly a 7 to 1 ratio!

I loved campaigning, meeting the voters, discussing the issues, and working with great people. I thought perhaps running for Congress would give me a greater voice to call the army together to go out and mentor kids.

I was also ready to take a break from the day-to-day administration and fundraising of the nonprofit. I loved developing programs and sharing the vision. Even though I had great assistants, the daily administration and accounting was wearing on me, particularly the federal grant that had consumed us with paperwork. It seemed 50 percent of the federal funds went to accounting and case management. Leading a nonprofit organization is a very consuming job, and on top of the politics on the school board, which were also demanding, I needed a rest. Yes, I know it sounds crazy. It's a bit crazy to think of running for Congress to get some rest. I was ready for a change.

Soon after I signed up to run the Republican leaders decided not to fund the election. It turned out to be a tough election year for the Republicans with presidential candidate Barack Obama, the community organizer, working the inner cities. My race was a tough one against Representative Loretta Sanchez, who was a prolific fundraiser. Many had tried to unseat her before, and were unsuccessful. The party felt that other congressional races were vulnerable and needed extra funding. We continued hoping something might change. At the end, when I hoped funds would come, Vice Presidential candidate Sarah Palin was called in, and much of the fundraising in Orange County went to Senator McCain's newly energized presidential campaign. I could not afford to send mailers to the voters. Needless to say, I did not win the election.

We continued the campaign just in case something changed. Since we had committed to run, it seemed like the right thing to do. We gathered about 300 names of people who indicated they wanted to volunteer, but never were able to activate them. It saddened me because leading grassroots efforts was generally my strength. I loved the energy and comradery it produced.

On election night, our campaign team gathered together to see the results, which were not good. The next morning, my husband was tiptoeing across the entry toward the front door. He was holding a large box. I asked him what was in the box. He turned and looked at me and sheepishly said, "It is fireworks, I was going to light them when you won." That is my husband. When I first won the school board election, as you will recall, he gave me a beautiful picture with a cup of coffee, glasses and a newspaper on a lacy tablecloth that expressed a cute sentiment that he was surprised. It read, … "Behind every successful woman is a man who is surprised." Now after winning four elections, he was again surprised, but this time because I did not win! He has become my greatest supporter.

It takes three things to win campaigns. You need a great candidate, a good ground game to connect with the individual voters, and thousands of dollars for mailers and signs. Just one mailer to my congressional area can cost $44,000 or more! All three elements are essential. It takes a team to win elections, and everyone on your side has to be on board. All things are possible when you are united.

I have seen candidates who have the funds to run, but they are not presentable, have difficulty communicating, or lack political principles. I have seen those who are great candidates, have the financial backing, but lack the people skills or ability to organize and inspire volunteers to work hard. Sometimes candidates are lazy, and their volunteers end up saying, "Why should I go out and walk a neighborhood when he is at home watching the game?" It takes all three: a quality candidate, financial backing, and inspired, hardworking volunteers. When one is missing, it is almost impossible to win.

At the end of the campaign, my campaign remnant of dedicated volunteers wanted to stay in my campaign headquarters on historical Main Street in Garden Grove. "Rosie, Alan Keyes says the next campaign starts the next day. We need to stay together and do other things!" said Johanna. "It sounds good, but, look," I told them, "I have raised five children, worked as a school board member for seventeen years, ran a nonprofit organization for twelve years, and now I have just finished a race for U.S. Congress. I am tired. I just want to go home, lie down, and have someone feed me."

Three weeks after the campaign, I fell and broke my hip! I guess God thought I needed six months to a year of rest. It was heaven sent! I had an excuse to "veg-out" on the couch. And I had time to write down some of my experiences on the school board, my vision and our work with inner city youth for this book.

During the congressional campaign, I was in a fancy suit speaking to wealthy women at the Balboa Bay Club in Newport Beach, and now, a month later, I was exhausted, playing ball with a hundred-year-old woman in a convalescent rehabilitation center. Life is strange. "Well, I guess it is time to learn about health care and, particularly, care for the elderly," I quipped to my visitors.

But I learned much more. My roommate had five children in the Santa Ana School District. I had to watch Spanish novellas (soap operas) every night. "Now I know why I told my children they were not allowed to watch soap operas!" And Spanish ones were even worse. Yet, as a close-knit family all of her high school–aged children came to the hospital to watch the shows. While I was hiding my eyes under the blankets hoping not to see what was on the television. It was hard to understand how that after watching a rape, the kids could walk out of the room with smiles on their faces. Sadly, we have all been desensitized watching so much violence and sex on TV and in the media.

One of her boys was a great baseball player, and he was invited to go on to the minor leagues. But he decided to give up this opportunity and stay with his family. Some Latino families hesitate letting their children go out of the area, even off to college. It is hard for them to leave the area; many stay in the same neighborhood all of their lives.

The father was very close to his brother. Both families lived together and shared the same house. While on a business trip to Florida, the brother was shot and killed. The police did not do much to find the killer. Due to the grief of losing his brother, my roommate's husband started to drink a lot. My roommate told her husband she would leave him if he did not stop drinking.

He quit mourning, armed himself, and drove to the East Coast to find the person responsible for killing his brother. He apprehended the killer and turned him over to the police. In third world countries it is not uncommon to have people killed without a police investigation. My own uncle, in Guatemala, was shot as he came out of work and no one ever investigated the homicide. Often people feel that if they want justice they have to take matters into their own hands. The father also told me later that he had given his son a gun so he could watch his back at school and in the neighborhood. After years on the school board and having to expel high school students for possession of a fire arm, it was interesting to learn about this so called "act of protection" by a father.

The mother, who shared the room with me, was Anglo,

a blue-eyed blonde, and the father was Hispanic. I sensed that the kids did poorly in school. The father lamented to me, "I thought she would teach them English and I would teach them Spanish. But instead she just wanted to learn Spanish, so we all spoke Spanish at home." Perhaps her Spanish, like that of many of our teachers, was not that developed, and it gave the children a disadvantage when entering school. The children were probably placed in a classroom that used the failed bilingual methods, teaching children in Spanish for the first four years and then slowly transferred them into English in 4th grade. Having the children enter intermediate school with a second grade English reading vocabulary.

Evidently, I learned more than just getting to know the health care system.

During this time when I broke my hip, I was still serving on the City's gang prevention commission. I had been looking for an opportunity to share some ideas with the commission members. I was dismayed to learn that at the next meeting there was a perfect opportunity to do so. But I was still staying at the rehab center. I asked Johanna, a friend from the Congressional campaign, to help me get to the meeting. She came and checked me out from the center for three hours. I was surprised they let me leave. We left quickly hoping they would not change their mind. As we snuck out the door, Johanna pushed my wheel chair along. I had the sense that I was in an *I Love Lucy* television show adventure. It seemed that Ethel Mertz instead of Johanna was pushing the wheelchair. And I was just hoping I would not fall out as we went down the slanted ramp.

It was Johanna who insisted we stay at the campaign head-quarters after the race for Congress was done. She had enlisted ten people from the campaign team to each give monthly for the rent of our headquarters. Soon our new little group decided to open up a vintage boutique, a classy thrift store.

With the economic crash in 2008, I was not sure it was the

right time to open a business. But it would be great to see what it is like to own a small business. We had a very enthusiastic team. I also learned I could consult from my hospital bed with a Blackberry cell phone. This was a new step in my training. In the past when starting programs, I was very hands-on at the beginning, setting up the structures for the programs. I began to realize that I did not have to do it all, or at least I did not have to do so much of the work. I could consult and direct. And with a great team, it all just came together!

Then it dawned on me. "There was one more program from our non-profit incorporation papers that we had not accomplished." That was a workplace training program and an entrepreneurial academy for older youth, ages sixteen to twenty-five. It seemed God had given me some needed rest and provided a new team for the last project.

We were very excited to learn how to start a small business, a unique boutique. We had eight on our sales team. Every sales team member brought in things to sell, helped pay the rent and utilities, and got a check each month for their sales. With so many team members we had enough help so that everyone only needed to come in one day a week. This schedule was great, not only for the team, but it also brought in new sales items almost every day. Carol Bowen, the store manager, worked more, of course, and I worked on developing a workplace training program and a youth center. Our team met weekly to discuss the business and members took turns double-checking the accounting.

It was a great team. Carol, the store manager, had been my campaign treasurer. She had a master's in management and had experience leading a sales team of sixty people. Another political friend joined the team later. She had a master's in business administration. And I, with my master's in organizational leadership, developed a second nonprofit organization to serve older youth. Other sales team members, the Garcias, were experts in selling. They had sold at swap meets and special events and were our best sellers. Others, like Yolanda, were great in merchandizing, creating attractive displays, and organizing the store. We provided youth interns with hands-on workplace experience with a different adult mentor each day. We gave letters of reference to enhance their résumés, tried to help the interns set goals, and provided educational classes.

We called our venture an entrepreneurial academy. Our sales team loved selling and enjoyed the pride of business ownership, and after about a year or two most of the team members went off to start their own businesses. From that one business, we saw six other businesses start. We proved we could help others start and run a small business!

When the team left to establish their own entrepreneurial enterprises, my son, an art major from Biola University, who had been involved with the store from the beginning, decorating the education room, and volunteering as a clerk, came to manage the store. Later my daughter helped us start a second boutique. This one was a high-end artisan shop in a very popular mini mall, called The OC Mart MIX.

My son not only managed the vintage store, but also transformed it into a youth center having approximately fifty youth events each year. There were music concerts, art lessons, Open Mic, poetry slams, comedy nights, art exhibitions, and fashion shows, drawing in older youth, sixteen to twenty-five years of age. While we started mentoring inner-city Hispanic young people, I grew to love these passionate artists who, due to their creativity, felt a bit disenfranchised from the world, full of talent, waiting to be recognized, but insecure as to how to use those creative gifts. We were giving them a loving, safe place to practice and see how they were received. We loved them. And they loved us. Basically, they felt encouraged to develop their passions and talents, turning them into money-making ventures, through my son's support.

While we started out working with older Hispanic young

people and then moved to working with young artists, in the end we really learned about the homeless. Several homeless people regularly visited the resale shop. But one older man in particular was there all the time. He started volunteering, and slowly he became a consigner, buying unique items and selling them at the store. Then we moved him to clerking for us. He was grateful to have a place to stay during the day, lots of old books to read, and music to listen to. He was very good at selecting and finding unique antique items to sell and was a great help because he knew what they were worth. He had helped at other antique shops in the past.

He had four adult children who also struggled, but one in particular had a drug addiction, was homeless, and was constantly in and out of jail. She had a precious little girl who was one year old, and she was now expecting a boy. She had intended to give the baby to her sister to raise, but her sister moved to the east coast. I was trying to encourage this frightened mother and counsel her on her different options. In short, she was going to go to the hospital alone on a bus to have the baby. I said I would take her. "I want to see that little baby get born!" I was there in the operating room when the baby boy entered the world by a cesarean section birth.

The sweet little boy had a club foot. At the hospital, social workers who were concerned about the mother were alerted. The county agents visited the mother at the hospital and told her they might take her children away from her. I thought this was a bit cruel. "She had just had an operation! She was trying to bond with the baby!" When I drove the mother and the darling little boy home, I pulled up into the motel driveway. I had a compulsion to announce his birth, so I rolled down my window, and yelled out, "Daniel Thomas is born!" "Daniel is born!" No one was outside. "Daniel Thomas is here!" I shouted. Soon a young tattooed man appeared in his blue jeans with no shirt. He was just another homeless resident. "What?" he yelled down

from the second story of the motel. "Daniel Thomas is born!"
I yelled back. "Oh, the baby is here!" he shouted back. He put
his hands up in the air and shouted, "Yeah!! Yeah!!" I finally got
someone's attention. "Yes, the baby is here. He is here!"

The mother went home from the hospital on Friday and had
to appear in court on Monday. I found this to be cruel. With
her record, the children were taken away from her. There she
was, holding the baby, crying, "Rosie, please take the babies;
don't let them go into foster care. Please take them." What could
I do? I took the babies.

The mother was taken away from her parents at age seven and
grew up in foster care. She had four different foster parents from
age seven to eighteen. She was crying from her own experience.

I called home. "Honey, I am bringing home some babies!" "I
think it is for a short time; we will use the guest room attached to
the main house," I tried to encourage him. Instantly we became
foster parents. Three of my older daughters rallied, got on Facebook, and we had everything we needed: cribs, changing tables,
diapers, clothes. It was an outpouring of support. Two days after
the babies came, with loss of sleep, my middle daughter and I
looked at each other. How do people do this?

Our daughter organized us into shifts and managed the operation. My oldest daughter came in the afternoons at three after
she taught autistic preschoolers. Her husband came on at 6 p.m.
to help her. They left at 9 p.m. My other daughter took the
late-night shift, and I came on at four in the morning. During
the day, we juggled the care of the children, depending on our
schedules. One daughter was our substitute. And now, gloriously,
my oldest daughter and her husband have adopted them. What
a happy day it was when these two beautiful amazing children
officially became our very own!

A home Bible study group from The Rock Church of Anaheim adopted us for Christmas giving us $150 worth of gift
certificates and some beautiful gifts. Mariners Church provided

an amazing nine-foot noble fir Christmas tree, and volunteers from other churches came to sing carols and pray for us. Many friends quickly rallied in so many ways. One of my daughter's friends even paid for the circumcision and came with us to the procedure. We had support.

When we started the vintage boutique, little did I know how it would change my life and my family. I was to learn about the homeless; life in motels, the foster care system, the court system, and the adoption process. The grandfather of the babies who volunteered at the shop had grown up in an orphanage. The babies' mother, his daughter, was taken away from her parents at age seven and grew up in the foster care system, where she had four sets of parents in 10 years. But now her two children will be safe and loved. The little boy has therapy, the children are in swimming lessons, and the one-year-old sweet little girl, now three years old, will soon have dance lessons. The cycle of homelessness has been broken, at least for these two amazing, precious babies!

"How do people do this; how could a single mother handle two babies without all of the support?" It takes a lot of support, grandmothers, grandfathers, aunts, uncles, and church friends to raise a child. I had been working on structures so we could all be a father to the fatherless. But now I understood firsthand what it means that we need to visit the single mothers in their affliction. It is hard, if not impossible, to go it alone.

Chapter 30

Overcoming Apathy

I visited an outreach of New Song Church, and they were all talking about "Lava Love." "What is Lava Love?" I asked. "Lava means 'wash' in Spanish. We take rolls of quarters down to the local laundromat and pay for people's laundry to be washed and dried." What a blessing.

I remember washing clothes with my mother at a laundromat when our washing machine broke. We often had to sit there and watch the clothes while our parents did other things. We needed to be there when the machines stopped so our clothes would not get stolen and so that others could use the machines. At home when I was young, I loved hanging out the clothes to dry on the clothesline. They smelled so clean. I would sing little songs to God while I hung up the clothes.

At a Vineyard Church, a man invited other church members to join him in washing cars for "our hardworking Hispanic neighbors." It seemed like "washing their feet," a symbol of serving, a custom in the Bible.

At the Rock of Anaheim, they were recruiting folks for a citywide "Day of Kindness" encouraged by the mayor. Hundreds of church members showed up to distribute bags with hygiene items for the homeless.

More and more are realizing that we have to go outside the walls of our churches and engage the community. Young people are more civic and community minded. They want to do something. They want an authentic faith. Schools require community service and encourage the students to volunteer and make a difference in their community. Many take up causes like sexual trafficking, graffiti removal, or the homeless. This generation of young people, soon to be leaders are cause driven. They have been taught to be global and community citizens.

There are churches and organizations that are ministering in low-income neighborhoods on a daily basis, investing in the lives of these children and families. We have always had the rescue missions, Salvation Army and Teen Challenge. In Santa Ana, we have Kid Works that emphasizes academic tutoring, and Victory Outreach and Lives Worth Saving who work with gang members. In the next town over, in Costa Mesa, there is Mika, an organization that works in the neighborhoods developing community leaders. Mariners Church, a large church in Newport Beach, has had a tutoring program in an apartment complex in Santa Ana for twenty-five years. Laurie Beshore, the pastor's wife and outreach director, wrote Love Without Walls, a book that shares their experience engaging the community.

Almost every church is involved with some outreach efforts: visiting prisoners, passing out turkeys on Thanksgiving, encouraging foster care, and feeding the hungry. With churches becoming more and more interested in making a difference in their community, it is time to mobilize an army of mentors.

There are excellent program models. There are experienced outreach leaders in our churches and established nonprofit organizations who know how to connect mentors with children and their families. Through our two nonprofits, we have set up structures for youth from five years old to twenty-five with our elementary and intermediate school-based character clubs, teen neighborhood sport centers, and older youth workplace sites. Many of our mentors have led an after-school club for more than ten years. One of our volunteers has been teaching for fifteen years. Once they start, they do not want to quit. We know how to place people in their callings. We know from experience that we can make a real difference in the lives of others.

Now many of our programs are under individual churches. At one of the elementary after-school clubs there are 100 children who attend each week, Calvary Chapel regularly sends 20 or more teenagers from their private high school to play sports and make friends with the children. Other church members also come along side and assist with Christmas parties, camping experiences, and outings such as fishing trips, a night out to a professional baseball or soccer game, or visiting the elderly.

Many churches feed the people who are homeless. My daughter, who first volunteered with a feeding program, has annually organized a Christmas party for the homeless. She enlists church groups to bake cookies and send music groups to sing. Others are working to create "check-in centers" for people who are homeless, so they can keep a few belongs in a safe place and be free to go to workplace training classes, doctor's appointments or job interviews without carrying their belongings. There is so much we can do.

Because the vision is big, it involves a large mobilization effort. Generally nonprofit organizations find that getting volunteers is difficult. We are discouraged. Something is holding us back.

Many have asked, "What makes you think you can get thousands of volunteers? They are hard to get and hard to keep!"

Everyone agrees the need is great. Our inner cities are spiraling out of control. Families are hurting. Our society is crumbling! Yes, there is a cause. Our foundations of religion and morality are destroyed. There are so many needs, we can't meet them all. And we do not know where to start.

We are commanded to go and share the good news of God's love, to feed the hungry and clothe the naked. We know God said to preach the good news to the poor, set the captives free, and bring liberty to those who are bruised. We know we need to love our neighbors. So why aren't we moving?

Apathy is holding us back. What is apathy and how do you get rid of it? Apathy is defined as "a lack of interest, enthusiasm, or concern. Not being willing to make the effort to change things."

We know that "the cares of this world and the deceitfulness of riches choke out" what God is telling us to do. Yes, life is tough, and we have our own personal problems to deal with. We all have challenges, family situations, and concerns that weigh us down. We are very busy; our schedules are full. We have a lot of stuff to take care of, our houses, our yards, our garages need organizing, and we have trips to plan. These are definitely obstacles that keep us from going out into the community. So how do we get ourselves going?

We have the Great Commission that tells us to go and the great commandment that requires us to love our neighbor as our selves. It could not be clearer! We need to go, to teach, and to love. How do we overcome apathy toward the real important work that has to be done?

We have great examples to encourage us. God continually reset the culture in the Book of Judges. Nehemiah mobilized the people to rebuild the walls in Jerusalem. When it was time to build the temple everyone gave willingly. In fact, they had to ask the people to stop giving, they had too much money. That is my favorite part.

I love the following quote by the famous historian Arnold Toynbee because it shows us just how to get rid of apathy:

"Apathy can be overcome by enthusiasm, and enthusiasm can only be aroused by two things: first, an ideal, with takes the imagination by storm, and second, a definite intelligible plan for carrying that ideal into practice."

Yes, apathy can be overcome! It can only be overcome by one thing: enthusiasm!

Now that makes sense. I do not think you can have both apathy and enthusiasm at the same time. It is one or the other.

And according to Toynbee, to have *enthusiasm*, you need two things:

1) an ideal that takes the imagination by storm
2) a definite intelligible plan for putting that ideal into practice

Okay, it takes an ideal, but you also have to have a plan. Otherwise it is only a pipe dream.

If you have a fantastic ideal, I mean a really great idea that takes everyone's imagination by surprise, some new thought so amazing that no one has really thought of it before, then you have an ideal that takes the imagination by storm. Perhaps it is an ideal that takes your breath away. "Wow! Is that really possible? It would be amazing if that could happen!" I think something that takes your imagination by storm is like a sudden change in the weather, like a flash flood, perhaps. Everyone has to run for cover. It moves people. Everyone has to do something different. It is an ideal that rushes in and people think it is amazing. The ideal is an answer to all of our problems, fulfilling our greatest desires.

But an ideal is not enough. There has to be a workable plan to carry out that ideal. If the ideal is astounding and the plan is doable, then people will take it seriously. Everyone can see that it can really happen, and when something amazing happens, people will become enthusiastic. They will get excited, be full of anticipation, desiring it to unfold. They will want to be a part of it, part of the big change.

And when enthusiasm arrives, apathy leaves. How great is that!?

This book is about the ideal that will take our imaginations by storm and a tangible, workable plan that will make the ideal a reality.

What is that ideal? What if we could take our nation and our culture back quickly? What if we could turn the world upside down? What if we could truly make a permanent difference? What if the Church rose up all at once and marched in like a mighty army and destroyed all of the works of the Devil, kicked open the Gates of Hell, broke the chains off the people, and set those that are held by addictions and past trauma free? What if God would really reset the culture!

Imagine if every child in our country, or in our county, had a nurturing family or wonderful caring mentors in their lives. Imagine drug abuse gone or at least cut down by 70 percent. Imagine if we could reduce the sexual abuse of children, and end the horrific sex trafficking, the savage raping of young girls. Imagine a world that is not inundated by pornography. Imagine if the Mexican or

Columbian drug cartels lost most of their customers in America. Their stashes of drugs would be worthless. Imagine if every child was encouraged and shown how to live an ethical lifestyle. Imagine if we could close our prisons due to vacancies! We have seen this before, during great awakenings. This can be our reality!

The ideal is that our efforts can make a difference. That God can reset the culture instantly. It is a belief that we can actually get the job done, fulfill the commission we have been given, and truly love our neighbors, obeying the greatest commandment.

It is the vision of a church that freely gives a "heavenly father" to a fatherless child and visits the struggling single mothers. James 1:27, in the Bible, states, "*Pure* religion and *undefiled* before God and the Father is this, to visit the fatherless and widows in their affliction, *and* to keep himself *unspotted* from the world." Hopefully this is what Christ will find when he returns— a pure and undefiled bride ready to meet her bridegroom?

The truth is, we do not believe it can be done. We say, "The problems are so big it will take years to solve them. The church is so weak, our statistics are no better than the world's." And many of us have not seen it done.

Others of us have seen revivals, and we know it is a move of the Spirit. So we think we just have to wait for the Spirit to move. We just have to wait for the waters to move, and then we can jump in. There is nothing we can do about the problems we see. It is up to God, and evidently, God is not working. It must not be time. Times are supposed to be wicked. It is the end times. Our cities are going to hell in a hand basket, and our nation is disintegrating. It was predicted. It is over!

You may be thinking, "Didn't Jesus say that the harvest is great and the laborers are few? Didn't he say that the poor you will always have with you? Didn't God say that there would be evil in the last days, and things would get worse? Isn't it time for God to just wrap this up? We are waiting for God."

No, No! God is waiting on us. He gave us the commandment to

go, he told the rich young ruler to give up his possessions and give to the poor and to go and love his neighbor. We have the marching orders; go, teach, and love. When we move in obedience, he will flood our hearts with the love we need and the power of the Holy Spirit to get the job done.

Yes, the harvest is ripe, and the laborers are few, but Jesus did not say, "Let the harvest drop off the trees and plants and let it rot." No. He said, "Get the laborers and get the job done." He, in fact, told us just how to get the laborers. He said to "pray the Lord of the Harvest that he would send forth laborers." Evidently, if we need thousands of laborers, the Lord of the Harvest, the Holy Spirit, will send them. That is, if we ask for them. We have to pray for them to be sent. We do not ask because we do not see the harvest. We are too into ourselves, our house, our cars, our vacations. We do not see the needs around us.

That is why Christ said, "Lift up your head, Open your eyes, Look at the fields! They are ready now to harvest." He says not to wait; he says go!

Since the Holy Spirit lives inside of believers, I think he knows just how to move and call people to the work. If we see the need, then it is up to us to pray. Ask the Lord of the Harvest to send out the laborers. How can we pray for laborers if we do not see the need, have a vision, a plan, a task, or a job description? And how can people change their lives if mentors are not sent out? How can people be sent if there are no leaders to send them?

At our nonprofit, I would say don't just pray for volunteers. Pray specifically! Ask for a mentor who wants to tutor on Tuesday from 3 to 5 p.m. Pray for a soccer player to come on Wednesdays in the afternoon. Pray for men who like fishing to volunteer to take kids fishing. First, identify your need, and then ask God to meet that specific need.

One time we spoke at a large men's group and thirty-one men volunteered, but most could not come during our after-school hours. And others were not available to attend events we had planned ahead of time for the children. We were just shooting bullets everywhere. People had a heart to serve, but it was hard to plug them in.

In the end, we had three that stayed and worked in our clubs. They were great volunteers, started a new club, and one ended up taking the kids to camp year after year. It is time to get serious about meeting the needs.

Once we learned to pray more specifically, it was amazing that we just ran into the right volunteers who were available at the needed time and had the right skills. For many, this is hard. It is difficult to tell the Holy Spirit just exactly what we need because we think it will make it harder for him to find the right person. So we try to make it easier on him. When you think of it, it is a little silly. He knows just where the person we need is. But when we pray specifically, it is joyous to see just how perfect the volunteer is for the spot. Praying specifically is for us. It encourages us to know our prayers are heard. It makes us partners.

In Mathew 24, Jesus told the disciples that the end would not come until the gospel, the good news, was preached to the entire world. Isn't that one of the end-time characteristics? So we better get to it.

Jesus told us to love our neighbor as ourselves. We also know he wants us to be a father to the fatherless and to visit the single mothers or widows in their afflictions. We are also told that others will know we are Christians by our love. And he told us that just as he is in the world, so should we be in the world. He came to preach the gospel to the poor, to set at liberty those who are bruised, and set the captives free. He told us what to do. I think he is waiting for us.

As has been mentioned, in I Samuel 30, David returned to Ziglag and saw that his family was taken captive. His men were angry and wanted to stone him; judgment was eminent. He asked God what he should do. Additionally, he asked God if he would be successful. After he got a strategy from God, he and his men ran after his enemies to rescue the wives and children. Isn't it about time we do the same thing? How long will we allow our children to be destroyed by our culture and deceived in our schools?

After he heard God and obeyed the instructions, God gave David everything he needed to get the kids back. When we hear from God and do what he says, we have guaranteed success! We have his power. We have his authority. We have his resources. We have his Word and his promises. He even promised to be with us in the battle. What more do we need?

Nehemiah wept over the broken walls in Jerusalem, and organized the people to rebuild the walls. He told them, "Fight for your friends, your families and your homes!

Here is what we need. We need enthusiasm to dispel our apathy; we need to stir ourselves up.

Knowing *what* we have to do is not enough. Knowing *how* we are to do it is not enough. We need our hearts to say, "Yes, I will go!" Samuel, the prophet said, "Here am I, send me!" We need our hearts to be in it. Sometimes it is hard to get started, but when we do, then we get energized. We need a vision, an ideal, that takes the imagination by storm, and we need a winning plan.

Aren't you tired of fighting to merely *contain* the enemy and having to fight the same battles over and over? Aren't you tired of *co-existing* with the Devil, enduring his destructive attacks? Aren't you tired of the live-and-let-live, *détente* mentality? I am. We have been so passive.

We need a big vision, an ideal that stirs our hearts, something amazing! And we need a workable plan. We need a good offense! We need a winning strategy. We need the will to win. We need to understand the enemy and know that the enemy has been defeated. Let's go set the captives free!

Chapter 31

The Winning Plan

One day, Brian, a leader from Rick Warren's Saddleback Church, came to my office. The church wanted to do an event for the residents of Santa Ana. "Great!" I said. "We usually start off the school year with a big event to welcome the kids back to our tutoring, sports, character clubs. Coach Mike Hoover does track and field sports, a soccer game, and some family fun events. Do you want to put it on this year?"

"That sounds great," Brian said. "I will get Jose Menaldo, our volunteer leader, to join us. Can you show us some different locations where we might put the event on?" I was happy to show them around. We selected Santa Ana High School because it was right downtown on First Street and had a field facing a busy street. I showed them how to get the school permits for the event, and they went off to plan.

Time went by. I had not heard from them. I was concerned, "Don't they know it takes a lot of planning? Don't they know that we have to get an invitation out soon? We need lots of meetings. I had better call them," I decided.

I was a little anxious as I called. Jose answered the phone, "I will send you the draft of the invitation tomorrow, and you can come to a planning meeting at the church." At the meeting, there was a large group, a policeman from the church had large charts with all of the traffic patterns, each committee leader reported on their progress, and I felt relieved. Really, you might say I was amazed!

I did very little, and the day of the event, I was totally blown away! We had invited the leaders of the PTA to have a table there, and they had declined. But as I arrived, I saw Teresa Mims, the PTA president, at the front entrance to the event. "Rosie, Wow, this is amazing! If you would have told us what it was going to be like, we all would have been here!"

How could I have told them what it would be like? I could never have imagined what I saw that day! Families from the community were lined up for hours waiting to get in. The first 200 received a family box with four lunches. Each box had four sandwiches, four apples, four cookies, and four bags of chips. The entrance to the event had a large orange, yellow, green, and brown fall-colored balloon arch. As you entered, bales of hay lined the entrance area on both sides. Nestled in the bales of hay were large wooden half barrels full of candies, apples, and small toys. The sign said "Country Store. Take whatever you like. It's free!" Kids and their families entered and filled their pockets with candy and treats. Now that was a great beginning!

The bands played on the stage, the motorcycles on the huge motocross ramps roared as the bikes took a spin up into the air, the boxing rink was up, and boys were sparring. Balloons flew in the air. Children were enjoying craft projects, fun carnival games, and book tables. All of the usual fair events were assembled, clowns and ladies painting faces. But there were new venues: free haircuts, free family photos, and free foot and back massages. It was awesome! Here ladies from the church, some blond high-class ladies, were massaging the feet of hard-working immigrant men and women. It was a beautiful sight! Family members were on their cell phones calling all of their children, cousins, and grandmas to come over for a free family picture. The field was full. Excitement was in the air.

People were not only given a box of lunches for the family when they arrived but also, at dinner time, the volunteers fired up the grills and served free hamburgers and hotdogs. If there was ever a company party, this was it!

The event was called "Family Success." The Saddleback team had chosen Santa Ana High School not only for its great location in the heart of the city but also because there were classrooms nearby. They had classes for parents on domestic violence, keeping your kids out of gangs, how to teach abstinence to your children, and preparing your children for college and life. With such relevant classes, many parents attended! Hispanics are family-oriented, and their children are their treasures. Representatives walked through the crowds with fliers inviting the parents to the "family success" classes.

When the event was over, large trucks pulled up, and each family left with a box with special gifts to take home: pots and pans, food, toys, and a copy of the book, *The Purpose Driven Life*, in English and Spanish.

The Orange County Register newspaper article was glowing, stating that "for one day, families in Santa Ana could forget the hardships of life, relax and truly enjoy themselves." What a beautiful gift to the community!

It was an incredible event. Six thousand members of the community came, and there were more than a thousand volunteers!

What made this event so special? First, it was big! It was exciting! The minute you arrived, you felt energized. It was well planned. It was relevant, meeting the needs of the people. The volunteers were excited, they were prepared, and each had their part to play. It was fun to be part of a big project. Saddleback leaders laid out an exciting vision for its church members. "Let's go down and bless the inner-city families!" The enthusiasm caught on. Church families sacrificed time, gathering things for the gift boxes. They had given of themselves! The volunteers experienced great joy putting the boxes together and personally giving them away. Love was in the air! And it felt good.

How different this event was from the event we had done a few years before. We spent $5,000 for an event planner to put on a fair. We sent out Victory Outreach people to sell tickets in front of grocery stores. A thousand tickets sold, so we prepared for more. But only about thirty to fifty people showed up. The tickets were sold all over Orange County, not right in the area. Most people who bought a ticket thought they were just giving a donation to a tattooed ex-drug addict who was seeking to better his life. They had no plans to come to our inner-city fair. We had so much food left over. There was no excitement. It was a lot of work for our little group, and it ended in disappointment.

What made these events so different? We both set out to do the same thing.

Saddleback Church leaders laid out the vision for their members. The volunteers gathered in one place, at the church. Great talent was pooled together. People with organizational skills and those versed in traffic control were involved. Children's workers, hair stylists, photographers, and cooks were ready to share their area of expertise with the community. Parent classes were relevant, meeting real needs. Teachers were passionate about their subject matter, hoping to bring true family success to the people. The volunteers had an allegiance to their church, they were committed to the cause and wanted the church to make a difference. Vehicles of communication were in place: church bulletins, video production, and church facilities to work from. Yes, they had a large vision, the expertise, the resources, and volunteers to accomplish a great work.

Today nonprofits struggle trying to recruit volunteers for their organization. Resources are hard to come by, and they lack all of the expertise they need. They have small offices and work in inexpensive, out-of-the-way places. Church leaders are overworked and understaffed and busy with all of the church programs and discipleship needs in the church.

If a nonprofit asks to speak at a church meeting, the leadership hesitates...and rightfully so. "If I let him speak, everyone else will want time for their project. There is limited time, and it will take away from our teaching time. And if they talk about the homeless or tutoring, maybe one or two will be interested in helping. It isn't worth the effort or time. Besides we have our own outreach department, our own projects that need the volunteers." Those with a mission and a passion for the needs of the community have to move on and try to find volunteers and resources elsewhere.

Pastors are busy preparing messages, teaching, meeting with staff, talking to members, preparing for board meetings and sharing their own church vision. They have to focus their energy on the people who are already in the church. Each pastor has a calling for their church that they have to move forward.

Yes, they realize the church needs to go out and help others. So they appoint an outreach leader, pay him very little, and tell him to go change the world. If he was in jail or on drugs at one time, he might start a jail ministry or a drug addiction support group. If he worked with children, he might emphasize tutoring in the community. As he goes out, he is inundated with needs. Voices pull him in all directions. "Let's do a homeless outreach; let's get a warehouse and feed the poor." "My uncle is in jail. What, you do not have a jail ministry? Didn't you read that we are to visit people in jail?" Other larger churches have lists of volunteers but are not sure how to get them out there serving the community. We have been doing things the hard way—and the ineffective way, I might add.

Thinking about the old civic center YMCA building in downtown Santa Ana and the Young Men's Christian Association's mission of ministering to mind, body, and spirit, I have often wondered, "What inspired community leaders in 1924 to build and invest in such a large magnificent building? How did the movement raise the money and enlist thousands of volunteers? The YMCA movement grew to reach billions of young people around the world. What in the first half of the 1900's generated that kind of excitement?"

In John R. Mott's two-page article, "Lessons I Learned in Over Fifty Years in Helping to Establish National and Worldwide Movements," there are some clues.

One of the lessons John R. Mott learned was:

"A large, exacting undertaking is easier than a smaller one."

It is hard to get people behind a small vision. When our vision is big, exciting, and doable, everyone will want to get behind it. We need an ideal that takes our breath away, takes our imagination by storm. When everyone is working together, there is a synergy. Synergy means that our combined efforts are greater than the sum of our individual parts. The Encarta Dictionary describes it as "the working together of two or more people, organizations, or things, especially when the result is greater than the sum of their individual effects or capabilities." I think synergy is a bit like exponential power. "One can take 1,000, but two can take 10,000." It is not like addition and multiplication.

When our vision is large, it is obvious that we cannot do it alone. We need others to get it done. It is a God kind of vision. Large undertakings require a greater pool of talent and experience to get it done right. At the school district when we built high schools, we needed to go outside of the school facilities department for talent. We needed civil engineers, architects, project managers, lighting experts, color designers, and, of course, lawyers.

Completing large successful undertakings, one after the other, creates momentum. It's like wow, Wow, WOW! They are on to something. Once it gets going, more and more want to join in. I learned that running political campaigns. As a candidate, you had to build momentum.

A large undertaking requires a great ideal. It requires a vision worth doing. It causes people to sacrifice and give their all.

When it comes to restoring America, is there not a cause? Our futures are at stake. Whether we live in freedom or under a tyrannical regime depends on whether Americans are good people and self-governed. "America is great, because America is good." "Religion and morality are our pillars, our foundation," believed our founders. If the foundations are destroyed, what are the people to do?

They have to rebuild the foundations. That's what the people have to do! And that is what we need to do today.

There is much to lose and much to gain in this battle for the hearts and minds of men. The cause is great and our enemies are strong. In rebuilding the walls of Jerusalem, Nehemiah had his enemies and said to the nobles, to the leaders and to the rest of the people, "Do not be afraid of them. Remember the Lord, great and awesome, and fight for your brethren, your sons, your daughters, your wives, and your houses."

Many believe we are in the end times. In the book of Malachi, the last book of the Old Testament, in the last chapter, we are told that God will send Elijah, or the spirit of Elijah. "Behold, I will send you Elijah the prophet before the coming of the great and dreadful day of the Lord, and he will turn the hearts of the fathers to the children, and the hearts of the children to their fathers, lest I come and strike you with a curse." Before Christ came the first time God sent John the Baptist, who was said to come in "the spirit of Elijah." It seems that before the end, when God comes to judge the earth, he wants to again send the spirit of Elijah, but this time the spirit of Elijah will restore the image of the father, a loving provider, strong protector and caring mentor, who instructs his children.

Interestingly, the verses before ask us to "Remember the Law of Moses, my servant." Perhaps it is time to teach the Ten Commandments again to our children. Sounds like a big mentoring movement to me!

The judges in Israel realized there was a cause when their society had left God's way. Nehemiah wept over the broken walls. God gave them a vision and a strategy and a well-thought-out plan. They had a winning plan.

Look at the great event the church members put on! The church people all came together in one place and moved out, each one to do their individual job. The leaders cast the vision and the people responded. They pooled their expertise together, over one thousand church members volunteered! They had sufficient resources for their large-exacting effort. They worked united, in a coordinated way, each one using their gifts, following a God-given specific strategic plan. They were enthusiastic and their enthusiasm pulled others into the effort.

As in the days of Acts the people were united, in one accord, of one spirit and one mind and they turned the world upside down!

When King David lost his family, he encouraged himself in the Lord. He asked God, "Will we succeed?" God said, "Yes, you will be successful." God gave him a plan. He called his warriors together and they went off. When Israel marched forward towards the Promised Land, God gave them a winning plan for each battle.

The winning plan includes a big amazing vision and a workable plan. It has to be something worth working for, something that energizes you and excites others. It includes getting started, bringing people together, and taking the first step. While our vision is large we have to be willing to start small and allow God to teach us and guide us step by step. It requires a clear plan with a mission, purpose and goals, and the commitment to seeing them come to pass.

And in this case taking back our children, our families and our nation is a big vision. Mobilizing thousands to share the good news of God's "father" love is exciting. And how amazing will it be to see our churches aflame with righteousness once again!

But just how do we that?

Part VII
How We Win

The Superhero Arrives

"If your actions inspire others to dream more, learn more, do more and become more, you are a leader." —*John Quincy Adams*

"Look!" He said. "The people are united, and they speak the same language. After this, nothing they set out to do will be impossible for them!"

—*Genesis 11:6*

"So all the people **gathered together as one man...**"
"...**all** the people **arose as one man...**"
"...**all** the men...gathered against the city, **united together as one man.**"

—*Judges 20:1, 8, 11*

Chapter 32

Leadership

Charles Finney, a great revival preacher from the early 1800's, who inspired a large benevolent work called the Benevolent Empire, stated, "When sinners are careless and stupid, and sinking into hell unconcerned, it is time the church should bestir themselves. It is as much the duty of the church to awake, as it is for the firemen to awake when a fire breaks out in the night in a great city."

I am sure there are many firemen who hate being awakened in the middle of the night. But duty calls. It is his job to answer the call. Let us stir ourselves out of our sleep!

But before we can stir ourselves up, we need leadership! We need someone to ring the alarm. How will people know when to wake up? Someone has to sound the alarm. Someone has to call the people to arise. Someone has to share the vision that will spark the imagination, create enthusiasm, and build momentum. We need leaders who are excited to get the job done!

We need leadership. But before leaders call the people, the leaders need a tangible, offensive plan! We need a winning plan. We will lose if we rise up only to contain the problem. We need to stop playing defense and rally the troops into offensive action. And the gates of Hell will not prevail against us. It is time to kick the gates down.

We need leaders that will lead the charge! Enlist the troops. Blow the trumpets in Zion! Sound the alarm! And call the soldiers into action.

It is time for us to awaken out of our sleep and see the desperate condition we are in. Our enemies are at our door. Our enemies are within our nation and also without. Time is running out. We have only a window of opportunity to arise. In a sense, the alarm has already sounded; we are in danger. The foundations are destroyed, our freedoms are at stake, the mothers are crying, teen boys are angry, and the children are confused. Let us rouse ourselves and put out the fire!

Ted Cruz, a candidate for president, recently said, "The whole world is on fire!" It caught national attention when a four-year-old girl in the audience repeated the phrase turning it into a question, "The whole world is on fire?" Cruz attributed the fire in the world to leaders who lead from behind. We need bold leaders who will take the lead in this critical hour.

Who should lead the troops?

Some might say it is Jesus Christ. Yes, that is true. He is the Commander in Chief. He has already given the command to go! He has already equipped us for the battle. He has already shown us how to love others on his behalf. He is next to God right now praying for us.

He has left the job to us. He needs people to blow the trumpets. He needs someone to sound the alarm, to call the people to the battle. Who are the leaders? The pastors, our spiritual leaders, need to sound the alarm, tell the people to go, teach, and love. The people look to them for leadership.

To the pastors who are leading the flocks, can't you see that the people are waiting? They are waiting for you. They are waiting to be sent out. They have gifts and talents they want to use. They are unfulfilled just sitting in the pews. They want to do what they were created to do. It will give them great joy to be used and to see changed lives. They are waiting for the alarm to sound.

Let's take the city by storm. Let's make a radical difference in our communities. Let's turn things around. Let's really turn the world upside down. Let's flip America around and start caring for and valuing the individual. Let's change lives, build up individual people, and empower them to be good, to be successful, to fulfill their greatness in life.

In America, it is "we the people." If the people are strong, then the nation is strong. If the people are good, then America will be great again. And if our foundations of religion and morality are repaired, we can stand. And if we obey God, we will be blessed. If we don't go, if we disobey, we will be held accountable. God has given us so much. This is the moment. We have to choose: obedience or judgment.

God loves the individual. God loves the poor. He loves the hurting. His heart is full of compassion for them. They are sheep without a shepherd, children without fathers. He says, "Seek my face." Can you see how much he cares? How he wants to impart truth and healing to those that are hurting!

He begs us to go. He gave us everything we need. We have the power of the gospel to change lives. We have the power of the Holy Spirit to be witnesses of the good news. We have the truth of God's Word that will set men free. God wants to raise up an army to move out and share his love. God's love moved him to send his son to die in our place so that we can be free from the punishment of sin. We can now experience his peace, his presence, his provision, and his loving care. Let's share the good news!

Orange County, here in California, has some of the largest, most effective churches in the world. We are known for our mega churches. We have thousands of people who gather in one place. They are poised to be sent out. They are waiting for the call to go out.

We have all of the expertise we need. In all of these churches, there are experienced outreach leaders who know how to lead others in ministry. We have the expertise to build buildings, to develop programs, to teach, to feed the hungry, to help people leave gangs, to set people free from addictions, to administrate, to organize, and to serve and love the community.

The theme in the book of Judges is, *When leaders lead, followers follow*. If our pastors give the charge, the people will follow. God has blessed our great leaders, given them favor with the people, and enlarged their work. According to Scripture, "To whom much is given, much shall also be required."

If anything, we have church members who are full of the Word of God, going to church, and listening to Christian radio all day long. As I mentioned earlier, when Fievel, the cartoon mouse in the Disney movie by that name, came to America, he saw danger and shouted, "There are cats in America!" I, too, began to see the cats in America...the dangerous fat cats. No, it is not the fat cats on Wall Street that are the problem. It is not the fat cat drug pushers on Main Street. It is the fat cats in our pews, who eat and eat and go home to eat some more. They do not exercise their faith, they are not sharing their faith, and they are not serving the poor. The fat cats consume instead of give; they prefer to curl up by the fire in comfort and sleep most of the day. And consequently they are not making a difference.

I think a lot of us in the pews would be surprised to hear what the sin of Sodom and Gomorrah was. Ezekiel 16:49–50 warns, "Now this was the sin of your sister Sodom: She and her daughters were arrogant, overfed and unconcerned; they did not help the poor and needy. They were haughty and did detestable things before me" (NIV).

Yes, Sodom and Gomorrah did do detestable things, and that is what we usually think of when their cities' names come up. But as this verse points out, long before they were destroyed, they had become arrogant, prideful, and very self-indulgent. They thought more about food and possessions than they did the poor and needy. They were self-centered, not caring for others. They were too busy keeping up with the Joneses. Perhaps it was their self-indulgent ways that caused their children to rise up and do detestable things. "If it feels good, do it," seems to be our culture's mantra. "Whatever makes you happy," appears to be the advice of the day. Happiness and pleasure have become our gods.

As American people, we have coveted material things. We wanted what the Joneses had. We loved our careers and our houses over our children. We have rejected his gift of children and limited our families. We rejected God's plan for the family. Raising godly seed was no longer the central purpose of our homes. We did not follow God's ways. We lost our marriages. Our children lost their dads. As husband and wife roles blurred, some lost their gender identity. Our self-indulgent lifestyle coupled with broken relationships led to an insatiable hunger for pornography and for all matter of perverseness, including sex trafficking of young girls and sodomy. Pleasure became our goal. "If it makes me happy, then it must be OK," we tried to tell ourselves. We no longer cared what God thought.

We have become so self-absorbed and self-indulgent that we have no regard for others, for their suffering, and their pain. We have neglected the poor. God is awakening us, but the world is already yelling at us for not caring for the poor. Let us not have God say about us that we are arrogant, overfed, and unconcerned. Let it be said that we humbled ourselves, were concerned for others, rose up, and helped the poor and needy.

It is time for leaders to lead.

Chapter 33

Turning

If you took the globe in your hands and asked, "What is the richest part of the planet?" one might answer Beverly Hills or Dubai. No, it would not be Beverly Hills or Dubai; it is right here in Orange County, California. The world knows about us as "The OC" from the high school television series by that name. In other places, there are a few with great wealth, but in Orange County, we have many people with wealth and, thus, we are the richest place on the planet.

In the heart of Orange County, many people face great hardships. Santa Ana, California, ranked number one among eighty-six of the country's largest cities for "urban hardship" in a 2004 study by the Rockefeller Institute of Government. We have great resources and great hardship!

We have all of the ingredients for a powerful move of God's love. We have a great vision to transform individual lives with the gospel, amazing leadership, megachurches, television stations, radio stations, outreach ministry expertise, thousands of potential volunteers, abundant resources, and we have the poor and needy. This is the "perfect storm" for dynamic change.

Andrew Murray, one of my favorite writers, in the last book he wrote, *The State of the Church,* stressed that all revivals must be a move of God, a move of the Spirit. The book further explained that his brother, a theological professor, believed a restoration of the knowledge of God would create revival. But Andrew differed; he believed it must be a work of God's spirit!

Charles Finney believed we need to stir ourselves up. He

was influenced by John Wesley, who was very organized and methodical. Bill Bright, the founder of Campus Crusade for Christ, in his book, *The Coming Revival,* said he did not think we needed to wait for God.

Everyone can't be right. So what is it? Is it the Word, is it the Spirit, or is it our stirring ourselves up out of our sleep? Yes, everyone is right. How can people stir themselves up without the preaching of the Word and a renewed knowledge of our call? And how can we move out and be effective without the power of the Spirit? And how can God move if we do not stir ourselves up and become obedient to what he said? If we hear God's commandment to go, teach, love, obey, and stir ourselves up, the Holy Spirit will come in like a flood and empower us. And when he moves, many respond, and communities are transformed.

Let us humble ourselves and recognize that we have not been obedient. Let's pray and ask God to show us what he cares about. Let's seek God's face and feel his heart. He will give us insight and individual instructions. Then let us step out and obey those instructions. All we need to do is take the first step, and he will take us the rest of the way. Let's turn toward God's will and away from our usual ways. This is what will heal our land.

During the Jesus Movement, Pastor Chuck Smith's wife Kay Smith saw the hippies hitchhiking, and her heart was burdened for them. She began to pray for them. Soon they met Lonnie Frisbee, a hippie minister who introduced Chuck and Kay to other hippies. They invited these strange-looking fellows to their church. Church members were shocked that these bare-foot young men were putting their toes in the communion cup holders. It was uncomfortable and caused a stir that the girls came to church in short shorts. And some hippies preferred sitting on the floor than in the pews. But Pastor Smith told his deacons not to worry, but to accept the young people the way they were. The hippies felt unconditional love and turned their hearts to Christ. They felt the love and felt so at home. God moved on their hearts and they wrote new music. They wanted to sing their songs at the church. When Pastor Chuck heard their simple, heartfelt songs, he cried and let them sing. And from these beginnings, the music in all of our churches changed. And the rest is history. A tremendous movement started and moved around the world.

The 60's Jesus Movement began with someone seeing a need and praying. It started with a heart for the disenfranchised young people.

God took the first step and said, "Go!" He gave us the Great Commission and the Great Commandment. Then it is our turn to take one step forward. It could be simply praying or renting a small nonprofit office. Then it is God's turn, and he rushes in with the resources to pay for the office. I think it is a partnership. We walk together with God, step-by-step. He instructs us and we obey. We obey and he provides. We are coworkers, working together. We do what only we can do, and he does what only he can do. God stirs our hearts, we respond, and he provides. And together we get the job done.

In 2 Chronicles 7:14, God gave us the pathway to healing our nation. "If my people, who are called by my name, will humble themselves and pray and seek my face and turn from their wicked ways, then I will hear from heaven, and I will forgive their sin and will heal their land" (NIV).

I drove behind a truck that had this verse written on the back window, except the "turn from their wicked ways" part was missing. I have seen the same verse quoted by famous leaders in Christian books with the last part missing. Why was *turn from their wicked ways* missing? Maybe the verse is too long. There just wasn't enough room on the truck window. Maybe they just accidently misquoted it. Or maybe we were not ready. Perhaps we were still in the praying mode or needing to seek his face part...not quite ready to turn.

In the '80s, Bill Bright from Campus Crusade for Christ wrote a book called *The Coming Revival,* America's Call to Fast, Pray, and "Seek God's Face." Bright shares how 600 Christian leaders, representing more than a hundred denominations and religious organizations, gathered in Orlando, Florida, on December 5–7, 1994, to actually fast and pray, not just talk about it. He also mentions that 110,000 young people gathered to pray with a new youth prayer movement, The Call. There have been many prayer gatherings in Washington, D.C., such as Washington for Jesus and America for Jesus in 1980, 1988, and 1996, with a total of a half a million or a million in attendance. Concerned women started prayer chapters, meeting in homes to pray, and 500,000 women joined in. In Kansas City, there is a prayer center called the International House of Prayer (IHOP), which trains people in prayer and has a prayer meeting going on continuously around the clock. It seems that we have prayed, fasted, and sought his face. So what is the hold up?

I think it is time to "turn from our wicked ways." Then, and only then, will he hear from heaven, forgive us of our sins, and heal our land.

Plain and simple, prayer has gone up, time to turn.

Perhaps we are waiting for fornicators, drunkards, and gang members to turn, and then once they quit doing what they are doing, God will heal the land. That is a good question. Are we waiting for the world to turn to God? But how can they turn if no one shows them God's love? We are the ones who have been told to go. "Go out into the highways and byways and invite people to come in." How can the world hear and turn without someone being sent to show them the way, and how can people go if they do not have the resources or if a leader does not ask them to volunteer?

We have to go, and we have to send people to go. There is no getting around it. It is up to us. He said go, so let's get moving!

The verse in 2 Chronicles shows us the process we have to go through. There are steps to getting America back on track. But if that verse does not get you moving, perhaps this one will. Psalm 50:22–23 warns us, "Now consider this, ye who forget God, lest I tear you in pieces, and there is none to deliver…to him that orders his conduct aright will I show my salvation." Wow! I was not sure if I wanted to share that with you. But I think this is how He feels about us.

If the next step is to turn from our wicked ways, what are our wicked ways? We do not feel like we are wicked. For the most part, we are trying to do the right thing, attending church, reading our Bibles, and listening to Dr. Dobson on the radio and trying to raise our families well.

I live in south Santa Ana, a middle-class neighborhood, near a beautiful shopping mall. In fact, South Coast Plaza Mall is the most successful mall in the United States. It has Saks Fifth Avenue, Bloomingdales, Macy's, Victoria's Secret, Nordstrom, Coach, and Gucci. It is a beautiful place and has a wonderful merry-go-round. That is where I took my children. I spent a lot of time at the mall, mainly having ice cream and riding the merry-go-round.

Then something happened. The AIDS epidemic came on the national scene. Young men were dying and it was spreading. California then mandated AIDS education for every child in public schools. Some of us mothers wondered how that would be taught.

One of the ladies urged us to go down to the school district to find out. As it turned out, a group of us spent close to three years there, attending school board meetings. First us "grizzly moms" we worked on sex education, and then we took on school-based clinics. After going to so many school board meetings, I was encouraged to run for the school board and was elected as a member of the Board of Education.

I used to drive to Bristol Street, near my house, and turn south toward the mall. Now as an elected school board member, I found myself having to turn north on Bristol, spending more and more time driving toward downtown Santa Ana seeing low-income neighborhoods. As a consequence, I was turning less towards the south, spending less time at the mall. Over time I stopped thinking about the Gucci bags, the Bergstrom's children's store, and the Gap, and started thinking more about gang members, poorly achieving students, and grieving mothers. As I drove north, I saw small homes with iron bars covering the windows, high-density apartments, fruit trucks at the corner, and lots of people walking. I saw the poor of Orange County. Each day I could drive to Bristol, the main street in town, and I had a choice. I could drive either to the mall or to the barrios.

Then I understood what turning meant.

It was not that being wealthy and enjoying nice things are wicked. They are in fact the blessings of living in America—the prosperity God promises to the nation who follows his rules and principles. Our founding principles of hard work, honesty, thriftiness, and initiative paid off with great prosperity. We are privileged to enjoy such blessings and have nice things.

It is not so much what we were doing; it was just what we were not doing or what we still needed to do. We were not preaching to the poor, not setting the captives free, and not spending time encouraging those who are bruised. We were ignoring our neighbors, perhaps hoping they would go away. We do not love our neighbors as we love ourselves. Our sins, our wicked ways, weren't in what we were doing. It was in our disobedience to God's command. We were distracted by riches and cares and all the stuff we had to do.

We were just not going. We were still sitting on the couch listening to Christian radio or on the merry-go-round at the mall. We worked very hard, perhaps too hard. We had a reason to "veg-out" in front of the TV. Our schedules are tight: we have to work out at the gym, meet our friends for lunch, shop, get our nails done, volunteer in the church nursery. These are all good things, but perhaps not the most important things.

It became clear. Turning from our wicked ways meant getting in the car and turning north on Bristol. The fatherless children were waiting for us, and single mothers or widows, in their affliction, needed a visit.

I saw a video, a DVD, on charter schools. The film featured a young black boy who never knew his father, and his mother had died recently. He was being raised by his grandmother. The grandmother learned about a charter school and wanted the boy to attend. It was a residential school, and he would have to move away from his grandma's house. They applied and he was selected.

The video showed this small handsome boy all dressed up in his new school uniform, packing his bags, and going off to the charter school. When they arrived, he was shown his room. There were three beds—one was a bunk bed and the other a regular bed. He was given the choice of the bed he wanted. First he picked the single bed. Then he changed his mind. He chose the top bunk and crawled up the ladder. Then he curled up like a ball and faced the wall. I thought, "Poor boy, he has no mother and no father, and he is now leaving his grandmother. He now has to adjust to this new place and new roommates." Then he grabbed a picture out of his jacket and taped it on the wall. I thought it would be a picture of his grandmother, perhaps his mother. But, no, it was a picture of his dad holding him as a baby. I started to cry. Yes, of course, all boys and girls hunger for their father. He is the protector.

While some of us may have missing fathers and understand the pain. It is good to know that all of us can enjoy talking to our Heavenly Father, going to him for comfort, for advice and for wisdom. We enjoy spending time with him, singing about him and talking with him. We enjoy just knowing he is around and available when we need him.

And if the truth were known, figuratively speaking, there is a whole room full of gift boxes with individual heavenly fathers, one for each child. Yet the fatherless children wait, while their father sits in the warehouse. We do not realize that the trunks of our cars are filled with these boxes marked with names. We just drive around, we take them to work and we take them to the mall. But we will not drive north and deliver them to the waiting boys and girls. So the boys and girls crawl up like little balls, face the walls, and hang up a picture of their missing dad. And tears roll down their faces.

I think that is our wicked ways. We will not deliver the dads. We will not fulfill the Great Commission to go and the greatest commandment to love others as we love ourselves. We will not give them the Heavenly Father. And God cries too. He longs to be a father to these children, but he has no one to make the delivery.

Chapter 34

The Power of Unity

I hate the starfish story. Some nonprofits like to give out starfish pins to their donors. The story goes like this: "Someone walks on the beach and sees hundreds of starfish out of the ocean lying on the beach. They will soon die and dry up outside of the water. So a passer-by picks one up one, one starfish, and throws it into the water. Someone watches and asks him, "Why did you do that? Don't you know there are all of these starfish that will be dying?" He says, "I know I cannot save all of the starfish, but I can save this one."

I hate it. I want to save them individually, but I also want to save them all. I want to make a huge impact. If we had enough people who cared, called them all to come, I know we could throw many of the starfish back in the water. We do not have a lot of time. Saving one or two or three is not enough. We have to save them individually, but we have to save as many as we can.

The frustrating thing is I know how to do that. We just need the leaders to share the cause, the experts who know just how to throw the starfish in quickly, the resources, maybe for boats and nets to get them out there, and enough volunteers to do the job. What if hundreds or thousands of volunteers showed up on the beach to throw the starfish in? We would at least save more than one or two or five. We could save a lot of them.

Some could put the starfish in baskets, others could carry the baskets to the boats, some volunteers could paddle the boats out to sea and another person in the boat could throw the starfish into the water. We could have several boats and several teams. With a coordinated effort, with each one doing their job, we could save many star fish.

And it would be an exciting project, not a lonely task. We could eat pizza afterward together and celebrate our work. Can you see thousands of volunteers, wet and tired, raising their arms, shouting "Hip, hip, hooray! Hip, Hip, Hooray!! We saved the starfish." Afterward all of the volunteers would be asking, "What can we do next?"

The negative changes in our society did not happen overnight. Our enemies gradually took more and more territory. It has taken about forty (perhaps seventy) years to destroy our families—a generation. It seems our churches are irrelevant. It almost seems that we are too late. When I recognized the educational goals and the system they brought in, I had a deep sense of urgency. I despaired. Then I got mad, and God gave me instructions. "Raise up an army; tell the truth with genuine compassion. Go save the children and restore the families!"

You might think it will take another generation to restore what has been lost, to get our nation and our families back. But that is not true. We can act quickly and rebuild the foundations. It took Nehemiah fifty-nine days to rebuild the walls. We have to push the reset button. We can restore America. Here is the plan. To turn a big ship around, it takes a lot of pressure and force. To turn a nation around, it will take a lot of force. It will take power that we do not have today. We are divided and scattered. It will take the power of unity.

Together we are more effective. I cannot lift a heavy couch alone. Two of us may be able to move it slowly with some grunting and sighing. But if six people come to help and lift the couch, it can be moved out very quickly. There is amazing power in unity. We can do what we never felt we could do alone. New possibilities are opened. Once we unite our efforts, a new strength will enter the church.

You may have seen the television infomercials that show us how, with a simple sliding pad, one person can move heavy furniture or even a car. Amazing! With simple strategies like this, we can do so much more than we thought we could. And God has a strategy for each battle.

In the time of the judges, when it was time for the people of Israel to reset their culture, the judges or leaders called the people together to fight the evil in the land. In Judges 19 and 20, there first was a moral outrage, a cause. A young woman had been raped all night and left to die. Her husband wanted the other tribes to avenge him and put a stop to this. He cut her body in pieces and sent a piece out to each tribe. This got the leaders' attention.

Alarmed, the people of Israel arose and went to war. In verse one, "*all* the children of Israel came out and the congregation *gathered as one man.*" In verse 8, "So *all* the people *arose as one man,*" and said, "None of us will go back home. We are committed to the effort." Then in verse 11 we read, "So all the men of Israel were gathered against the city, *united together as one man.*" They united under one effort to take a city. They "*arose and worked as one man.*" All the people came out, they gathered together *in one place,* they showed up. Then they arose, offered themselves. They were united under one cause.

In verse 18, they inquired of God. They got the battle strategy. "Send Judah first!"

This is the winning plan. First, we need a moral outcry. We need to care. God has to touch out hearts. Then we need to arise. Leaders have to call and assemble the people in one place. The people need to make themselves available; leave everything behind and be committed to the cause. Then with God's winning strategy and instructions we need to move out together, at one time, as one man. As we move out together under God's direction, he comes in with the power we need to win the victory.

Joshua who led Israel into the Promised Land told his men,

"One of you will chase a thousand, for the Lord your God is He who fights for you, as he promised" (Joshua 23:10). In the book of Deuteronomy, it is asked, "How could one chase a thousand, and two put ten thousand to flight?" (Deut. 32:30). Why didn't it say one could take one thousand and two could rout two thousand? That would still be very powerful. That would be addition. No, it said, one could take a thousand, but two could take ten thousand. Now that is powerful! That is exponential power!

While it is not stated, I ask, could three take one hundred thousand, and could four take one million? Could four people really defeat one million of their foes? When we work together, we do not add merely to our strength; we have exponential growth! It is explosive! In Acts 1:8 we read about the power we need to share God's love. It is called *"dunamis"* power, a word for dynamite. God's spirit wants to give us explosive power to be his witnesses. We have his power and strength. And when we come together and light the fuse, it is explosive!

Now I have talked about calling thousands and thousands to come to fight. But as you can see with exponential power, it might not take that many. (As you have read in this book, even just five angry women can make a big difference.) Like Gideon, a judge and deliverer in Israel, we may need to send some people home. He started with 10,000 men and ended up using just 300. The men took clay pots with fiery torches inside, at just the right moment they broke the pots and their enemies saw the fire. They thought there were thousands of them. It only took a few people to confuse the enemy. Just think, the 300 men defeated 135,000 of their enemies! Sometimes a great strategy or the perfect instructions brings an amazing victory.

In the Book of Acts, it was said they were "in one accord," "of one soul, one mind." And what did they do? They turned the world upside down! They flipped their world around.

When Jesus prays, we need to take note. What did he pray

for? In one of his last prayers, he prayed "that we would be one." "One," just like he and the Father are one. How close is that? They are as close as "One," as in one person. In Judges, it says "they worked as one man." They moved out together, with one mind, and worked as though they were "one man."

In Rome, when it was time for war, all of the new recruits had to give their allegiance to their leader. They had to sign an oath, called a Sacrament, to do whatever their leader said to do. Later the ritual of baptism was called a sacrament, signifying that believers were now willing to follow Christ. In the United States, our leader in war is the president of the United States, the commander in chief.

And in this battle, Christ is our commander in chief. We have to give our allegiance to him and listen to his instructions. We are called the "Body of Christ." And hopefully the body has only one head. With lots of heads, it is confusing, and it can make us look like a monster. In fact, sometimes we are made to look like monsters in the media.

Jesus Christ is the head. The head gives the orders to the body. The body is made up of many parts. Some are the eyes, some the ears, some the lungs, some the heart, some the fingers, and some are the toes. Each part is needed. Without one part we might die, or we might just hobble around and not be as effective as we could be. All of us need to come under the headship of Christ and move out under one command.

The church is weak and ineffective because the church is "carnal" and divided. We have many vying to be the head. Being carnal means we are not spiritual. We are not in tune with the Holy Spirit.

The Bible puts it this way: "For where there are envy, strife, and divisions among you, are you not carnal and behaving like mere men? For one says, 'I am of Paul,' and another, 'I am of Apollos,' are you not carnal? Who then is Paul and who then is Apollos, but ministers through whom you believed, as the

Lord gave to each one? I plant, Apollos watered, but God gave the increase. Now he who plants and he who waters are one, and each one will receive his own reward according to his own labor. For we are God's fellow workers; you are God's field, you are God's building." (1 Cor. 3:3–9).

During the 1960s Jesus Movement, there was an outpouring of love, a desire to help the disenfranchised youth, the hippies. But it was also a movement that united the Body of Christ. Pastor Chuck Smith disliked all of the denominational divisions in the church. He wanted them to be united under the Word of God.

For almost forty years, the Sunday church bulletin at Calvary Chapel reflected this founding principle. "We are not a denominational church, nor are we opposed to denominations as such, only their over-emphasis of the doctrinal differences that have led to the divisions of the Body of Christ."

Pastor Chuck called the people to unite around the Word of God, a simple teaching of God's Word from Genesis to Revelation, verse by verse. He felt if the whole Word was taught from start to finish, we would not divide into factions emphasizing only one part of the message. It was a powerful movement. It changed many lives, and it created a new music. Many churches took down their Baptist or Lutheran shingle and put up nondenominational signs. Many churches became just "Bible-believing" churches.

And while it has been over forty years, this movement of love is still having rippling effects today. Yet, sadly, it seems we have been drifting apart again. Once again we need to reach out to this generation of young people, and we need a new movement of unity.

The early church was in one accord. In the Book of Acts we read, "They were in one accord in prayer," "They were in one accord, in one place," "continued daily in one accord," "raised voices in one accord," and so it goes (Acts 1:14; 2:1; 2:46; 4:24). They even shared their funds and belongings. They were filled with the Spirit and become one family. They were united in purpose.

Strife and division kills, and unity gives life. We need a new dynamic move of God. We desperately need to see God's glory again. It is time to turn from our carnality, from our divisions, from strife and envy. It is now time to unite again.

In Ezekiel, another book of the Bible, it talks about dry bones coming to life. There was a cute song, "Dem Bones," written by James Weldon Johnson, an African American, in 1928. "The hip bone connected to the leg bone." "The leg bone connected to the foot bone." "Now hear the word of the Lord." You could just see all those dry bones coming together "to work as one man." As a young kid, I thought it was an exciting song. It can be exciting to see something that was once dry and lifeless come to life again.

We need to change what we have been doing. Insanity is sometimes defined as doing the same thing over and over again and expecting a different outcome. We have been doing outreach the hard way. We need to do it the easy way, with a coordinated effort. It will take a large exacting undertaking that unites our expertise, our volunteers and our financial resources. We need an exciting ideal that sparks our enthusiasm and a well thought out plan that when carried out creates momentum.

In the Old Testament, God gave a different strategy for each battle. The leaders had to have their ears open to the new instructions so they could lead the people into the battle with an assurance of victory. God has something big on his mind. I don't think anyone has seen or can fully comprehend what God is planning now!

I kind of think it is his last hurrah! It will be kind of like the Grand Finale at the Disneyland fireworks show when all of the fireworks go off at the same time.

One thing is for sure, in this cultural battle we cannot keep on playing defense, reacting to our enemy's agenda, fighting every battle again and again. A defense is not enough. We need a great offense! We have to take territory, and we have to score, if we are to win. We have to exert force, using exponential power, to turn things around.

We have to present a great vision, a truly magnificent ideal that takes everyone's breath away. That will create enthusiasm. We have to unite people behind that vision and mobilize the troops out into the battle. That will bring power.

We have to work quickly. We have only a limited time. There is a sense that there is only a window of opportunity. It is our hour. We can take back our inner cities, introduce the poor to their Provider, heal the broken hearted and set the captives free. The power of the gospel changes us. It is astounding how God's love for each of us can utterly transform individual lives.

Government programs enslave us to a life of dependency, while God's love and provision sets us free to be all we can be. It is that transformation of individual lives that will heal our land. We can repair our nation's cracked foundation. We can restore the two pillars of religion and morality upon which our national freedom rests. We can truly make a difference! That is the good news!

Look at how fortunate we are. We have an all-knowing commander in chief. Who needs the CIA or the FBI? The Holy Spirit can tell us what our enemies are talking about in their chambers. He can crack their double-speak secret code for us. He knows just what to do. And he wants to lead us. We have the answer. We must unite! There is power in unity. We are more than conquerors. The hour is urgent. We must mobilize now!

Chapter 35
The Perfect Church

If apathy stops volunteers from volunteering, and division or carnality stops pastors from working together, what hinders churches, groups of people with distinct callings, from actually working together? First it is hard to work together; often we feel like it is easier to just do it ourselves.

Marriage may be the ideal, but it is a lot of work to make two people one. Most often in marriage opposites attract. That can create conflict, but it is also good to have our gifts and weaknesses complement each other. Most of the time, one is better at budgeting, or the other partner is a better communicator. We rub each other the wrong way, creating friction, but in the end, the family has all of the strengths it needs.

Like individuals, every church family has a unique gift to give to the Body of Christ, a unique calling. In fact, it is our opposite or particular unique gifting that makes us more effective and complements the work. For years, churches in our area have been perfecting their distinctive callings. Meet the seven churches in our area:

1) One church stresses the teaching of the Word and sound doctrine. This church wants to teach the *"Logos,"* the whole Word of God from Genesis to Revelation. Bible knowledge is key.

2) Another church wants the people to apply the teaching and "Build Solid Lives." They encourage people to read God's Word, be willing and obedient to experience God's blessing.

3) A third church has an entrepreneurial spirit. They are the

high achievers in our area and love vision. Their gift is to organize people in teams, develop programs, and start new works.
By creating the right processes they give the work sustainability.

4) Yet another church emphasizes worship, taking their people
into God's presence to hear a *"Rhema"* word from God to meet
a present need. They love providing food for those who are
hungry and are in tough times, wanting to be there, to pray for
others at their point of need.

5) Another church has a lot of strong young people. They do
not know how to start businesses or programs, but they love to
serve, and have annual "Serve Days" where they come alongside
established ministries and set up for community fairs, provide
a BBQ, or paint a house.

6) Yet another church sees things globally. They seek to relieve
human suffering whether it is at home with AIDS, obesity or
mental health issues, or in places like Africa, especially Rwanda
where thousands were massacred.

7) There are many other wonderful churches in our area with
amazing areas of expertise. Actually there are too many to mention. Number seven includes your church.

The perfect church should do all of these things—teach the
Word, help people apply its wisdom, provide for immediate
physical and spiritual needs, organize new programs, serve other
organizations and the community, and relieve human suffering.
Many try to be the ideal church. But the reality is we cannot do
everything. And thank God we are not called to do everything!

But here is the question? Do we want to be a perfect church?
Yes, indeed!

The good news is God has created a perfect church. We are
the perfect church when we work together!

The apostle Paul wrote that some plant and some water. We
may have different callings, yet we are all on God's team. God has
given each church distinct gifts and distinct functions. As we learn
to appreciate each other, God is glorified. He is glorified because

we are recognizing his work in each of us. When we look down at parts of his family, he takes it personally, he feels rejected.

We need to be united in our purpose. And we also need to see ourselves as part of what God has done in the past with other great movements. We are His workmanship created for good works.

Wouldn't it be wonderful if all the churches got together to do outreach together? We do not need to lose our distinctions. We do not need to change what God has called us to do. We need to keep on doing what we are doing. We just need to unite in outreach so we can be more effective and powerful.

The world needs to see us working together, united, loving, and appreciating each other.

Perhaps there are seven churches in every area, city, or county in America that will want to form a coalition. But even if two or three churches could catch the vision, it would be a wonderful start. Pastors would agree to send out their people to work together on projects or programs. Pastors also need to release their outreach pastors to lead the volunteers.

Pastors who decided to unite their efforts could form a board of professionals to oversee the coalition work. Each pastor who committed to the work could appoint board members. One scenario could be a board with 12 or even 24 members. In the case of 24 board members, three would be appointed from the seven churches in the area making 21 members, plus three corporate officers.

The coalition will be made up of outreach leaders or nonprofit leaders from each church. These ministry experts will be the generals or captains in the army. They will lead the troops (volunteer mentors) out into the field to do a specific work such as an after-school tutoring program, a homeless check-in center, a sport program, or teen counseling program. Individual churches could set up their own after-school character clubs, sport centers, or entrepreneurial work training sites.

The board of directors may decide on an annual schedule.

One idea is for pastors to call their members to volunteer in the month of May. During May pastors would stress the importance of fulfilling the mission to go and teach and obey the command to love our neighbors as we love ourselves. They could show their members how to recognize their particular gift and calling and teach them how to hear God's voice.

The pastors, the spiritual leaders, are the ideal ones to share the exciting vision of working together to get a job done. The greatness of the task makes the vision that more compelling. The ideal of making a quick turn-around in our nation and community will bring excitement and ignite enthusiasm. The people will be energized as pastors urge their people to go out and work in the community using their unique gifts and passions for this great endeavor.

Just imagine, all of the pastors, with one mind and one purpose, all doing the same thing at the same time, calling the people to the work of rebuilding our communities. Each one will be repairing the broken walls in the community near where they live. How exciting that would be. I can already hear that trumpet sound!

Once the pastors have sounded the trumpet and called the people to the work, church members will be given a complete list of ministry opportunities and the dates of their Open Houses. The people are called in May, they select programs to work in and attend Open House events in June. At these events they can meet the ministry leaders, volunteers, and hear about the work they have been doing. After visiting three Open Houses, the potential volunteer selects where they would like to work and applies to join the effort.

In July, volunteer applicants are screened, accepted and assigned by outreach leaders. Outreach leaders can interview and accept the volunteers that are needed for each program. In August and September, each volunteer is required to attend four weeks of intensive training prior to going out into the community to work.

After the training, volunteer mentors begin their nine-month "service learning" assignment, which begins in October and ends with a celebration Open House event in June. In May, the calling, selecting, applying, screening, training, and working cycle can begin again. Each year more and more recruits will join the effort.

As you can see, the work is similar to a university, where people are recruited, accepted, and taught how to be effective. But in this model, rather than staying in classrooms, they will be out on the field learning how to mentor and disciple people. In the education world, this is called "service learning."

The board of directors, made up of recognized spiritual leaders with professional skills, will then decide if the work needs a large headquarters, such as the old YMCA building or the First American building, or a smaller location for a mentoring university. At the site, volunteers will be processed, trained, and equipped. Leaders or instructors will follow up with the volunteers, evaluating the effectiveness of the work.

While out in the community, serving at a site, each volunteer will be working under an outreach ministry leader who runs the programs and reports to the coalition. During the summer special interns will be invited to provide special programs such as DVBS, reading or sport clinics.

The coalition of outreach leaders will receive ongoing training and support so they can increase their capacity to receive and monitor more and more volunteers for this larger work.

Well, that is how I see it. And I am sure once we all get together, ideas will flow, and new structures will be set up to facilitate the work. Working together is hard, but it is easier and more powerful than doing it alone.

As you can see this is not an ecumenical movement, where we seek to make all the churches one or the same. Instead we love and respect each of the individual characteristics of the church families. We celebrate our differences. We want to bring them together to use their strength to get a particular job done. We want the world to see the church in all its glory, fully functioning. The definition of a coalition is for different groups to come together, often temporarily, to accomplish a specific task.

How can we truly unite our efforts and avoid conflict? In our nonprofit organization, we have a saying, "Stay in your lane." We need to have clear job descriptions, evaluate regularly and set up good communication methods to quickly deal with situations that come up. We get in trouble when we try to do another man's job. Some call it crossing our boundaries. It makes the other person feel unappreciated and unneeded. We get excited and want to do everything, but we are not called to do everything. And when we try to do another person's job, we mess up. We need to do our part and function as we have been designed to function. Another way we get in trouble is when a team member is not doing his job. That weakens the effort and discourages the others. So we need to continually check if we are doing our job, identifying weaknesses, and fortifying the volunteers.

The heart is designed to pump blood to the body, and the lungs are designed to provide oxygen. Both are needed and are essential. As long as each one does its job, everyone is fine. But if we have air in our heart, it is painful, and if blood gets into our lungs, it too is painful. The heart and lungs are meant to do their own job, but by working side-by-side connected to each other they are more effective. The lungs cannot do what the heart does and the heart cannot do what the lungs do. They were not designed that way. Each church should do what they were designed to do and they need to appreciate others who have a different calling. We need to respect the distinct gifting of the other part, or person that is working right there next to us

The problem in the church is that we are trying to do everything ourselves and we cannot do it. We desire to be better than another part. This is pride and carnality. And we need to turn from it. Can't you see that the church is ineffective because we are not working together? We hobble around trying to get the job done with one foot, blind eyes or a collapsed lung. How foolish we have been. Most pastors and particularly outreach leaders are overworked and understaffed. Churches are strained trying to meet the discipleship needs of its members while meagerly, inadequately, doing outreach into the community. Is it any wonder why we are so ineffective?

What if churches united just for outreach efforts, pooled their resources, their expertise, and volunteers together? That is the only way we will be effective. This would free the church leadership, paid staff, and their volunteer teachers to concentrate on teaching, discipling believers, and building up families. All the other areas of the church: regular preaching, Sunday school, small groups, counseling, and youth groups would remain the same. In fact by calling out and inspiring volunteers, the churches would have even more help for their church programs. And with new members coming into the church, more and more church volunteers will be needed.

This work may not be easy, but it is rewarding. The song "Bringing in the Sheaves" is about working in the harvest when the wheat or fruit is ripe. The people may shed tears toiling in the fields, but they will come in rejoicing bringing in the sheaves, the harvest. There is nothing more thrilling and exciting than seeing others being transformed in front of your very eyes!

And knowing you had a part in it is a great reward. Changing one life brings changes to many lives.

Soon all of our churches will be filled with new members as more volunteers go out and bring others in. Church outreach directors or ministry experts, the captains in this effort, who oversee the new recruits out in the fields, will be liberated knowing they do not have to meet every need. They can now work on projects that are close to their hearts. They will also be relieved that the church will be concentrating on regular discipleship and caring for the new members they bring in. The mentors can bring the children they serve and their families into the church, then go back out and bring more in.

With the aging of America, seniors are looking for meaning and fulfillment in their retirement years. They want to leave a legacy. They want to make sure their life made a difference. And the best thing is they have time to volunteer. They are available during the after-school hours. They also have a wealth of life experience and great wisdom. They know how to teach values. We cannot let that go to waste. Our retired volunteers make excellent mentors and character teachers.

Young people need to be kept busy doing meaningful work. They need to learn to care for others. They also need the affirmation of older adults. By volunteering, young people can build valuable leadership skills and learn to take responsibility. Most teens are good at a specific sport or are gifted in technology or art. All of these great skills can make a character club fun and develop the skills and confidence in disadvantaged youth. Often these vulnerable young people do not have the opportunity to be involved in sport or extra enrichment classes.

Today's young adults are more socially conscious. They are looking for an authentic Christianity. They want to make a difference in the world. They are idealistic, energetic, and looking for places to build their résumés. Many are leaders and have management skills. They can assist seasoned outreach leaders, taking on administrative responsibilities. Their energy needs to be harnessed and used for God's glory. We cannot allow the social justice movement to take them in the wrong direction, denying the real power that transforms lives.

Homeschool families and other families are also looking for volunteer experiences for their children. Mothers who have raised their children have so much to give to the children in the community. Men get so busy and work long hours, they need an excuse to go fishing, take a young person along for golf, or share their interests in miniature trains. Older men with boats would probably get great satisfaction taking ten young people out to sea as a reward for memorizing the Ten Commandments, the Twenty-Third Psalm, and the Golden Rule. And how special would these outings be for the young people, particularly if you never knew your father. Having an older man pay attention to you can give you confidence that you are indeed special.

There are so many possibilities; it is a perfect time to mobilize the church out into the community.

We have a choice. Do we want to continue to do ministry the hard way, the disjointed way, the slow way? Or as John R. Mott from the YMCA movement stated, do we want to do ministry *the easier way?* "A large exacting work is easier than smaller ones."

This winning plan calls for a large exacting work, a professional well-planned effort. The exciting thing is that it will be much easier than what we are doing now. But most importantly, what we do will be more effective; it will produce results. Why work with little results when you can work in unity and get great results—explosive exponential results!

Remember one successful program, and another successful effort, and another successful event builds momentum. And momentum builds enthusiasm. And you know what that means. Enthusiasm destroys apathy. Enthusiasm and an effective successful work will bring such great joy! It will energize us.

Best of all, as we do the good works that we are called to do God will be glorified! He will be seen in all of his splendor as a great and loving Father, the Provider and the one who can set us free! And the world will finally know we are Christians by our love for each other.

At church, many of us sing a beautiful song, *"Your Great Name,"* by Natalie Grant. A line particularly touches me: "the fatherless; they find their rest." The words come alive because I think of David and Pedro and Lucinda. How amazing it will be when we can give each child a wonderful constant spiritual father who loves them unconditionally, comforts them, and provides for their every need.

Malachi 4 states that in the last days, "the hearts of the children will be turned towards their fathers and the hearts of their fathers will be drawn towards the children." Fatherhood will be restored.

And you know it will not only be the fatherless who find rest but also God, our loving heavenly "Abba" Daddy Father will too find his rest. He is longing to hold us in his arms, smother us with kisses, and be a father to us. He longs to counsel us and teach us the ways of life. He looks at everything we do and has great joy in our accomplishments.

God is glorified by our unity. He is given proper credit when we acknowledge his work in each of us. He can do so much more when we work together in unity to reach the lost, to complete the mission.

We have everything we need, all of the resources, and the promise that if we give, he will give us more to give. There is a never-ending source of resources when we help the poor. Lend to the poor, and I will repay, God promises.

God not only repays what we give to the poor but he adds other promises, that "we will be blessed, have treasure in heaven, will not lack, and that he will remove our curses (our troubles)" (Prov. 22:9; Matt. 19:11; Prov. 28:27; Ps. 41:1). What a great investment. It is like getting our money back with interest. While we help others, we are also blessed.

In 2001 and in 2008, we had stock market crashes and many lost some of their wealth. With such a high national debt and instability in the world, some fear we may again experience a financial crash. Wouldn't it be sad if we lost half of our wealth and had not shared with the poor? And if we give, perhaps God will bless our work and protect our funds so we can give again and again.

We have unlimited financial means for a great mobilization effort. Across America, in our own cities, we have thousands of mentors waiting to be put to work. We have the power and the authority to do the work. We have respected spiritual leaders to call the workers out into the fields. We have a message that is powerful. It can transform individual lives and turn whole nations around.

We can ADD more programs to our churches to attract more people. We can also MULTIPY our efforts by adding more locations. But why settle for addition and multiplication when we can have EXPONENTIAL POWER!

The Bible says in John 14:12 that we "will do greater works" than Jesus. How can we do greater works than Jesus? He was the Son of God. He was God! No one can do greater works than Jesus. But if the whole Body of Christ arises, using every part together, we can do great amazing things. What are the greater works? It is everyone arising, *"working as one man,"* the man Christ Jesus. It is one big Jesus!

Chapter 36
Here He Comes to Save the Day!

Often we think that we can solve the nation's problems with the next election. Yet presidents from both parties come and go, and we are still spiraling downward, out of control. The national debt continues to climb at an alarming rate. More and more people are incarcerated. And families are still under siege. Of course, good leaders and angry mothers make a real difference, and I hope this book illustrated that. But our problems are deeper than the next election.

When we had a skateboard competition event, we gave T-shirts to the children. Soon I noticed several of the children had on two T-shirts, hoping I would not notice. A highlight of the event was a demonstration by a professional skater. The skater was excited he was going to film a commercial for more than a thousand dollars right after he judged the skateboard competition. While judging their routines, he left his skateboard near the table where he was sitting. Soon he discovered the skateboard was missing. He panicked. "I need that skateboard for the commercial!"

Someone told him they thought a boy took it and went down the street to the left. The skater looked around, and then took off on a small bike to find his skateboard. The event stopped. The police were called. And just in time they found the stolen skateboard, and he took off to do the filming. While these may seem innocent or an everyday occurrence in the inner city, perhaps a few years from now these same children will be stealing cars or burglarizing stores and end up spending part of their lives in prison. That is unless they are mentored now and shown a better way.

Politically, we lament that the Ten Commandments are being removed from our public schools and our courthouses. And it should sound a national alarm. But here is the question. "Who is going to put the Ten Commandments into the children's hearts?" This is where they belong. How many young men sit in prison day after day, year after year, because no one taught them, "Thou shalt not steal" or "Thou shalt not covet." How many live their entire lives in prison because no one impressed upon them, "Thou shalt not murder." The Ten Commandments belong in the hearts and minds of boys and girls.

When we look at the problem, particularly the lack of character among our youth, it seems so great that it cannot be solved overnight. The enormity of the situation demands an enormous effort—a united effort. We will not solve it alone.

We continue to spend more and more money on welfare programs, food stamps, enterprise zones, Weed and Seed gang reduction measures, mental health identification programs, and still our inner cities waste away. Government solutions, while well-intentioned, just make the problems worse. The reason is that government was not created to solve all the social problems. It is only one of our three institutions. The church and the family are the institutions that are best equipped to tackle these problems. And with families in disarray, it is up to the church.

Community organizers work the inner city streets, getting more and more people to register to vote. But how will they vote? Will they vote for principled candidates with high moral values when they themselves do not know what that is? Or will they vote for more free government programs? Will they vote just so they can keep their free Obama cell phones?

What our nation needs is fundamental change. If we are truly a government of the people and by the people, then we are as good as the individuals in the nation. Our welfare programs help people survive. But is that what we want? Do we want the poor hanging on by a thread, surviving, or do we want them to thrive and become competent adults who know how to work and can provide well for the needs of their families? Perhaps God has been good to let them survive on welfare until we, the church, come knocking at their door with a bag of groceries. We need to bring the groceries, but what they really need is their "daily bread," from the hand of a personal, loving heavenly father.

As many of us who have been politically active know full well, not everyone is called to be involved in politics. Everyone should vote and give to Caesar what is Caesar's, but not everyone has the calling to serve in the political area. For those of us who have a calling and a passion for our nation, this is hard to understand. The battle is intense; we think everyone should get involved politically. But we cannot save America with just political action. We also have to be involved where the rubber meets the road, in the chaos, in the prisons, in the inner cities, in our community.

Nehemiah was an assistant to the King, but when he realized the walls of Jerusalem were broken down, he wept. He assembled a team, went quietly at night, surveyed the situation, and set out a plan. He involved the people. They were asked to each fix the wall nearest their home. He, too, had enemies so the people not only worked on the walls with their trowels but also carried a sword.

Some are critical of political activists. They think those engaged in political activity give Christians a bad name, always calling out what is wrong, and pointing to our traditional form of government. These critics point to the Silent Majority of the '80s and say that political activism has not changed the culture. While gains are being made in some areas like abortion, political action has not dramatically turned the tide. Political activism is good, we must push back. We must slow down the destruction of our freedoms and point to a better way. But it is not enough. They take three steps forward and we push them back two steps. They continue to gain ground. This is also because, as Superman put it, it is "a never-ending battle for truth and justice and the American way," and each generation has to fight the battle for freedom. Political activism is like the Dutch boy in the story who has his finger in the hole of the dam, holding back the flood. Someone has to do it. But there comes a time when there are too many holes in the dam.

In an article on Christian engagement or activism, "Three Ways Christians will Address Cultural Issues in the Coming Years," Ed Stetzer, President of LifeWay Research, suggests we need three kinds of people involved: culture defenders, creators, and engagers (www.edstetzer.com). And I agree we need all three. In my view, culture defenders are those who defend America's historical Judeo-Christian values and history. We need to point to the values that made us a great nation: our trust in God, self-government and limited government. We have to provide that moral compass. We also need to warn the American people of the evils of tyranny.

We need culture creators to provide alternatives, make relevant uplifting movies for the big screen, write good inspiring children's books, and create uplifting music. But most important we need those who will engage the culture. Culture engagers are out on the front lines, getting to know the people in their communities, teaching them how to live by walking beside them, feeding the hungry, addressing homelessness, visiting prisoners, tutoring and mentoring young people, and encouraging needy, struggling families.

What is exciting is that these three callings, all important, show us that God is working today. This to me is encouraging. Before Christ came, first John the Baptist had to come. Like the political activists, he pointed out what was wrong and called the people to turn—not too popular a message I might add. And look what happened to him! After John the Baptist came, Christ showed up and glorified the Father with his good works, showing God's love and compassion for the people. It is time for Christ to show up again. Then perhaps those of us, political activist, can take a break!

Today we need thousands who will show the people God's love and compassion. It was the great awakenings in America that brought dramatic cultural change in our nation.

Whatever your calling, everyone is needed! It is time to arise!

So kiss your political activist friends who are standing up for righteousness, limited government, and freedom. They carry a heavy burden. They are fighting "a never-ending battle for truth, justice, and the American way." Like Superman, they are our superheroes! But their efforts are not enough. They have played mainly a defensive role, holding back the tide, trying to contain the enemy. What we need is a good offense!

We also need to kiss all of those who faithfully teach Sunday school, who quietly teach character to the next generation. They, too, are our superheroes. But, sadly, not everyone is coming to Sunday school. We need to pray that many will be sent out into the streets, to the schools, to community centers, to sport centers to lift up our young people giving them hope and purpose and the strength of character that they need to meet the challenges they face. We need to strengthen the single mothers who are going it alone. We need to support hungry, needy families who are facing hard times. But most of all, we need those who will hand deliver a personal heavenly father to the hurting boys and girls.

Frankly, those of us in the battle are weary; we need the cavalry, like in the cowboy movies, to swoop down from the top of the mountains and come fight in the valley where our enemy is killing and destroying the people. We are in dire need for everyone to join the battle. We are in critical times. Our nation is about to be sawn in two, divided, and then captured.

All the people who have good values and understand how to successfully live life must enlist in this great effort. We have to restore the pillars on which our nation rests. For our

Constitution and the freedom it guarantees is only good for a religious and moral people. We can only live in freedom if we have strong individuals who are self-governed and are trying to live out ethical lives. We cannot wait on the schools to teach our children. Those who know the truth must teach the truth. Those who understand how to build character are the ones who are needed on the front lines. We are the ones who have to be the change agents. As Abraham Lincoln said, "The philosophy of the school room in one generation will be the philosophy of government in the next." It is up to us to educate the next generation.

This has to be a united effort. We must all fight in this cultural war, in the political arena, in the media, and in low-income areas. We are called to preach to the poor and bring liberty to the captives and encourage the brokenhearted. We are not being asked to pick up arms, to fight a new American Revolution. We are being asked to get up, move our feet, get going, and fight in a revolution of love, teaching truth with real compassion.

Let us stir our hearts for the hurting, the weak, and the captive. The Bible says to stir yourself up, to stir up the gifts that are in you. Come to the inner city, come and see the needs, come and meet the wonderful people who live there. We must see God's heart for the poor. We are told that he, God personally, takes up the cause of the widows and the orphans.

In the final judgment according to Mathew 25:39–40, we will be asked about those that were strangers, naked, sick, or in prison. He will say, "Assuredly, I say to you, inasmuch as you did it to one of the least of these My brethren, you did it to Me." He intimately identifies with the poor among us.

I am not talking about being "a bleeding heart liberal." I have sat with them in boardrooms while they advocate for the poor. It is easy for them to give away other people's money while they ignore the statistics that show that the government programs just make the problems worse. At least their conscience is clear.

They feel like they did something. They care about the needs of people, and for many of them, government redistribution of the wealth and resources is the solution for humanity. They voted to help the poor. And for many, that is all they know how to do. They do not understand the difference God's love can make.

Yet it saddens me because after their votes are cast, the poor are made poorer, their fates are sealed, while their dignity and initiative are drained.

We are different. When our hearts are stirred, we move out. We invest ourselves. We write checks from our own personal labor. We travel to the need and make a personal commitment of our time and effort. We are God's hands and feet. We are his mouth to encourage and his shoulder to cry on. He only has us. But with him in us, it is enough. It is more than enough.

The early church turned the world upside down. They flipped the chart. They shared willingly, with joy, of their own substance with those who had needs. We can flip America around. It is time to value freedom and reject tyranny. We can again value the individual. If the individual person and his needs are not important to us, we have lost America.

We have given up our right to freedom. Freedom demands that we believe in the redemption of the individual. God loves each and every one of us. He gave his own son for us. We do not work for some collective concept of the poor, for some imaginary utopia. We really love people because "God's love is shed abroad in our hearts." (Romans 5:5). We love those that are bruised by a hateful world. We truly care about their pain and about their futures.

The world planners know the power of unity; they are working quickly to bring in a seamless, united, integrated system, a "One World" government. The Communists believe that there will not be peace on earth until all are under their Socialistic government-managed, centrally planned society. They are dedicated, but where is our winning plan?

Creating a one-world system is nothing new. In ancient times, a rebellious people wanted to unite the world. They built the tower of Babel, a stairway to Heaven, a utopian dream. And it is said that once they would be united, nothing would be impossible to them. But God knew how to stop them. He stopped the project. He confused them. Let's do it again.

Today the church is divided, and nothing seems possible. We are not changing the culture; the culture is changing us. We play defense while our enemies unite the world to save the planet. But if we unite, their agenda will be undone. "United we stand, and divided we fall," it has been said. We won World War II because we were united, and we lost Vietnam because we were divided.

Lies and deception enslave, but truth sets people free. If we share the truth, we will be free indeed!

Perhaps we will be that "rock" that, according to Daniel, the prophet, rolls in and destroys the last government system. Perhaps we will be the rock that ushers in God's true Kingdom on earth. When Jesus returns, we will have a true just society based on love, not based on government tyranny.

Once again, I can see the damsel in the Mighty Mouse cartoons. She is tied to a log and floating down the conveyor belt. She is moving toward the blades of the saw that will soon saw her in half. We watch in desperation; we wring our hands; we want to save her, but we feel helpless.

Then out of the blue in flies Mighty Mouse. The music plays. "Here he comes to save the day." Here comes Mighty Mouse, the superhero. He will cut the cords, sweep the damsel in his arms, and carry her away to safety.

Can you hear the music now? Listen! I can hear it: "Here he comes to save the day." Here he comes! As he comes closer, I can see him. No, it is not Mighty Mouse.

Who is it? Who is coming to save the day? I feel the wind blowing. He is coming! It is not Mighty Mouse. And—it is not Superman. Yes, I know Superman stands for Truth and Justice and the American Way, but it is not him that will save us. It is not Superman!

Who is it? Who will save America? Who will save our inner cities? Who will save the children? Here he comes! Yes, now I see him. It is only Jesus Christ, who alone can save us, transform our lives, and restore America. Yes, Jesus is the Superhero who can save the day!

Jesus came once before, taught us how to live and returned to heaven, and at an unexpected time, he will return again. But for now, we are his representatives. We, the church, are his body. We are awakening. We are stretching. We are rising up. He is here, not in his own physical body, but with our flesh and bones, with each of us doing our part.

Can you see all of the different parts, united, "working as one man"? It is his body that has come to save the day. It is you! And it is me. It is all of us. Only we can save the day!

We are the Superhero.

It is time to join the army that will save the day!

Let us arise, and our enemies will be scattered!

ACKNOWLEDGEMENTS

I would like to thank my husband, Jim, for his encouragement and support in the writing of this book. A big thank you goes to my sister, Veronica, who has published two books, and has given me invaluable counsel and a listening ear. And I thank my mother who has had to share her time with my computer, who also came along on our wonderful visits. I love you for your gentleness and for teaching me to trust God. You have led with your great example.

But none of these stories would have been possible if I did not have such wonderful friends to fight these battles with me. I thank Bob and Bev, and Abie and Denise, Ted, Anne, Carol, Stan and Marva, Margie, Viola, Rachel, Jennifer, Brian, Tim, Lupe, Gwen, Luis, Eddy, Steve, Gloria, Elaine and Judy, and all the rest of you who worked so hard to get me elected, and the many who stuck with me through the battles on the school board, and worked tirelessly volunteering and building our nonprofits. I would include your last names but I do not want to get you into too much trouble. You know who you are. You were there for me, and I love you for it. Together, as a team, we did great things.

I want to thank all the rest of you who lived my life with me, my beautiful children and grandchildren, who have blessed my life. I know you had to share me with the community, but I trust it made you better people for it. You are caring people who see the needs of others around you. It is my hope that this book will help you also better understand the warfare we are in. But most importantly, I hope you will be inspired by what I have learned along the way.

Writing a book is a large and challenging project, and I am so grateful to those of you who took the time to read it and give me your feedback. Thank you, Orlean, Viola, Terri, Nelson, Veronica, David and Steve. Thank you, Amy Leonhardt, for the copy editing and thanks to Steve Weregland for his research and final review.

And a great big cheer goes to my artistic team, Bethany Guajardo who designed the book cover and formatted the inside and for Jordan Avila who did the original artwork for the cover. Bethany, you are more than a graphic artist but a partner in the project. I appreciate your technical skill. You made the book look good! Together we can all be proud. May all of our efforts make a difference for our great nation. It is my greatest hope that this book will help restore America and make her great again. At the very least, my children, grandchildren, and great grandchildren will be able to see some of the things I saw.

ABOUT THE AUTHOR

Rosemarie "Rosie" Avila has been married for forty-two years to Jim Avila. Together they have five children, five grandchildren, and three great-grandchildren, including the twins. Rosie was born in Guatemala, Central America, and came to the United States two days before her sixth birthday. She spoke Spanish before she learned English in the schools.

In high school Rosie was in student government, on the cheer squad as a flag twirler, and a homecoming princess for the homecoming football game. Rosie attended Biola University and earned a BA in social science and missions with a minor in Latin American history. She also earned an elementary teaching credential. She graduated from Biola Cum Laude. In both high school and college, she was an honors student, ranking academically in the top 2 percent of her class in both graduations.

Later, in 2002, Rosie earned a master's degree in organizational leadership from Biola University. By this time, she had founded a 501(c)(3) nonprofit organization that provided elementary and intermediate school-based after-school clubs, teen sport centers, and teen entertainment events for inner city youth.

When she left the staff in early 2008, she was overseeing 18 programs, with an enrollment of 800 students, and a weekly average attendance of 667. All programs provided academic tutoring, sports instruction, and character development. She was able to apply her non-profit experience to her studies in organizational leadership. In 2008, she founded another nonprofit organization, establishing a vintage boutique, to provide older youth workplace skills as well as training in starting and operating a small business. From the one store, six additional businesses were started by individuals in the entrepreneurial academy.

Medically, she and her husband were not supposed to have children, but miraculously they had five beautiful children, including their second child who was born with cerebral palsy. After substitute teaching for several years, she enjoyed staying at home with her children. As the scriptures say, "the barren will be a contented mother of children."

Rosie Avila was elected to the Santa Ana School Board in 1991 and served until 2008, after serving for seventeen years, having been elected to four terms. She also served as a Trustee of Biola University for almost twenty years. Both the Santa Ana Unified School District, which served 60,000 students and employed 4,000 people, and Biola University, a hundred-year-old Christian liberal arts institution, with served over 5,000 students annually, provided Rosie Avila a broad view on governance, education, and an understanding of the inner management of large organizations.

Rosie Avila was appointed by President George W. Bush to the President's Commission on White House Fellows, where she helped select the final top twelve applicants from thirty finalists, who would serve under president cabinet positions. In 2008, Rosie Avila was a candidate for the United States Congress. She also was appointed by Congressman Bob Dornan to serve as a RENEW Woman Advisor to Congress. Rosie was appointed and served on the city's gang prevention commission (EPIC: Early Prevention and Intervention Commission). She has received many awards, including the Excellence in Education Award by the California School Board Council, and a Friend of the Family Award from California's Capital Resources. Rosie also received the City of Santa Ana's Parks and Recreation Community Award for providing recreational activities for young people.

CONNECT WITH ROSIE

To get in touch with Rosie, or to submit your thoughts and comments, visit *rosieavila.com*.